Financial Accounting

C I *M* A

Published in association
with the Chartered
Institute of Management
Accountants

Other titles in the CIMA series

Stage 1

Economics for Accountants
Keith West

Quantitative Methods
Kevin Pardoe

Stage 2

Accounting Information Systems and Data Processing
Krish Bhaskar and Richard Housden

Management
Cliff Bowman

Cost Accounting
Mark Inman

Stage 3

Management Accounting Techniques
David Benjamin and Colin Biggs

Advanced Financial Accounting
Peter Taylor and Brian Underdown

Company Law
Julia Bailey and Iain McCullum

Stage 4

Management Accounting: Control and Audit
Jeff Coates, Ray Stacey and Colin Rickwood

Management Accounting: Strategic Planning and Marketing
Patrick McNamee

Financial Management
Paul Collier, Terry Cooke and John Glynn

Public Sector Accounting
Maurice Pendlebury (Editor)

Revision Guides

Quantitative Methods Revision Guide
Paul Goodwin

Cost Accounting Revision Guide
Colin Drury

Company Accounting Revision Guide
Peter J. Taylor and Brian Underdown

Economics Revision Guide
Keith West and Rob Dixon

Business Law Revision Guide
Stan Marsh

Advanced Accounting Techniques Groups and Special Transactions Revision Guide
Peter J. Taylor and Brian Underdown

Financial Accounting

Stage 2

Peter J. Taylor and
Brian Underdown

HEINEMANN : LONDON

Heinemann Professional Publishing Ltd
22, Bedford Square London WC1B 3HH

LONDON   MELBOURNE   JOHANNESBURG   AUCKLAND

First published 1987

British Library Cataloguing in Publication Data
Taylor, Peter, *1929–1987*
    Financial accounting.
    1. Accounting
    I. Title   II. Underdown, B.
    657'.48   HF5635

ISBN 0 434 91920 9

Printed in Great Britain by
Redwood Burn Ltd, Trowbridge, Wiltshire

Contents

Preface

The purpose of this book is to provide students with a contemporary and comprehensive course of study in financial accounting. Knowledge of the material contained in this book should enable students to carry out the financial accounting function in industrial, commercial and service organizations in both the private and the public sectors, as well as introducing them to the internal audit function in such organizations.

Financial accounting is in a constant state of evolution. Although this book reflects current theory and practice it also examines the major developments which have taken place in recent years. Four of these developments are reflected in the structure of the book. First the traditional accounting principles and practices underlying the preparation and presentation of financial reports have come under increasingly close scrutiny by the accountancy profession and others who are interested in, or affected by, financial disclosures. Amongst other things this resulted in the establishment of an accounting standards setting body in the UK. The accounting standards which have been issued are designed to improve financial reporting but they have themselves led to controversy and have called into question the relationship between legal regulation through company law and the self-regulatory mechanisms of the accountancy profession. We consider in detail the nature and role of accounting standards in the UK and the requirements which they place upon the preparers of external financial reports in different types of organization.

Second, developments in company law, especially those arising from the UK's membership of the European Economic Community, have not only expanded the scope of the disclosure requirements placed on companies, but have changed the nature of those requirements. The greater degree of detail which is now required by law and the prescription of formats for financial reports are examples of significant changes, and these, together with the other accounting requirements of company law, are thoroughly examined in this book.

Third, the general economic influence of pressure on material resources has had a marked impact upon financial reporting. As well as placing greater emphasis upon efficient resource allocation in the private sector, with attendant implications for financial reporting, economic stringency has created demands for greater value for money from public sector organizations. This has resulted in a greater interest in improving the accountability, and consequently financial reporting systems, of public sector organizations. From being almost an exclusive preserve of private sector organizations external financial reporting is of growing importance in the public sector. The lack of a public sector equivalent of the Companies Acts together with the greater economic diversity of public sector organizations has meant a great diversity in financial accounting and reporting practices in the public sector. Financial accounting and reporting by public sector organizations is reviewed in this book.

Finally, just as the pressure on resources has had external accounting implications, it has had important effects on internal accounting systems in organizations. Internal auditing has experienced an unprecedented growth recently. Over the years the primary role of internal auditing has moved away from the detection and prevention of fraud and errors towards an emphasis upon reviewing systems of internal control. In its various roles internal auditing relates closely to the financial accounting function and it is considered here.

In preparing this book we have sought to present the material in ways in which it will succeed in developing in readers four types of ability. The first of these is appreciation: students of accounting must first appreciate what a topic, problem or technique is, so that they may understand it themselves and communicate it to others. The second type of ability is knowledge: students should have sufficient knowledge of a topic or technique to be able to give advice in a professional capacity. The third type of ability is skill: accountants should possess sufficient skill to allow them to use techniques to solve problems. Finally, the most important ability is application: accountants must be able to apply their knowledge to unfamiliar situations, involving the selection of relevant data and appropriate techniques using professional judgement. We hope that the text, the worked examples used in the chapters and the end-of-chapter problems will develop these four skills. Most of the self-study problems are drawn from the examinations of the various professional accountancy bodies and thus give a good guide to the type of question which may be expected in such examinations and the level of attainment which must be achieved for success.

In writing the text we have made two assumptions. The first is that readers have already studied accounting at an introductory level. Hence, we do not deal with the mechanics of double-entry bookkeeping or with other basic accounting techniques. The second is that readers will have access to an up-to-date copy of current UK accounting standards and exposure drafts. Although these are dealt with in several chapters, notably Chapter 3, we do not reproduce the full texts of accounting standards and exposure drafts. These things said, *Financial Accounting* can be used as either a self-contained and comprehensive text on financial accounting and reporting or as a stepping stone to more advanced study of the subject.

Peter J. Taylor
Brian Underdown
June 1987

Acknowledgements

We express appreciation to Tony Hughes, Bill Jarvis, Mike Nardone and John Goulding for giving us the benefit of their experience and knowledge.

We gratefully acknowledge permission to quote from the past examination papers of the following bodies:

Chartered Institute of Management Accountants
The Institute of Chartered Accountants in England and Wales
The Institute of Chartered Accountants of Scotland
The Chartered Institute of Public Finance and Accounting

Peter J. Taylor
Brian Underdown

1 Financial accounting and reporting: an overview

Introduction

Financial accounting and reporting exist to provide information about the financial characteristics of organizations to individuals and groups interested in those organizations. The processes of financial accounting and reporting do not take place in a vacuum. They are significantly affected by the economic and social environment in which they are conducted, they are a reflection of prevailing notions of accounting theory, and they are strongly influenced by the regulatory system which operates to control them. In this chapter we shall briefly review these three sources of influence on financial accounting and reporting.

Environmental influences

The development of accounting has been greatly influenced by changes in social and economic conditions. The origins of the stewardship function of accounting can, for example, be traced back to the feudal system, and double entry book-keeping associated with the growth of market economies and the needs of trade. The more recent appearance of cost accounting is generally believed to have occurred as a response to the need to price products produced by the emerging mass production methods of the Industrial Revolution.

In more recent times the evolution of financial reporting has been in response to four major forces:

First, the shift from the *laissez faire* of the nineteenth century to broader notions of social responsibility in the twentieth century has had important implications for financial reporting. The development of a wider social awareness during the present century initially focused attention on the role of financial reports for encouraging the efficient

1

allocation of capital resources by private sector organizations. Later, the social impact of companies came to be seen as extending beyond this limited role to encompass employment, pollution and effects on consumers. With this changed perspective came a recognition that groups other than shareholders, for instance, employees and local communities, had a right to receive financial reports from businesses.

Second, the growth in the number and complexity of private and public sector organizations necessitated developments in financial reporting. The growth of companies increased the size of external financing requirements. Before the Industrial Revolution, the predominant source of finance for business enterprises was internal and, consequently, financial statements served only the needs of the proprietor – manager. As the Industrial Revolution progressed, and as internal sources of finance proved insufficient to meet the needs of increasingly large scale industrial enterprises subject to rapid technological change, external financing became more important. With the development of the joint stock company, a new group of people having an interest in the affairs of the enterprise emerged, namely shareholders. Management and ownership were divorced and financial statements became important vehicles for the provision of information to actual and potential shareholders. Acquisitions and mergers increased the complexity of business organization and created a need for group accounts to report the activities of large and diverse business units.

Similarly, the increased scale and complexity of government heightened the demand for accountability and resulted in more attention being given than previously to the financial reports of central and local government agencies, nationalized industries and the other bodies that constitute the public sector.

Third, greater pressure on resources and concern with resource allocation between the major sectors of the economy led to demands to analyse and question the economic activities and effects of public sector organizations. Debate within government and amongst the public at large has been directed to issues such as the efficiency and effectiveness of public bodies as well as their policies and legal obligations.

Fourth, scandals and business failures have led to changes in financial reporting practices. As many authors have pointed out, the company legislation to 1948 was largely a response to scandals that led to public demands for regulation. More recently the setting up of the Accounting Standards Committee in 1970 and the development of guidelines for auditors have resulted from public criticism of financial reporting practices.

The role of accounting theory

The second influence on financial accounting and reporting is accounting theory. The previous section indicates that the system of financial accounting and reporting is not static but responds to the characteristics of the environment in which it operates. It must be stressed, however, that all changes in financial accounting and reporting do not occur in a random way. It is one of the functions of accounting policy makers such as the accountancy profession, accounting standards setting bodies, the formulators of company law, and bodies like the Stock Exchange to evaluate current practice and formulate and implement proposals for its reform. They are guided in this by accounting theory. Although there is no single, generally accepted body of accounting theory, much work has been done by academics and policy makers to develop accounting theory in ways which might facilitate the improvement of financial accounting and reporting. Such a body of theory is frequently termed 'a conceptual framework'.

The Financial Accounting Standards Board (FASB), the US accounting standards setting body, has been particularly active in the development of a conceptual framework. The FASB has defined a conceptual framework as:

> ... a coherent system of interrelated objectives and fundamental concepts that can lead to consistent (accounting) standards and that prescribe the nature, function and limits of financial accounting and financial statements.

Financial reporting objectives

The FASB has also undertaken a considerable amount of research directed at the identification of the objectives of financial reporting. This research culminated in the publication of Statement of Financial Accounting Concepts Number 1 in which three objectives were identified for financial reporting by business enterprises. These were:

1 The provision of information useful to present and potential investors, creditors and other users in making rational investment, credit and similar decisions. This information should be comprehensible to those with a reasonable understanding of business and economic activities.
2 The provision of information to help present and potential investors, creditors and other users in assessing the amounts, timing and uncertainty of prospective cash receipts from dividends, interest and the proceeds from the sale, redemption or maturity of securities or loans.
3 The provision of information about the economic resources of an enterprise, claims on those resources, and the effects of transactions, events and circumstances that change its resources and claims on them.

Although these objectives relate to business enterprises, the FASB subsequently stated its view that it was not necessary to develop independent objectives for any particular category of entity and concluded that essentially the same considerations were applicable to non-business organizations. Thus as the FASB observed in 1981:

Financial reporting by non-business organizations shall provide information that is useful to present and potential resource providers and other users in making rational decisions about the allocation of resources to those organizations.... Despite different interests resource providers of all entities look to information about economic resources, obligations, net resources and changes in them for information that is useful in assessing their interests. All such resource providers focus on indicators of organizational performance and information about management stewardship.

Hence, we may conclude that although the different characteristics of various types of organizations may affect the way accounting information contained in financial reports is used, the underlying objectives of those reports are to facilitate users' decisions, different though they may be. Thus, despite differences between organizations the objectives on which their financial reports are based are broadly the same.

Accounting concepts and assumptions

Although a statement of the objectives of financial reports provides the general framework for considerations of the form and content of financial reports, it gives little guidance on details. More specific accounting concepts and assumptions can be offered as detailed criteria to guide decisions on financial reporting taken by preparers of such reports or regulators of financial reporting. These guidelines concern which events should be included in financial reports and how those events should be expressed in accounting terms. They are based on the premise that financial reports should be useful to the user for decision making purposes and may be classified under three headings: environmental assumptions, operating concepts and qualitative characteristics as in Table 1.1.

Environmental assumptions reflect the constraints imposed on accounting by aspects of the environment in which it operates. The

Table 1.1   *A classification of accounting assumptions and concepts*

Environmental assumptions	Operating assumptions	Qualitative characteristics
Entity	Accruals	Comparability
Going concern	Cost	Completeness
Money measurement	Realization	Consistency
Periodicity		Materiality
		Objectivity
		Relevance
		Reliability
		Timeliness
		Understandability

entity assumption, reflecting the idea that accounting communication be confined to a specific accounting entity is fundamental to financial reporting. Some notion of the scope of the enterprise being reported on is a prerequisite to reporting the results of the economic events in which it has engaged. However, agreement on this assumption exists only at a general level. For instance, in the case of companies one might argue for the adoption of either an entity or a proprietary view. The latter reports the results from the point of view of the company's shareholders, while the former is concerned with the performance of the company itself. Similar considerations apply to public sector organizations. The scope of various classes of public sector organizations is susceptible to different interpretations. For example, a nationalized industry may be perceived as owned by central government and its financial reports may consequently reflect a modified shareholders' perspective. A broader, entity view would report the nationalized industry's operations as they affect various interest groups.

The going concern assumption allows preparers of financial reports to treat enterprises as having continuity. This facilitates the deferring of costs such as closing stocks, prepaid expenses and undepreciated asset balances which will be charged against future periods. This assumption also facilitates the use of cost based rather than realizable values.

The money measurement assumption is of self-evident use in providing a common denominator for financial reports but the assumption imposes limitations on the scope of financial reports for dealing with real-world events. Not all significant variables associated with an entity can be readily expressed in money terms. Although this has come to be increasingly recognized as a deficiency for company reporting it is a more serious problem for both government and business-type public sector organizations.

The events in which an entity is engaged occur continuously and most are the result of events which have occurred earlier or may have implications for events occurring subsequently. Periodicity allows these continuing and overlapping events to be divided into artificial time periods for accounting and reporting purposes. The periodicity assumption underlies the issue of accruals versus cash based accounting and illustrates an important point of difference between financial accounting in private and public sectors. Accruals accounting is the dominant method for private sector enterprises whilst cash based accounting is widely used in the public sector.

Cost, realization and accruals assumptions provide accountants with guidance on the recording and manipulation of data in accordance with the environmental assumptions. The traditional approach to accounting focuses on historical cost values. Accountants have been reluctant to depart from historical cost valuation because it is definite and determinable. As a consequence a substantial portion of the contents of financial reports is based on objectively determined amounts. However, the major criticism of historical cost valuation is that such values remain static when prices change and may, as a consequence, be of limited use for decision making purposes and may be inconsistent with capital maintenance based on concepts other than money capital.

Realization is the process of formally recording or incorporating items in the accounts and financial reports of enterprises. The concept states that revenue is recognized when the earnings process is complete or virtually complete, and an exchange has taken place. Critics of realization view it as a barrier to reporting since it precludes the reporting of increases in wealth which have not been confirmed by an external market transaction.

Whilst realization concentrates on external transactions as the way to identify revenues to include in accounts, the accruals assumption provides the equivalent criterion for costs. Accruals and realization together provide the two pillars of conventional financial accounting. The accruals assumption requires that revenues recognized in a particular period should have deducted from them the expenses associated with the generation of that revenue. According to many critics conventional financial accounting has been too concerned with the achievement of a good matching between revenues and costs based on realization and accruals rather than on the usefulness of the resulting information to financial statement users.

Qualitative characteristics are applied by accountants to the operating assumptions to ensure that their measurements exhibit characteristics appropriate to the objectives of the financial reports containing those measurements. In the context of the objectives of financial reports discussed above, the interpretation of these qualitative characteristics is clear. However, two problems limit the satisfactory application of the concepts as guidelines. First, they may conflict, for example, relevance may be in conflict with objectivity and therefore, tradeoffs are necessary when applying them. Second, lack of knowledge about user needs has restricted the development of the relevance criterion. Instead, accounting concepts have focused on the need for objectivity, realiability and comparability in financial reports. In the absence of agreed accounting concepts the content, format and basis of financial reports may vary considerably from one situation to another, from one time period to another and from one management source to another. Important accounting concepts are entity, money measurement, going concern, cost, realization, accruals, periodicity, consistency, prudence, materiality and objectivity.

The extent to which the accounting assumptions and concepts discussed above apply outside profit-organizations varies considerably. At one extreme business-type public sector organizations such as nationalized industries largely adopt the accounting conventions consistent with the framework of assumptions and conventions. At the other extreme, central government adheres to a system of cash accounting. Between these extremes varying degrees of conventional commercial practice are adopted. For example, the health service applies accrual accounting principles in its income and expenditure reporting.

The regulation of financial reporting

The third influence on financial accounting and reporting is the framework of regulations. The regulation of financial reporting in the UK has traditionally relied on two main foundations: a general framework prescribed by law and the professional judgement, conventions, recommendations and standards of accountants and auditors and others involved in the financial reporting process. This mix of legislative and professional influence is typified by financial accounting and reporting for companies but applies almost equally in the public sector.

Legal regulation of companies

The history of legal regulation of company financial reporting in the UK contains regular changes and developments not only in the content of financial reports but additionally in the emphasis and objectives of the statutes. Since the first general legislation on companies enacted in 1844, numerous companies acts have introduced varying amounts of change into the legal requirements for accounting disclosure. The current framework is the result of legislation over a period of almost forty years beginning with the Companies Act 1948 which was added to by subsequent acts in 1967, 1976, 1980 and 1981. More recently, the Companies Act 1985 was enacted with the objective of consolidating these different statutes into a unified piece of legislation.

The introduction of the Companies Act 1948 marked a radical departure from the approach adopted in previous legislation. For the first time emphasis was placed on the importance of providing information in financial reports to assist in investment decisions. Amongst the major provisions of the act were: the subjection of the profit and loss account to audit; the requirement for group accounts; a considerable extension in the requirements regarding individual items of information which should be disclosed; and most importantly for subsequent developments in company financial reporting, the requirement that auditors report whether financial statements present a 'true and fair view' of the Company's financial position and profitability. The criterion of a 'true and fair view' superseded that of a 'true and correct view' which first appeared in 1844. The Companies Act 1948 provided that the 'true and fair view' shall override all other requirements of the Companies Act as to matters to be included in a company's financial reports. Despite its overriding importance the interpretation of the 'true and fair view' has not been without its difficulties.

In 1983 the Accounting Standards Committee (ASC) obtained a written opinion from counsel on the meaning of 'true and fair' with particular reference to the role of accounting standards. The ASC intends to take account of the opinion in all its future work. The opinion states that financial statements will not be true and fair unless the information they contain is sufficient in quantity and quality to satisfy the reasonable expectations of the readers to whom they are addressed. But the expectations of the readers will have been moulded by the practices of accountants because, by and large, they will expect to get what they ordinarily get and that, in turn, will depend upon the normal practices of accountants. Therefore, the courts will treat compliance with accepted accounting principles as prima facie evidence that the financial statements are true and fair. The opinion states that since the function of the ASC is to formulate what it considers should be generally accepted accounting principles, the value of a Statement of Standard Accounting Practice to a court is:

(*a*)   A statement of professional opinion which readers may expect in financial statements which are true and fair.
(*b*)   That readers expect financial statements to comply with standards.

The opinion concludes, therefore, that financial statements which depart from standards may be held not to be true and fair, unless a strong body of professional opinion opts out of applying the standard.

Legal regulation of public sector organizations

The law plays an equally important role in regulating the financial reports of public sector organizations. The central services of government departments are mainly provided for by supply grants voted annually by Parliament and are accounted for in annual appropriation accounts which set out the actual payments and receipts associated with the relevant service.

Although time has conferred a traditional character on the financial reports of central government the statutory basis for the accounts is provided by the Exchequer and Audit Department Act 1966 which prescribes that the system of cash amounting rather than accrual accounting is used in government departments.

Local authorities not only produce accounts but also provide considerable information to central government for its own purposes. Currently, the Local Government Act 1972, the Accounts and Audit Regulations Act 1974, the Local Government Planning Act 1980 and the Local Government Finance Act 1982 all make prescriptions about local authority accounts. The latter Act provided the basis for the auditor to state an opinion that the relevant financial reports 'present fairly' the income and expenditure position of the authority. This development promoted the concept of accounting standards in the financial accounts of local authorities.

Nationalized industries (including the water industry) each have their specific statutes in the form of Nationalization Acts. These acts have generally recognized the essentially commercial nature of the industries concerned by requiring their accounts to follow best commercial practice. This suggests that nationalized industry accounts should contain, as a minimum, the same kind of information as required by the Companies Acts and as enhanced by accounting standards. This tends to be confirmed by the practice of private sector auditor firms which audit nationalized industry accounts.

Health authorities are required by the National Health Service Act 1977 to submit statutory accounts to central government. These accounts are more similar to capital and revenue out turn forms submitted to central government by local authorities, than to financial reports presented to the public. However, reports of the latter kind are becoming more common as voluntary disclosures.

Accounting standards

Accounting standards, promulgated by the Accounting Standards Committee which was established in 1970, represent the latest element in private sector regulation of financial reporting. Although the accountancy profession had a lengthy history of interest in attempts to influence financial reporting standards, it was not until the 1940s that any significant action was undertaken. The quickening of interest by the accountancy profession (in the form of the Institute of Chartered Accountants in England and Wales (ICAEW)), was in response to the setting up by the Government of the Cohen Committee of Enquiry into company law. The ICAEW formed the opinion that the Cohen Committee was likely to propose a significant increase in legal regulation of financial reporting unless the accountancy profession took it upon itself to make improvements. The response of the ICAEW was to set up a Taxation and Financial Relations Committee in 1942 which, in the same year, published the first of twenty-nine Recommendations on accounting topics, the last of which was issued in November 1969. These Recommendations were not mandatory upon members of the ICAEW and frequently contained alternative approaches. The ICAEW stated that, even with the publication of the Recommendations, it remained '... a matter for each individual member to consider his responsibility in regard to accounts presented by directors'.

Although there is evidence that the Recommendations series succeeded in improving practice, there was continuing concern expressed about the variety of practice which the Recommendations allowed. The problems which might arise from a permissive attitude to accounting practice were highlighted by the accelerating volume of takeover activity in the 1950s and 1960s. A series of highly publicized takeover battles put public and government confidence in the accountancy profession under increasing strain and culminated in a crisis of confidence over the accounting implications of the GEC – AEI merger. The ICAEW reacted to the extensive criticism and the threat of legislation to tighten controls on accounting by issuing a 'Statement of Intent on Accounting Standards in the 1970s' which announced the setting up of a committee to set accounting standards.

In establishing the committee the ICAEW stated its intention to advance accounting standards along five lines as follows:

1   Narrowing the areas of difference and variety of accounting practice. This was to be achieved by publishing authoritative statements on best accounting practice.
2   Disclosure of accounting bases. This was to be required when accounts include significant items whose values depend upon judgement.
3   Disclosure of departures from established definitive accounting standards.
4   Wider exposure for major proposals on accounting standards.
5   Continuing programme for encouraging improved accounting standards in legal and regulatory measures.

In order to direct action along these lines of development, the committee was given the following terms of reference:

1   To publish consultative documents with the objective of maintaining and advancing accounting standards.
2   To publish consultative documents with the objective of maintaining and advancing accounting standards.
3   To propose to the councils of the governing bodies statements of standard accounting practice.
4   To consult as appropriate with representatives of finance, commerce, industry and government and other persons concerned with financial reporting.

Subsequently, the ICAEW was joined by other UK and Irish accountancy bodies in its standard setting activity, and together the professional bodies established the Accounting Standards Committee (ASC), known at first as the Accounting Standards Steering Committee.

In seeking to meet its terms of reference the ASC has set Statements of Standard Accounting Practice (SSAPs) by a process which has entailed effectively four elements: research; drafting; evaluation; and approval. Although significant changes have been introduced into the standard setting process in recent years these elements have been present in standard setting since the inception of the committee. Similar characteristics are to be found in the preparation of another type of document recently introduced by the ASC, the Statement of Recommended Practice (SORP). SORPs are designed to apply to matters of less general applicability than SSAPs and may be produced by the ASC itself or by groups of organizations representing an economic sector. In the case of the latter, if SORPs are judged to have been properly prepared, they will be 'franked' by the ASC.

The characteristics of the standard setting process, together with their institutional status, make SSAPs authoritative statements of financial accounting practice. Statements of Standard Accounting Practice, although prepared by the ASC, are issued by those professional accountancy bodies which provide members for the ASC. These bodies require their members to apply accounting standards in their work either as preparers of accounts or as auditors. Consequently, failure to meet this professional responsibility opens up the possibility of disciplinary sanction by an accountancy body.

It has been widely assumed that SSAPs are primarily applicable to company financial reports. This view is encouraged by the explanatory foreword to all SSAPs which states that the standards '... describe methods of accounting for application to all financial accounts intended to give a true and fair view of financial position on profit and loss'. Since 'true and fair' is strictly applicable only to companies, SSAPs may seem inapplicable to other organizations. However, there is growing evidence of the application of SSAPs to not-for-profit (NFP) organizations in recent years, as well as an increasing acceptance of the appropriateness of such applications. As one authoritative view has expressed it: 'It is our opinion that as far as possible all SSAPs, excluding of course those not relevant, are intended to apply to all enterprises, including charities and other non-profit organizations'. (Bird and Morgan-Jones, 1981.) 1982 saw the setting up of a sub-committee of the ASC to reconsider its approach to the setting of standards in the public sector. As a result of this sub-committee's recommendations, the ASC decided:

1 To initiate consultation with principal reporting groups and user groups within the public sector, as a basis for formulating a framework for developing accounting standards in the public sector.
2 To ensure that a statement is issued by authoritative persons within the public sector about the role of the ASC in such matters.
3 To issue a statement itself about its policies and objectives for facilitating the publication of accounting standards tailored to the requirements of principal divisions within the public sector, including the use of a system of franking.
4 To formulate a programme of work taking into account that already undertaken by the Public Sector Sub-Committee.

Some progress has already been made in the chosen direction, and it is now evident that NFP organizations have begun to accelerate the rate at which SSAPs are influencing their financial reports. These matters are discussed further in Chapter 10. At the time of writing the ASC has issued twenty-three SSAPs although not all remain operative. The requirements of nine of these accounting standards are considered in Chapter 3 with others being considered elsewhere in the text.

Questions

1 Discuss the main factors that have influenced the development of financial accounting.
2 Compare and contrast the characteristics of profit and non-profit organizations.
3 Discuss the role of accounting concepts and assumptions. How may they be classified?
4 What is meant by a 'true and fair view'?

5   Discuss the aims and purposes of the Statements of Standard Accounting Practice and the duties of members of the accounting profession in relation thereto.   (*15 marks*)

Institute of Chartered Accountants in England and Wales, Professional Examination I: Financial Accounting I

2 Companies – characteristics and disclosure requirements

In Chapter 1, we saw that the growth of the company sector played an important role in the development of the law regulating the form and content of published financial reports. The purpose of this chapter is to examine the classification, formation and disclosure requirements of the Companies Acts. Many of the topics introduced in this chapter will be considered in greater detail in the chapters that follow.

Classification of companies

The earliest companies which were formed required a royal charter to establish their existence. In the nineteenth century, as the company form became more common, they began to be established by a special Act of Parliament. Early water and electricity companies were established in this way. Today, by far the most usual and important form of company is one registered and incorporated under the provisions of the Companies Acts 1948–85.

Companies incorporated under the Companies Acts may be of three types:

(a) Unlimited in respect of its member's liabilities to contribute to the company's debts in the event of liquidation. This form is used by professional firms who want the tax advantages of incorporation and wish to avoid the need to render accounts for public inspection.

(b) Limited by shares, in which a member's liability is restricted to the amount unpaid on his shares.

(c) Limited by guarantee, in which a member's liability is restricted to the amount which he has guaranteed.

Unlimited companies and those limited by guarantee are comparatively rare and will not be dealt with in this book.

Until 1980 company law required that companies be either public or private. Over 90 per cent were private and such companies were defined by the Companies Act 1948 as those whose constitution:

(a)   Restricted the right to transfer shares.
(b)   Limited membership to fifty.
(c)   Prohibited public invitation to subscribe for its shares or debentures.

Any other company was held to be of the public variety and, therefore, the public company category was the residual one. The Companies Act 1980 reversed this residual role and laid down specific requirements for a public company and made any other company a private one. This follows the Second Directive on Company Law of the EEC in seeking to make public companies conform to a set of minimum standards not previously found in English law. To be registered as a public company the Companies Act 1980 required of a corporation that:

(a)   It should have at least two directors and a secretary.
(b)   The last three words of its name should be either 'public limited company' or the abbreviation plc, or their Welsh equivalents.
(c)   It should have a memorandum stating that it is a public company.
(d)   It should have an authorized share capital of at least £50,000 or such figures as the Secretary of State may specify.

In addition, for a company to do business and exercise its borrowing powers, it requires a certificate from the Registrar of Companies showing its compliance with requirements as to allotted share capital. The nominal value of this capital must not be less than that in (d) above, with not less than one quarter, plus the whole of any share premium, being received by the company (in cash or otherwise).

The characteristic features of the public company following the 1980 Act are, in addition to the minimum share capital requirements noted above, restrictions on the paying up and maintenance of capital, and prohibitions on the company entering into certain transactions with associated parties, such as directors. The key feature of the private limited company is that it is prevented from offering its shares or debentures for public subscription.

The new division of companies was introduced in 1981–2. Existing private companies which wished to continue as such were not required to take any action. 'Old' public companies, 'old' private companies wishing to become public, and 'old' public companies wishing to become private were all required to re-register.

A further distinction between companies was introduced by the Companies Act 1981 (CA 81) which classified them by size. *Small and medium-sized companies* are exempted from certain disclosure requirements, as considered later in this chapter.

Formation of companies

Before incorporation can take place two documents must be filed with the Registrar of Companies – the Memorandum of Association and the Articles of Association. The first lays down the rules which govern the company in its relations with the outside world. It contains the company's name, its registered address and objectives, a statement that the liability of its members is limited, and the total amount of share capital the company is allowed to issue. The second document is more concerned with the internal management of the company, setting out rules concerning the issue of shares by the directors, the conduct of meetings, the voting rights of shareholders and the declaration of dividends. Unlike partners, the members of a company are not involved in the day-to-day management of a company nor do they have the power to bind the company in contracts. Instead, the members appoint directors to act on their behalf and one purpose of the Articles is to define the rights and duties of directors.

Characteristics of limited liability companies

The main differences between the financial accounts of a company and those of a sole trader and partnership arise from the following:

(a) A company is a legal entity separate and distinct from its members. It may contract, sue and be sued in its own name.
(b) The equity capital is typically subscribed by shareholders who receive rewards in the form of dividend payments.
(c) Shareholders have the right to transfer their shares. Because the life of a company is not affected by changes in individual shareholders it is said to have perpetual succession.
(d) The privilege of limited liability means that once shareholders have paid the full nominal value of the shares they have agreed to take, they cannot be held responsible for any of the debts of the company which cannot be met from the company's assets.
(e) The management of a company is delegated to a board of directors.
(f) Each company has its own individual regulations registered in the form of its memorandum and articles of association.
(g) The profits of a company are subject to corporation tax.
(h) The affairs of a company are regulated by the Companies Acts.

Under these Acts, every company is required to keep proper books of accounts in respect of money received and expended, sales and purchases and assets and liabilities. Final accounts, comprising a profit and loss account and balance sheet, must be approved by the directors and signed on their behalf. These accounts must be 'delivered' to the Registrar and, in the case of public companies, 'laid' before the members in a general meeting. They must be accompanied by the report of the auditors and the report of the directors although the latter is not required for 'small' companies. Every public company is required to hold an annual general meeting in each year and not more than fifteen months must elapse between the date of one annual general meeting and the next. The period allowed for delivering and laying accounts is seven months after the end of the accounting reference period, or ten months in the case of a private company. An extension of three months may be granted by the Registrar to companies carrying on business or having interests outside the United Kingdom. Where at the end of the financial year a company has subsidiaries, accounts dealing with the financial performance of the company and its subsidiaries are required, and will normally take the form of group accounts, as discussed in Chapter 8.

A 'true and fair view'

As we saw in Chapter 1, disclosure in company accounts has been dominated by the requirement that they present a 'true and fair view'. Three major influences have dominated such disclosures:

(a) Company law which has prescribed legal requirements for a minimum level of disclosure in company accounts, and which provides the basis for this chapter.
(b) Stock Exchange requirements relating to listed companies only. These are contained in the Stock Exchange Listing Agreement which companies must sign before their securities can be given a Stock Exchange listing. These requirements are not considered in this book.
(c) Statements of Standard Accounting Practice (SSAPs) containing accounting and disclosure requirements approved by the professional accountancy bodies. Some of these are considered in Chapters 3, 6, 7, 8 and 9.

A 'true and fair view' is related to the full disclosure concept which holds that management should disclose all significant financial data on the premise that an informed person will not be misled. Therefore, any additional information necessary to give a true and fair view must be included in the accounts and, exceptionally, where compliance with any of the specific requirements of the Companies Acts would not give a 'true and fair view' the directors must depart from the requirements in order to do so. In such cases, particulars of the departure, the reasons for it and its effects must be disclosed in a note.

The development of company law

Although joint stock companies have a long history it was not until the mid-nineteenth century that legislation allowed them to become the dominant form of business organization. From the mid-nineteenth century there has been a regular succession of Companies Acts which have gradually extended the regulation of companies generally, and in particular, their accounting and financial reporting. Especially influential have been the Companies Acts 1948, 1967, 1976, 1980 and 1981. In addition to Companies Acts, the legal framework for company disclosure is provided by Statutory Instruments which are issued from time to time to modify or supplement existing Companies Acts. The five Acts just referred to were consolidated into one piece of legislation in the Companies Act 1985. In what follows we shall refer to the part of the 1985 Act in which particular legal requirements introduced by earlier legislation are now contained. Also, where appropriate, we shall indicate the earlier Companies Acts from which certain requirements are derived.

Two Companies Acts in particular are relevant to this book, those of 1980 and 1981. The main accounting requirements of the 1980 Act are considered in Chapters 4 and 5 as they refer to share capital and distributable profit. The 1981 Act will be considered next.

The influence of the Companies Act 1981

The Companies Act 1981 was a very influential piece of legislation as far as company financial reporting is concerned. The Companies Act 1981 (CA 81) implements the European Economic Community's Fourth Directive, which sought to harmonize the legal regulation of accounts in EEC member countries. This Directive applies only to the accounts of individual companies; group company accounts are dealt with by the Seventh Directive. However, CA 81 requires that group accounts should be prepared as far as possible to comply with the accounting rules laid down for individual companies. Accounting for groups is considered in Chapter 8.

CA 81 introduced four major changes in British company legislation. First, precise formats were prescribed for the first time in UK law and required disclosure of considerably more detail than was previously the case. Second, fundamental principles (i.e. concepts) for the preparation of published accounts were prescribed. Third, valuation rules were laid down for certain items included in published accounts. These rules allowed for the continued use of historical cost but alternative valuation rules were included for companies wishing to prepare statutory accounts on an inflation adjusted basis. Fourth, a distinction was drawn between the publicity and filing requirements of different companies according to their size. It should be noted that the fundamental principles and rules did not differ from those generally followed in practice; they merely represented a shift from non-statutory to statutory regulation.

We shall now briefly consider the main aspects of these four changes as they are now represented in the Companies Act 1985 (CA 85).

Prescribed formats for annual accounts

Section 227 of CA 85 requires that the directors of every company prepare a profit and loss account for the company's accounting period, together with a balance sheet as at the last day of the company's financial year. The accounts prepared to satisfy this requirement must, following CA 81, conform to the requirements of Schedule 4 of CA 85. Schedule 4 CA 85, which also covers any additional information which may be provided by way of notes to the accounts, contains four formats prescribed for the profit and loss account (illustrated in Figures 2.1, 2.2, 2.3 and 2.4, and two formats prescribed for the balance sheet (illustrated in Figures 2.5 and 2.6).

According to Schedule 4 the following rules must be adhered to:

(a) Every profit and loss account and balance sheet of a company must show the items listed in one of the formats prescribed.

(b) When a format has been chosen the directors of the company must adopt the same format in preparing the financial statements for subsequent financial years unless in their opinion there are special reasons for the change. Such reasons must be explained in a note to the accounts.

(c) Items may be shown in greater detail than that required by the format adopted.

(d) Other items may be included if not covered by any of the headings listed in the format, although restrictions are placed on specific items being treated as assets in any balance sheet. These are considered below.

(e) The directors of a company are required to adapt the arrangement of headings and sub-headings, as well as the headings and sub-headings themselves, where the special nature of a company's business requires it.

(f) Items to which Arabic numbers are assigned in any of the formats may be combined in a company's accounts for any financial year if either:

(i) Their individual amounts are not material to assessing the state of affairs or profit and loss of the company for the year or,

(ii) The combination facilitates that assessment.

But in the case of (ii) the individual amounts of items so combined shall be disclosed in a note to the accounts.

(g) A format heading shall not be included if there is no amount to be shown for that item in respect of the financial year to which the profit and loss account and balance sheet relates.

(h) For every item in a company's profit and loss account corresponding items must be shown for the financial year immediately preceding. If items are not comparable, those for the preceding year must be adjusted and the reasons for adjustment disclosed in a note to the accounts.

(*i*) Amounts representing assets or income may not be offset against items representing liabilities or expenditure or vice versa.

Accounting principles

CA 81 required that the amounts included in respect of all items shown in a company's accounts should be determined in accordance with five accounting principles. These principles are set out in Part II of Schedule 4 of the CA 85. The principles are as follows. First, the company shall be presumed to be carrying on its business as a going concern. Second, all accounting principles shall be applied consistently from one financial year to the next. Third, the amount of any item shall be determined on a prudent basis, and in particular:

(*a*) Only profits realized at the balance sheet date shall be included in the profit and loss account.
(*b*) All liabilities and losses which have arisen or are likely to arise in respect of the financial year to which the accounts relate, or to a previous financial year, shall be taken into account, including those which only become apparent between the balance sheet date and the date on which it is signed on behalf of the board of directors.

Fourth, all income and charges relating to the financial year to which the accounts relate shall be taken into account without regard to the date of receipt or payment (i.e. the application of the accruals concept).

Fifth, in determining the aggregate amount to be shown in respect of any item in the accounts the amount of each individual component asset or liability must be determined separately.

The first four of these principles, going concern, consistency, prudence and accruals are the four fundamental accounting principles contained in the Accounting Standards Committee's Statement of Standard Accounting Practice Number 2, *Disclosure of Accounting Policies*. In conjunction with other accounting standards SSAP2 will be examined in Chapter 3. As we noted at the beginning of this chapter the overriding requirement governing the preparation of company accounts is that they present a true and fair view. Section 228 of CA 85, together with Paragraph 15 of Part II of Schedule 4 to CA 85, permit the directors of a company to depart from any of the requirements relating to the balance sheet and profit and loss account in order to present a true and fair view. If this is done, it is necessary to give particulars of the departure and the reasons for it in a note to the accounts. The Department of Trade and Industry, the government department responsible for company matters, has stated that departures from statutory requirements are not permissible to facilitate compliance with accounting standards.

Valuation rules

CA 81 reaffirmed that historical cost of purchase or production was the primary basis of valuing assets but introduced alternative accounting rules to historical cost. The historical cost accounting rules are set out in Section B of Part II of Schedule 4 of CA 85 whilst the alternative accounting rules are in Part C.

Historical cost valuation rules

Separate rules are set out for fixed assets and current assets. For fixed assets valuation is based upon purchase price or production cost. Purchase price is defined to include expenses incidental to the acquisition. Production cost is defined to include all costs directly attributable to the production of the asset and may also include a reasonable proportion of indirect costs as well as any interest paid on money borrowed to finance the asset in question. The inclusion of distribution cost is specifically prohibited.

Fixed assets, in terms of the Act, include tangible assets and intangible assets such as deferred development costs and goodwill and also long-term investments. All fixed assets which have a limited useful economic life must be depreciated systematically over the period of the asset's useful economic life. Long-term investments may be written down to reflect current market value. Any fixed asset must be written down where the diminution in value is thought to be permenent, and such provisions, if any, must be written back when they no longer become necessary. Provisions made and amounts written back must be disclosed either in a note or on the face of the profit and loss account.

Development cost may only be carried forward as an asset in 'special circumstances' (which are not described). If amounts are carried forward as an asset, notes to the financial statements must disclose the period over which the capitalized costs are written off and the reasons for capitalizing them. Where goodwill acquired by a company is shown or included as an asset in the company's balance sheet it must be reduced systematically by provision for depreciation over a period chosen by the directors but which does not exceed its useful economic life. The period chosen and the reasons for choosing it must be disclosed in the notes. This provision does not apply in goodwill arising on consolidation which is discussed in Chapter 8. Other expenses, such as preliminary expenses, expenses in connection with a share or debenture issue and costs of research, must not be capitalized.

Current assets should be stated at the lower of purchase price (or production cost) and net realizable value. Provisions for reduction to net realizable must be written back to the extent that they are no longer required. The Act specifies that stocks should be valued using a method thought appropriate to the circumstances of the company by the directors and drawn from a list comprising FIFO, LIFO weighted average cost or any other similar method. Any material difference between the revaluation of stock resulting from the chosen method and its current replacement cost must be disclosed.

Alternative valuation rules

Alternative valuation rules which essentially adopt current cost methods are permitted. The rules are as follows:

(a)   Intangible fixed assets, other than goodwill, may be included at their current cost.
(b)   Tangible fixed assets may be included at a market value determined as at the date of their last valuation or at their current cost.
(c)   Investments may be stated at market value at the date of their last valuation or at a value determined on any basis which appears appropriate to the directors. If the latter is adopted details of the valuation method must be disclosed together with the reasons for choosing it.
(d)   Stocks may be included at current cost.

In any of the above cases disclosure must be made of:

(a)   The items affected and the basis of valuation adopted.
(b)   The comparable historical cost amount for each of the affected items (except stocks) or the difference between the historical cost amount and the amount shown.

Where any asset's value is determined on the basis of the alternative valuation rules, that value must be the basis for the determination of depreciation provisions. If an asset is valued on the alternative rules, any profit or loss arising on this valuation is to be credited or debited to a special reserve known as the revaluation reserve. The revaluation reserve shall be reduced to the extent that amounts standing as credits to the reserve are no longer necessary for the purpose of the accounting policies adopted by the company, but amounts may only be transferred from the reserve to the profit and loss account if either the amount in question was previously charged to that account or it represents realized profit. The tax treatment of amounts credited or debited to the revaluation reserve must be disclosed in a note to the accounts.

Provisions on disclosure of modified accounts

CA 81 introduced provisions which allowed companies of different sizes to prepare and deliver modified accounts. These provisions are contained in Sections 247–50 of CA 85. Company law now allows small and medium-sized companies to file modified accounts with the Registrar of Companies, although they must still prepare accounts in full form for presentation to their members. To qualify as small or medium-sized, companies must meet two or more criteria both for the current year and the preceding one. The criteria are as shown in Table 2.1.

Table 2.1   *Criteria to qualify as a small or medium-sized company*

	Small company	Medium-sized company
Turnover not exceeding	£1.4 m	£5.75 m
Balance sheet total not exceeding	£0.7 m	£2.8 m
Employees less than	50	250

Table 2.2

	Small companies	*Medium-sized companies*
Directors' report	Not required	Required in full
Profit and loss account	Not required	May commence with 'gross profit' by combining: items 1, 2, 3 and 6 Format 1, items 1–5, Format 2
Balance sheet	Only main headings and amounts are required, but aggregate debtors/ creditors due after more than one year must be disclosed.	Required in full
Notes to the accounts	Only the following required: (*a*) Accounting policies (*b*) Share capital (*c*) Allotments (*d*) Particulars of debts (*e*) Basis of foreign currency translation	Analysis of turnover and profits not required
Particulars of salaries of directors and higher and employees	Not required	Required

The modified reporting available to companies meeting the criteria are set out in Table 2.1. The accounting items referred to in the table relate to the detailed reporting requirements required by law, and to which we now turn.

Detailed reporting requirements

Profit and loss account

As we noted above, four formats are specified for the profit and loss account (see Figures 2.1, 2.2, 2.3 and 2.4). The major difference between the formats is the method of classifying expense items. Formats 1 and 3 (Figures 2.1 and 2.3) analyse expenses on an operational basis (e.g. cost of sales, gross profit, distribution costs, administrative expenses). Formats 2 and 4 (Figures 2.2 and 2.4) analyse expenses by type of expenditure (e.g. raw materials and consumables, changes in stocks, wages and salaries). Schedule A to CA 85 stipulates that every profit and loss account of a company must disclose the following items even though they do not appear in the formats:

(a) Profit and loss on ordinary activities before taxation.
(b) Transfers and proposed transfers to and from reserves.
(c) The aggregate amount of dividends paid and proposed.

In addition to the items just noted, CA 85 specifies other items of information not included in the formats which must none the less be shown either in the profit and loss account or in the notes thereto. Where appropriate these will be referred to in what follows.

```
 1  Turnover
 2  Cost of sales
 3  Gross profit or loss
 4  Distribution costs
 5  Administrative expenses
 6  Other operating income
 7  Income from shares in group companies
 8  Income from shares in related companies
 9  Income from other fixed asset investments
10  Other interest receivable and similar income
11  Amounts written off investments
12  Interest payable and similar charges
13  Tax on profit or loss on ordinary activities
14  Profit or loss on ordinary activities after taxation
15  Extraordinary income
16  Extraordinary charges
17  Extraordinary profit or loss
18  Tax on extraordinary profit or loss
19  Other taxes not shown under the above items
20  Profit or loss for the financial year
```

Figure 2.1 *Profit and loss account – Format 1*

```
     1   Turnover
     2   Change in stocks of finished goods and in work in progress
     3   Own work capitalized
     4   Other operating income
     5   (a)  Raw materials and consumables
         (b)  Other external charges
     6   Staff costs
         (a)  Wages and salaries
         (b)  Social security costs
         (c)  Other pension costs
     7   (a)  Depreciation and other amounts written off tangible and
              intangible fixed assets
         (b)  Exceptional amounts written off current assets
     8   Other operating charges
     9   Income from shares in group companies
    10   Income from shares in related companies
    11   Income from other fixed asset investments
    12   Other interest receivable and similar income
    13   Amounts written off investments
    14   Interest payable and similar charges
    15   Tax on profit or loss on ordinary activities
    16   Profit or loss on ordinary activities after taxation
    17   Extraordinary income
    18   Extraordinary charges
    19   Extraordinary profit or loss
    20   Tax on extraordinary profit or loss
    21   Other taxes not shown under the above items
    22   Profit or loss for the financial year
```

Figure 2.2   *Profit and loss account – Format 2*

Turnover

Turnover is defined as the amounts derived from the provision of goods and services falling within the company's ordinary activities after deduction of trade discounts, value added tax and other sales based tax (e.g. excise duty). Therefore, it is not permissible to describe the amount of turnover inclusive of VAT merely as 'turnover' in the accounts.

The amount of VAT may still be shown in a note, if desired.

Cost of sales, distribution costs and administrative expenses

Formats 1 and 3 require the disclosure of cost of sales, distribution costs and administrative expenses as separate items. Cost of sales includes the cost of raw materials consumed, direct labour, fixed and variable factory overheads and depreciation of machinery. Distribution costs include sales salaries, advertising and promotional costs, warehousing costs and transportation costs (including depreciation on motor vehicles).

A   Charges

1   Cost of sales
2   Distribution costs
3   Administrative expenses
4   Amounts written off investments
5   Interest payable and similar charges
6   Tax on profit or loss on ordinary activities
7   Profit or loss on ordinary activities after taxation
8   Extraordinary charges
9   Tax on extraordinary profit or loss
10   Other taxes not shown under the above items
11   Profit or loss for the financial year

B   Income

1   Turnover
2   Other operating income
3   Income from shares in group companies
4   Income from shares in related companies
5   Income from other fixed asset investments
6   Other interest receivable and similar income
7   Profit or loss on ordinary activities after taxation
8   Extraordinary income
9   Profit or loss for the financial year

Figure 2.3   *Profit and loss account – Format 3*

Administrative expenses cover all items not already included in the cost of sales or in distribution costs. Typically, administrative expenses will include administrative and office salaries, administrative building costs (including depreciation and maintenance), legal expenses, amounts written off bad debts, and stationery and printing costs.

Staff costs
The aggregate of each of the following amounts must be disclosed in the notes if Formats 1 and 3 are adopted:

(*a*)   Wages and salaries
(*b*)   Social security costs
(*c*)   Pension costs

In Formats 2 and 4 these items are shown on the face of the profit and loss account.

Depreciation and other amounts written off fixed assets
Provisions for depreciation must be disclosed either in a note to the financial statements (under Formats 1 and 3), or on the face of the profit

A   Charges

1   Reduction in stocks of finished goods and in work in progress
2   (*a*)   Raw materials and consumables
     (*b*)   Other external charges
3   Staff costs:
     (*a*)   Wages and salaries
     (*b*)   Social security costs
     (*c*)   Other pension costs
4   (*a*)   Depreciation and other amounts written off tangible and
             intangible fixed assets
     (*b*)   Exceptional amounts written off current assets
5   Other operating charges
6   Amounts written off investments
7   Interest payable and similar charges
8   Tax on profit or loss on ordinary activities
9   Profit or loss on ordinary activities after taxation
10   Extraordinary charges
11   Tax on extraordinary profit or loss
12   Other taxes not shown under the above items
13   Profit or loss for the financial year

B   Income

1   Turnover
2   Increase in stocks of finished goods and in work-in-progress
3   Own work capitalized
4   Other operating income
5   Income from shares in group companies
6   Income from shares in related companies
7   Income from other fixed asset investments
8   Other interest receivable and similar income
9   Profit or loss on ordinary activities after taxation
10   Extraordinary income
11   Profit or loss for the financial year

Figure 2.4   *Profit and loss account – Format 4*

and loss account (under Formats 2 and 4). The provision of CA 85 that
'all fixed assets which have a limited useful economic life must be
systematically written off by provisions for depreciation made over
their estimated useful life' is fully consistent with SSAP12, *Accounting
for Depreciation*, which is considered in Chapter 3.

Other investment income
The four formats require income from other fixed asset investments and
other interest receivable and similar income to be shown separately.
Income from listed investments must be separately identified in the
notes if not in the profit and loss accounts, as indicated below.

Amounts written off investments
This item is required to be shown on the face of the profit and loss account by all formats. Where a fixed asset investment has diminished in value, a provision for the diminution in its value may be made. However, the Act states that where the reduction in value of any fixed asset (including investments) is expected to be permanent, a provision for the diminution in its value must be made. This rules that no asset may be stated at a net amount in excess of its estimated, recoverable amount. Where the reasons for any provision for diminution in value no longer apply the provision must be written back to the extent that it is no longer necessary.

Profit or loss on ordinary activities before taxation
At the beginning of this section we stated that this item must be shown on the face of the profit and loss account. The figure reported must represent the balance of all previously mentioned items including exceptional items (see below) that relate to the ordinary activities of the company, but excluding taxation and extraordinary items (see below).

Taxation
The issues raised by accounting for taxation are considered in detail in Chapter 6, and the disclosures required in notes to the profit and loss account are set out later in this chapter.

Appropriation of profit
The following items must be disclosed separately.

(*a*)   Any amounts that have been set aside for:
    (*i*)   The redemption of share capital.
    (*ii*)   The redemption of loans.
(*b*)   Any amount that has been set aside or withdrawn from reserves.
(*c*)   The aggregate amount of any dividends that have been paid and have been proposed must be stated.

    The treatment of dividends in the accounts and the redemption of share capital and loans are considered further in Chapters 4 and 5.

Notes to the profit and loss account

Paragraphs 53 to 57 of Schedule 4 of CA 85 require information which either supplements the information given with respect to particular items shown in the profit and loss account or provides particulars of a company's income and expenditure or information on circumstances affecting profit and loss account items.

Disaggregated turnover and profit
If a company carries on two or more classes of business that, in the opinion of directors, differ substantially, it must disclose:

(*a*)   A description of each class.
(*b*)   The amount of turnover attributed to each class.
(*c*)   The amount of the profit or loss before taxation that the directors consider is attributable to each class.

Where the company supplies markets that, in the opinion of the directors, differ substantially from each other, the amount of turnover attributed to each market shall be disclosed. 'Market' for the purpose of the Act means a market geographically delimited. Where the directors consider that disclosure of disaggregated information would be seriously prejudicial to the interests of the company, such information need not be disclosed, but the fact that the information is not disclosed must be stated.

Staff
In addition to the information on staff costs given on the face of the profit and loss account companies are required to disclose:

(*a*)   The average number of persons employed by the company in the financial year.
(*b*)   The average number of persons employed by categories of employment, which the directors are required to select having regard to the way in which the company's activities are organized (e.g. by geographic location or class of business).

Specific items of income and expenditure
A note to the profit and loss account should state separately the amounts for:

(*a*)   Bank loans and overdrafts, and loans made to the company (other than bank loans and overdrafts) which:
   (*i*)   Are repayable otherwise than by instalments and fall due for repayment within five years at the end of the financial year; or
   (*ii*)   Are repayable by instalments, the last of which falls due for payment before the end of that period.
(*b*)   Loans to any other kind of company.

In addition, information must be given about amounts set aside for redemption of share capital and loans, income from listed investments, and rents from land where they form a substantial part of the company's revenue for the year.

CA 85 also specifies that amounts payable for the hire of plant and equipment be disclosed, as must be the renumeration of the company's auditors.

Particulars of taxation
The notes to the profit and loss account must state the basis upon which the charge for UK corporation tax and income tax is computed, together with particulars of any special circumstances affecting liability

to taxation in the present year or in succeeding years. In addition, the following amounts must be stated:

(a) The charge for UK corporation tax, whether that amount would have been greater but for double taxation relief, and if so, what the charge would have been.
(b) The charge for UK income tax.
(c) The taxation charges imposed outside the UK.

Balance sheet

Two balance sheet formats are permitted by CA 85 and these are shown in Figures 2.5 and 2.6. Both require the same basic disclosure and differ principally in that Format 1 adopts a vertical presentation and Format 2 a horizontal presentation. The requirements relating to particular balance sheet items will now be discussed.

Fixed assets
Fixed assets are defined as those assets intended for use on a continuing basis in the company's activities. As we noted above, these assets may be valued under the historical cost accounting rules or the alternative accounting rules. Additional disclosures for fixed assets are specified for the notes to the balance sheet. These are discussed below.

Intangible assets
These must be included on the face of the balance sheet under this main heading, with the following sub-headings included either on the face of the balance sheet or in a note. The following intangible assets are defined in the Act: development costs; concessions, patents, licences, trade marks and similar rights and assets; goodwill and payments on account.

Development costs may only be included as an asset in 'special circumstances'. The CA 85 does not define these 'special circumstances'. SSAP13, *Accounting for Research and Development*, provides criteria for the capitalization of development costs and these include the clear identification of a project and the clear identification of specific related expenditure. If amounts are carried forward additional disclosures are required in the notes. These are considered below.

Purchased goodwill (excluding goodwill on consolidation) may be capitalized and treated as an asset. Where this is the case, goodwill must be written off over its useful economic life and the period chosen for its life together with the reasons for choosing that period must be stated. SSAP22, *Accounting for Goodwill*, follows these legal requirements.

Concessions, patents, licences, trade marks and similar rights and assets may only be included in a company's balance sheet if either the assets were acquired for valuable consideration, or they were created by the company itself.

A   Called up share capital not paid

B   Fixed assets

  I   Intangible assets
    1   Development costs
    2   Concessions, patents, licences, trade marks and similar rights and assets
    3   Goodwill
    4   Payments on account

 II   Tangible assets
    1   Land and buildings
    2   Plant and machinery
    3   Fixtures, fittings, tools and equipment
    4   Payments on account and assets in course of construction

III   Investments
    1   Shares in group companies
    2   Loans to group companies
    3   Shares in related companies
    4   Loans to related companies
    5   Other investments other than loans
    6   Other loans
    7   Own shares

C   Current assets

  I   Stocks
    1   Raw materials and consumables
    2   Work-in-progress
    3   Finished goods and goods for resale
    4   Payments on account

 II   Debtors
    1   Trade debtors
    2   Amounts owed by group companies
    3   Amounts owed by related companies
    4   Other debtors
    5   Called up share capital not paid
    6   Prepayments and accrued income

III   Investments
    1   Shares in group companies
    2   Own shares
    3   Other investments

 IV   Cash at bank and in hand

D   Prepayments and accrued income

E   Creditors: amounts falling due within one year

1   Debenture loans
2   Bank loans and overdrafts
3   Payments received on account
4   Trade creditors
5   Bills of exchange payable
6   Amounts owed to group companies
7   Amounts owed to related companies
8   Other creditors including taxation and social security
9   Accruals and deferred income

F   Net current assets (liabilities)

G   Total assets less current liabilities

H   Creditors: amounts falling due after more than one year

1   Debenture loans
2   Bank loans and overdrafts
3   Payments received on account
4   Trade creditors
5   Bills of exchange payable
6   Amounts owed to group companies
7   Amounts owed to related companies
8   Other creditors including taxation and social security
9   Accruals and deferred income

I   Provisions for liabilities and charges

1   Pensions and similar obligations
2   Taxation, including deferred taxation
3   Other provisions

J   Accruals and deferred income

K   Capital and reserves

 I   *Called up share capital*
 II   *Share premium account*
III   *Revaluation reserve*
IV   *Other reserves*
    1   Capital redemption reserve
    2   Reserve for own shares
    3   Reserves provided for by the articles of association
    4   Other reserves
 V   *Profit and loss account*

Figure 2.5   *Balance sheet – Format 1*

Assets

A Called up share capital not paid

B Fixed assets

  I Intangible assets

    1 Development costs

    2 Concessions, patents, licences, trade marks and similar rights and assets

    3 Goodwill

    4 Payments on account

  II Tangible assets

    1 Land and buildings

    2 Plant and machinery

    3 Fixtures, fittings, tools and equipment

    4 Payments on account and assets in course of construction

  III Investments

    1 Shares in group companies

    2 Loans to group companies

    3 Shares in related companies

    4 Loans to related companies

    5 Other investments other than loans

    6 Other loans

    7 Own shares

C Current assets

  I Stocks

    1 Raw materials and consumables

    2 Work-in-progress

    3 Finished goods and goods for resale

    4 Payments on account

  II Debtors

    1 Trade debtors

    2 Amounts owed by group companies

    3 Amounts owed by related companies

    4 Other debtors

    5 Called up share capital not paid

    6 Prepayments and accrued income

  III Investments

    1 Shares in group companies

    2 Own shares

    3 Other investments

  IV Cash at bank and in hand

D Prepayments and accrued income

Liabilities

A Capital and reserves

  I Called up share capital

  II Share premium account

  III Revaluation reserve

  IV Other reserves

    1 Capital redemption reserve

    2 Reserve for own shares

    3 Reserves provided for by the articles of association

    4 Other reserves

  V Profit and loss account

B Provisions for liabilities and charges

    1 Pensions and similar obligations

    2 Taxation including deferred taxation

    3 Other provisions

C Creditors

    1 Debenture loans

    2 Bank loans and overdrafts

    3 Payments received on account

    4 Trade creditors

    5 Bills of exchange payable

    6 Amounts owed to group companies

    7 Amounts owed to related companies

    8 Other creditors including taxation and social security

    9 Accruals and deferred income

D Accruals and deferred income

Note: Liabilities may alternatively be shown below assets or on a separate page.

Figure 2.6 *Balance sheet – Format 2*

32

Tangible fixed assets
The amounts of the following fixed assets must be shown either on the face of the balance sheet (or in the notes thereto): land buildings; plant and machinery, fixtures, fittings, tools and equipment; payments on account and assets in course of construction. The category 'land and buildings' must be sub-divided (in the notes) into freehold, long lease-hold (over fifty years) and short leasehold.

Investments
The formats show that investments may be reported either in the category of fixed assets or that of current assets. Investments intended to be retained by a company on a continuing basis should be treated as fixed assets while any other investments should be listed under current assets.

Stocks and work-in-progress
As we stated previously, the valuation rules require that current assets be included at the lower of purchase price or production cost and net realizable value. Also, they require that where current assets have been written down but where the reason for the write down no longer applies either in full or in part, the provision must be written back to the extent that it is no longer necessary. CA 85 defines 'purchase price' as the actual price of the asset plus any expenses incidental to its acquisition. The production cost of an asset is determined by including all production costs directly attributable to the costs of the asset together with a reasonable proportion of indirect costs together with any interest on capital borrowed to finance the production of the asset. Distribution cost must not be included in the production costs.

Stocks and work-in-progress should be sub-classified in the balance sheet (or in the notes) in a manner appropriate to the business, but must include: raw materials and consumables; work-in-progress; finished goods and goods for resale; and payments on account. This provision incorporates SSAP9, *Accounting for Stocks and Work-in-Progress*, which calls for an analysis of stock by categories. However, SSAP9 is more specific about certain requirements. CA 85 allows the use of FIFO, LIFO weighted average price, and similar methods for valuing stocks and the method chosen must appear to the directors to be appropriate. Whichever method the directors of a company choose any material differences between the amount stated and replacement cost or most recent actual cost (if this latter comparison is considered appropriate by the directors) must be disclosed.

Debtors
Debtors must be disclosed as a main heading on the balance sheet and the following items must be disclosed on the face of the balance sheet (or in the notes thereto): trade debtors; amounts owed by group companies; amounts owed by related companies; other debtors; called up share capital not paid; prepayments and accrued income. Additionally,

the aggregate of debtors is to be sub-divided between amounts due within one year and amounts falling due after more than one year.

Creditors
CA 85 requires creditors to be shown under the following sub-headings on the face of the balance sheet (or in the notes thereto): debenture loans; bank loans and overdrafts; payments received on account; trade creditors; bills of exchange payable; amounts owed to group companies; amounts owed to related companies; other creditors including taxation and social security; and accruals and deferred income.

The aggregate of creditors is to be sub-divided between amounts due within and after one year. The treatment of creditors differs from that of debtors since those of the former falling due within one year are to be shown as a deduction from current assets in Format 1, and creditors falling due after one year are to be deducted from total assets less current liabilities. The term 'current liabilities' disappears except in the balance sheet caption 'total assets less current liabilities'.

Provisions for liabilities and charges
This item must be shown on the face of the balance sheet as a main heading and the following sub-headings must be disclosed either on the face of the balance sheet or in the notes thereto: pensions and similar obligations; taxation (including deferred taxation); other provisions. The Act defines a provision of liabilities and charges as 'an amount retained as reasonably necessary for the purpose of providing for any liability or loss which is either likely to be incurred or certain to be incurred, but uncertain as to amount or as to the date on which it will arise'.

Share capital and reserves
This section is sub-divided under the headings of called up share capital, share premium account, revaluation reserve, other reserves (capital redemption reserve, reserve for own shares, reserves provided for by the articles of association, other reserves) and profit and loss account. The characteristics of share capital and reserves are considered in Chapters 4 and 5.

Notes to the balance sheet

Paragraphs 37 to 51 of Schedule 4 to CA 85 set out requirements for information which supplements information given for particular items in the balance sheet, or is relevant to assessing the company's state of affairs. The supplementary disclosures will now be considered under various headings.

Fixed assets
With respect to each item which is shown under the general item 'fixed assets' in the balance sheet the following information should be given in notes to the balance sheet:

In respect of each fixed asset item there must be shown: the aggregate cost or valuation at the beginning and end of the financial year; any revaluations during the year; acquisitions and disposals during the year; and any transfers to and from reserves.

Where a fixed asset is depreciated disclosure is required of: the cumulative provisions at the beginning and end of the year; the annual depreciation provision; any adjustment resulting from the disposal of assets; and any other adjustments to the provision.

Where fixed assets (other than listed investments) are included at a valuation the following information is to be given: the years in which the assets were valued; the amount of each valuation; the names or qualifications of the valuers and the bases of valuation used.

For every item shown under the heading of investments, whether fixed or current assets, disclosure must be made of the amount attributable to: investments listed on a recognized stock exchange; investments listed on any other stock exchange; and unlisted investments.

Where listed investments are disclosed, there must also be stated: the aggregate market value where it differs from the amount included in the accounts, and the stock exchange value, where this is taken to be lower than the market value.

Where, at the end of its financial year, an investor company holds more than 10 per cent of the nominal value of the allotted share capital of another company; or more than 10 per cent of the nominal value of any class of allotted equity shares in another company; or an amount of shares in another company which constitutes more than 10 per cent of the investor company's assets, the following information regarding the investment must be disclosed by a note to the accounts:

(a) The name of the company in which the shares are held.
(b) The country of incorporation of that company (or country of registration in the case of a company incorporated in Great Britain).
(c) The identity and proportion of the nominal value of each class.

Creditors
Additionally, the following disclosures are required:

(a) In respect of each item shown under 'creditors' in the balance sheet (whether due within one year or more), there must be stated:

   (i) The aggregate amount of any debts included under that item in respect of which any security has been given.
   (ii) An indication of the nature of the securities so given.

(b) In respect of each item shown under 'creditors' and falling due after more than one year there must be stated:

   (i) The aggregate amounts of debt which are payable or repayable otherwise than by instalments and fall due for payment or repayment after the end of five years from the end of the financial year; and payable or repayable by instalments any of which fall due for payment after the end of the period.

> (*ii*)   The terms of payment or repayment and the rate of interest payable on each date.

(*c*)   The aggregate amount which is recommended for distribution by way of dividend must be disclosed in a note to the profit and loss account. However, where arrears exist of fixed cumulative dividends the amount of arrears and the period for which they are in arrears must be disclosed in a note to the balance sheet.

With respect to debenture loans, the following items must be detailed: convertible loans must be shown separately, for any debentures issued during the year, the reason for making the issue, the amount, class and consideration received for the issue must be shown, particulars must be given of any redeemed debentures which the company has power to reissue, where any of the company's debentures are held by nominees of, or trustees for, the company, the nominal amount and the book value of the holding must be disclosed.

Share capital and reserves
Additionally, the following details are required:

(*a*)   The amount of allotted share capital and the amount of called up share capital which has been paid up must each be shown separately.

(*b*)   The authorized share capital and, where shares of more than one class have been allotted, the number and aggregate nominal value of share of each class allotted.

(*c*)   For any shares allotted during the year, the reason for making the allotment, the classes and number of each class allotted and their aggregate nominal value must be given.

(*d*)   For redeemable shares the earliest and latest dates of redemption, whether redemption is mandatory or at the option of the company, and the premium, if any, payable on redemption.

(*e*)   For options to subscribe for shares, the number, description, and amount of shares, period exercisable and price to be paid.

(*f*)   Where any amount is transferred to or from any reserves and the reserves are shown as separate items in the company's balance sheet, the following information is required:

> (*i*)   The amount of reserves at the beginning and end of the financial year.
>
> (*ii*)   Any amounts transferred to or from the reserves during the year.
>
> (*iii*)   The source and application of any amounts so transferred.

Where any asset is revalued under any of the alternative accounting rules, any difference between the revalued amount and the previous book amount must be credited or debited to a revaluation reserve. Only profits realized at the balance sheet date may be included in the profit and loss account.

Guarantees and financial commitments

The following information, if not included in the accounts, must be given in the notes.

(a) Particulars of any charge on the assets of the company to secure the liabilities of any person, including where practicable, the amount secured.

(b) The estimated amount of future capital expenditure.

    (i) Contracted but not provided for.

    (ii) Authorized but not contracted for.

(c) Pension commitments, both provided for and not provided for, giving separately details of commitments in respect of past directors.

(d) Particulars of other financial commitments which are not provided for in the accounts but which are relevant to assessing the company's state of affairs.

Particulars must be given of each 'other provision' included under this item in the balance sheet in any case where the amount of that provision is material.

The following information must be given with respect to any contingent liability not provided for:

(a) The amount or estimated amount of that liability.

(b) Its legal nature.

(c) Whether any valuable security has been provided by the company in connection with that liability and, if so, what. SSAP18, *Accounting for Contingencies*, adds to these disclosure requirements. This standard is considered in Chapter 3.

Loans and other transactions with directors and company officers

Schedule 6 of CA 85 requires the disclosure of information on loans or other transactions with directors, as follows:

(a) Full details of loans to and other transactions with directors and connected persons must be disclosed in accordance with the requirements of CA 85.

(b) The number of officers (other than directors) who were liable to the company, and the aggregate amount outstanding under the following categories: loans, quasi-loans and credit transactions. An amount not exceeding £2,500 in respect of any officer may be ignored.

(c) Where a company makes loans to employees (other than directors) or provides money in accordance with an employees' share scheme for the acquisition of fully paid shares in the company or its holding company, the aggregate amount of outstanding loans must be disclosed.

In addition to more detailed information supporting that disclosed in the balance sheet and profit and loss account, CA 85 requires:

(a) The accounting policies followed by a company in determining the amounts of profit and loss and balance sheet items must be stated. In particular, details are required of the policies adopted with regard to goodwill, the depreciation and diminution in value of assets, and the basis of translating foreign currencies into sterling.

(b) Corresponding amounts for the preceding financial year must be shown for every item in the balance sheet, profit and loss account and notes to the accounts. Where a corresponding amount would not be comparable with the current year item, an adjusted corresponding amount must be shown, particulars of the adjustment and the reasons for it being included in a note.

Directors' Report

In addition to the balance sheet, profit and loss account and notes thereto, a company is required to prepare a Directors' Report for each financial year. This must contain a 'fair review of the development of the business of the company and its subsidiaries during the financial year and of their position at the end of it'.

The company's auditors are under a duty to consider whether the information given in the Directors' Report is consistent with the accounts. Where the auditors are of the opinion that the Directors' Report is not consistent with the accounts, they are required to state that fact in their audit report. There are no formats specified for the report. The following information must be given:

Activities and results
(a) Principal activities of the company during the period and any significant changes in those activities.
(b) A fair review of the development of the business of the company during the financial year and its position at the end of it.
(c) The amount recommended to be paid by way of dividend.
(d) Proposed transfers to reserves.
(e) Particulars of important events which have occurred since the end of the financial year that affects the company (SSAP17, *Post Balance Sheet Events*, which requires additional disclosure of details relating to what are termed non-adjusting events, is considered in Chapter 3). This requirement may be given in the balance sheet section.
(f) An indication of likely future developments in the business of the company.
(g) An indication of any activities in the field of research and development.

Fixed assets
(a) Any significant changes in fixed assets during the period.
(b) Any significant difference at the year end between market values and book values of land and buildings.

Directors
(a) The names of any persons who were directors at any time during the financial year.
(b) For those persons who were directors of the company at the year end, the interests of each (including interests of spouse and infant children), in shares or debentures of the company or any group company at the beginning of the year (or date of appointment if later), and at the year end.
(c) If a director had no such interest at either date that fact must be stated. (The information in (b) and (c) may be given in notes to the accounts.)

Company's interest in its own shares
Where shares in any company:

(a) Are purchased by the company or acquired by forfeiture on surrender in lieu of forfeiture.
(b) Are acquired by the company's nominee or any other person with financial assistance from the company and in a situation where the company has a beneficial interest in the shares.
(c) Are subject to a lien or other change taken by the company, the following details must be disclosed:
   (i) The number and nominal value of shares purchased, the aggregate amount of consideration paid by the company, and the reasons for their purchase.
   (ii) The maximum number and nominal value of shares that have been at any time acquired or charged (excluding any shares purchased by the company) that the company or the other person held at any time during the financial year.
   (iii) The number and nominal value of the shares acquired or charged which were disposed of or cancelled during the year.
   (iv) Where the number and nominal value of shares are disclosed under (i) to (iii) the percentage of the called up share capital that the shares represent.
   (v) Where any of the shares have been charged, the amount of the charge.
   (vi) The consideration for any such shares disposed of.

Disabled persons
Where the company's average number of employees over the financial year exceeds 250, it is necessary to state the company's policy for

(a) The employment of disabled persons.
(b) The employment and training of persons who became disabled while in the company's employment.
(c) The training, career development and promotion of disabled persons.

Political and charitable donations
If political and charitable donations together exceed £200:
(*a*)   A separate total for each.
(*b*)   The amount of each political contribution over £200, naming the recipient.

Employee involvement
Companies whose average number of weekly employees exceeds 250 must include in their Directors' Report a statement describing the action that has been taken to introduce, maintain, or develop arrangements aimed at:

(*a*)   Providing employees with information of concern to them on a systematic basis.
(*b*)   Consulting employees or their representatives on a regular basis so that their views can be taken into account in decisions affecting their interests.
(*c*)   Encouraging involvement in the company's performance through an employees' share scheme or some other means.
(*d*)   Achieving a common awareness on the part of all employees of the financial and economic factors affecting company performance.

Auditing and company accounts

Section 236 of CA 85 requires a company's auditors to make a report to the members of the company on the accounts examined by them, and on the balance sheet and profit and loss account, the report should state:

(*a*)   Whether in the auditors' opinion the balance sheet and profit and loss account have been prepared in accordance with the CA 85.
(*b*)   Whether a true and fair view is given.

The CA 85 also sets out the auditors' duties and powers. In particular a duty is placed on auditors to carry out any investigations as may enable them to form an opinion on whether proper accounting records have been kept and whether the balance sheet and profit and loss account are in agreement with them. Auditors are given the right of access at all times to the company's books, accounts and vouchers, and are entitled to require any information and explanations which they think necessary from the company's officers.

Illustration

Better Products plc – Report and Accounts for the year ended 31 December 19X6

The following illustration conforms with the requirements of the Companies Acts except that comparative figures are omitted in the interests of clarity. Also, an Auditors' Report and a Directors' Report are not included. The illustration does not take account of the supplementary disclosures required by Statements of Standard Accounting Practice such as funds flow and current cost information nor of the Stock Exchange Listing Agreement. In this illustration the profit and loss account and the balance sheet follow Format 1.

Better products plc

Profit and loss account for the year ended 31 December 19X6

Notes		£000
2	Turnover	44,680
	Cost of sales	(31,564)
	Gross profit	13,116
	Distribution costs	(3,602)
	Administrative expenses	(3,943)
3	Operating profit	5,571
6	Investment income	35
	Interest payable and similar charges	(316)
	Profit on ordinary activities before taxation	5,290
7	Tax on profit on ordinary activities	(2,433)
	Profit on ordinary activities after taxation	2,857
8	Extraordinary items after taxation	(104)
	Profit for the financial year	2,753
9	Dividends paid and proposed	(1,200)
	Retained profit for the year	£1,553

Better Products plc

Balance sheet at 31 December 19X6

Notes		£000	£000
	Fixed assets		
10	Intangible assets		60
121	Tangible assets		15,656
122	Investments		300
			16,016

		£000	£000
	Current assets		
14	Stocks	3,148	
15	Debtors	2,872	
16	Investments	135	
	Cash at bank and in hand	127	
		6,282	
17	Creditors: amounts falling due within one year	3,680	
	Net current assets		2,602
	Total assets less current liabilities		18,618
18	Creditors: amounts falling due after more than one year	720	
19	Provisions for liabilities and charges	267	(987)
			19,605
			17,631
	Capital and Reserves		
20	Called up share capital		14,000
	Share premium account		246
21	Revaluation reserve		208
22	Profit and loss account		5,151
			19,605

Better products plc

Notes to the accounts at 31 December 19X6

1   Accounting policies   BOTH

(a)   Basis of accounting: The accounts have been prepared under the historical cost convention, modified by the revaluation of properties.

(b)   Depreciation: Depreciation is provided on all tangible fixed assets, other than freehold land, at rates calculated to write off the cost or valuation, less estimated residual value, of each asset evenly over its expected useful life, as follows:

Freehold buildings   ..   ..   ..   40 years
Plant and machinery   ..   ..   ..   10 years

(c)   Goodwill: Goodwill acquired for cash relating to a business purchased by the company is amortized over five years. In the opinion of the directors this represents a prudent estimate of the period over

which the company will derive a direct economic benefit from the products acquired as part of the business.

(d) Research and development expenditure: This is written off in the year in which it is incurred.

(e) Stocks and work-in-progress: These are stated at the lower of cost and net realizable value. In general, cost is determined on a first-in, first-out basis and includes transport and handling costs; in the case of manufactured products cost includes all direct expenditure and production overheads based on the normal level of activity. Net realizable value is based on estimated selling price less further costs expected to be incurred to completion and disposal.

(f) Foreign currencies: Assets and liabilities in foreign currencies are translated into sterling at the rates of exchange ruling at the balance sheet date.

(g) Pensions: Retirement benefits to the present employees of the company are funded by contributions from the company and employees. Payments are made to pension trusts, which are financially separate from the company, in accordance with calculations made periodically by consulting actuaries. The cost of these contributions and of providing pensions to some former employees is charged against the profits of the period.

2 Turnover   *P+L*

Turnover represents the invoiced amount of goods and services provided during the year, excluding value added tax.

The analysis of turnover and profits is as follows:

	Turnover £000	Profit £000
Class of business:		
Domestic appliances	32,008	3,906
Cycles and toys	12,672	1,384
	44,680	5,290
Geographical analysis:		
United Kingdom	15,346	
USA	4,685	
Europe	24,649	
	44,680	

3 Operating profit   *P+L*

Operating profit is stated after charging:

	£000
Depreciation	2,103
Amortization of goodwill	20

	£000
Hire of plant and machinery	85
Auditors' remuneration	22
Exceptional bad debt	14

4   *Employee information*   *BOTH*

(a) *Number employed:* The average number of employees during the year was as follows:

	000
Office and management	140
Domestic appliances	462
Cycles and toys	136
	738

(b) *Payroll costs:* The aggregate payroll costs were:

	£000
Wages and salaries	7,825
Social security costs	910
Other pension costs	376
	9,111

(c) *Senior employees:* The number of employees earning in excess of £30,000 was:

| £30,001 – £35,000 | .. | .. | .. | 4 |
| £35,001 – £40,000 | .. | .. | .. | 1 |

5   *Directors' emoluments*   *BOTH*

	£000
Fees	75
Other emoluments	563
Pensions to past directors	32
	670

The Chairman received emoluments of £42,000 and the highest paid director £46,000. The emoluments of the other directors were within the ranges:

£15,001 to £20,000	..	..	..	..	2
£20,001 to £25,000	..	..	..	..	4
£30,001 to £35,000	..	..	..	..	7

6   *Investment income and interest payable* *P+L*

	£000
Income from listed investments	35
Interest payable on bank loans, overdrafts and	
loans repayable within 5 years	34
on other loans	282
	316

P₊L

7 *Tax on profit on ordinary activities:* Disclosure requirements are considered in Chapter 4.6

8 *Extraordinary items*   *P₊L*

	£000
Redundancy and other costs relating to the closure of the Burnley factory	156
Less tax thereon	52
	104

9 *Dividends*   *P₊L* .

		£000
Ordinary dividend – interim (paid)	5.0p per share	400
– final (proposed)	10.0p per share	800
	15.0p	1200

10 *Intangible fixed assets*

	£000	£000
Goodwill		
Cost		100
Accumulated amortization at 1 January 19X6	20	
Provision for the year to 31 December 19X6	20	40
Net book value at 31 December 19X6		60

11 *Tangible assets*

Cost or valuation	Land £000	Freehold Buildings £000	Plant and machinery £000	Total £000
Cost:				
At 1 January 19X6	200	2,500	18,500	21,200
Revaluation surplus	208	–	–	208
Additions	63	175	1,600	1,838
Disposals	(30)	(200)	(560)	(790)
At 31 December 19X6	441	2,475	19,540	22,456
Depreciation:				
At 1 January 19X6	–	960	4,167	5,127
Provision for year	–	63	2,040	2,103
Disposals	–	(150)	(280)	(430)
At 31 December 19X6	–	873	5,927	6,800
Net book values:				
At 31 December 19X6	441	1,602	13,613	15,656
At 31 December 19X6	200	1,540	14,333	16,073

Part of the freehold land was revalued on 1 June 19X6 by Smith and Brown, Chartered Surveyors and Valuers. It was valued on 'an open market existing use basis' and resulted in a revaluation surplus of £208,000. This has been credited to a revaluation reserve in the balance sheet.

12   Investments

	£000
Cost:	
At 1 January 19X6	250
Additions	50
Disposals	–
At 31 December 19X6	300
Listed investments	280
Unlisted investments	20
	300

Valuation:
Listed investments at market value	420

The unlisted investment, comprises £20,000 ordinary shares in Molo plc, representing 15 per cent of the issued share capital of that company. Molo plc was incorporated in Great Britain which is the principal country of operation. Taxation of £15,000 would be payable if the investments were sold at valuation.

13   Stocks

	£000
Raw materials	815
Work-in-progress	565
Finished goods	1,768
	3,148

Current replacement costs exceed costs of the above items as follows:

Raw materials	12
Work-in-progress	8
Finished goods	24

14   Debtors

	£000
Trade debtors	2,164
Other debtors	595
Prepayments and accrued income	113
	2,872

15   *Investments*

	£000
Short-term deposits	135

16   *Creditors: amounts falling due within one year*

	£000
Bank loans and overdrafts	84
Trade creditors	572
Taxation and social security	2,210
Accruals	14
Proposed dividends	800
	3,680

17   *Creditors: amounts falling due after more than one year*

11 per cent debentures	720

The debentures are secured by a floating charge over the company's assets. They are repayable at the company's option between 1995 and 2000 with a final redemption data of 31 December 2000.

18   *Provisions for liabilities and charges*

These refer to provisions for taxation which are considered in Chapter 4.6

19   *Called up share capital*

	£000
Allotted, issued and full paid:	
Ordinary shares of £1 each	14,000
Authorized 16 m Ordinary shares of £1 each	16,000

20   *Revaluation reserve*

At 1 January 19X6	–
Amount set aside from profit of year	208
Balance at 31 December 19X6	208

21   *Profit and loss account*

	£000
At 1 January 19X6	3,598
Retained for year	1,553
	5,151

22   Post balance sheet events: Details of post balance sheet events are given in the Directors' Report.

23   Capital commitments
Contracted for but not yet provided	144
Authorized by directors but not yet contracted for	460
	604

24   Contingent liabilities: The company is being sued by an Italian customer for late delivery of goods. The company has denied liability under the contract. The maximum amount which could arise as a liability is £10,000.

Questions

1   Hyrax Ltd, a company manufacturing industrial shelving, has an authorized share capital of £375,000 divided into 125,000 8 per cent preference shares of £1 each and 1,000,000 ordinary shares of 25p each. The opening and closing trial balances extracted from the books of the company as on 1 May 19X5 and 30 April 19X6 showed the following position:

	1 May 19X5 £000	1 May 19X5 £000	30 April 19X6 £000	30 April 19X6 £000
Administration, distribution and factory expenses			1,099	
Bank charges			2	
Bank interest			19	
Bank account		30	47	
Capital reserves		25		25
Cash	1		1	
Corporation tax		140		4
Creditors		419		414
Cumulative depreciation		193		360
Debtors	592		622	
Depreciation charge for year			167	
Dividends		255	85	
Fixed assets at cost	733		893	
Goodwill	60		60	
Medium-term bank loan				100
Profit and loss account		786		786
Raw materials and consumables purchases			1,114	
Rental income				27
Salaries			285	
Sales				3,723
Share capital		325		375

	1 May 19X5		30 April 19X6	
	£000	£000	£000	£000
Stock of finished goods	270		270	
Stock of raw materials	337		337	
Wages			633	
Work-in-progress	180		180	
	2,173	2,173	5,814	5,814

You also obtain the following information:

(a) Depreciation which should be calculated at 20 per cent on reducing balance had been incorrectly calculated at 25 per cent on the assets held on 30 April 19X5. Assets purchased during the year bear a full year's depreciation in that year.

(b) The directors agreed to purchase a new heavy duty press at a cost of £150,000, the finance being raised by a medium-term bank loan received on 1 July 19X5 and the receipts from the issue of the remaining unissued share capital. The bank loan is repayable over a period of five years, in monthly instalments at a fixed interest rate of 14.5 per annum, the first payment being due on 1 July 19X7. The balance of the ordinary shares was issued at par on 1 December 19X5.

(c) The directors wish to provide for a general provision on doubtful debts of 3 per cent of the balance of debtors.

(d) The corporation tax payable on the profit of the year is estimated at £104,000.

(e) Stock of finished goods, raw material and work-in-progress on 30 April 19X6 are valued at £315,000, £368,000 and £262,000 respectively.

(f) The directors wish to write off all the goodwill.

(g) The first half-year's dividend on the preference shares and an interim ordinary dividend of 10p per share were paid on 1 October 19X5. The directors now propose a second half-year's dividend on the preference shares and a final ordinary dividend of 20p per share.

Requirement:

Prepare the company's financial statements excluding the notes to the accounts for the year ended 30 April 19X6 in accordance with generally accepted accounting principles and in a form suitable for presentation to the members. (*27 marks*)

Note: Ignore advance corporation tax. The information may be taken as if it included all that is necessary to satisfy the requirements of the Companies Act 1985. Ignore the requirements to show comparative figures.

Institute of Chartered Accountants in England and Wales, Professional Examination I, Financial Accounting 1

2   The trial balance of R Limited at 31 December 19X5 was as follows:

	£	£
Distribution costs	989,200	
Administration expenses	642,300	
Cash at bank	53,700	
Advance corporation tax suffered on franked investment income received	6,000	
Dividend received from listed investments, including tax credit		20,000
Sales		11,940,000
Profit on sale of plant		11,500
Preference dividend paid for the year	2,100	
Stock of goods for resale at 31 December 19X5	1,549,500	
Cost of sales	9,552,000	
Unsecured loan stock interest, gross	30,000	
Listed investments, at cost	235,000	
Provision for depreciation – buildings		26,500
Provision for depreciation – plant		804,000
Freehold land, at cost	56,500	
Buildings, at cost	340,000	
Plant, at cost	2,050,000	
Interim dividend paid	28,700	
Corporation tax, due 1 January 19X6		241,000
Value added tax		37,700
Social security owed in respect of employees' remuneration		31,500
Trade creditors		1,695,000
Provision for doubtful debts		6,000
Prepayments	33,473	
Other debtors	54,792	
Trade debtors	2,043,735	
Advance corporation tax recoverable	43,200	
Deferred taxation		66,000
Investment grants		6,000
10 per cent convertible unsecured loan stock 1994–2000		300,000
Ordinary share capital		1,025,000
6 per cent (now 4.2 per cent tax credit) redeemable preference shares		50,000

	£	£
Share premium account		210,000
Profit and loss account		1,240,000
	£17,710,200	£17,710,200

Other relevant information:

(a) The authorized share capital consists of £50,000 redeemable preferences shares of £1 each and £1,400,000 of ordinary shares of £0.25 each. During 19X5 the board of directors decided to redeem the preference shares after paying the dividends for the year. This was done during December, but as yet no entries have been made in the books of account. The preference shares were originally issued at par and have been redeemed at a premium of 5 per cent.

(b) The following purchases of fixed assets were made during 19X5: land and buildings £50,000 and plant £270,000. At 31 December 19X5, capital expenditure commitments totalled £585,000 of which £210,800 was covered by firm orders on suppliers. Various items of plant were sold during the year for a total of £34,500, the original cost of these items being £100,000. The profit on sale, which is considered to be a normal transaction of the business, is to be apportioned: administration expenses £4,500, distribution costs £7,000. Depreciation of £50,000 (buildings £4,000, plant £46,000) is to be charged for the year and is to be apportioned: administration expenses £20,000, distribution costs £30,000.

(c) The market value of the listed investments at 31 December 19X5 was £450,000.

(d) Transfers are to be made from:

(i) The investment grant account of £2,000. This is to be apportioned between administration expenses and distribution costs on the same basis as the depreciation charge in note (b) above.

(ii) The deferred taxation account of £4,000, the adjustment being necessary to cover the difference between the book values and the written down values for tax purposes.

(e) The directors are resisting a claim in the courts of £250,000 for damages against the company: the legal advice which has been obtained indicates that no liability is likely to arise from this claim.

(f) Provision is to be made for:

(i) Audit fees of £3,500, which are to be regarded as an administration expense.

(ii) Doubtful debts, increasing the amount to £8,000: this is to be treated as a distribution cost.

(iii) Corporation tax of £286,000 on the year's profit: the liability due on 1 January 19X6 has now been agreed at £240,000.

(*iv*) A final dividend of £0.035 per share.

(*g*) The administration expenses and distribution costs, in the trial balance include:

(*i*) £28,500 for the hire of computer equipment in the administration area.

(*ii*) £952,000 for wages and salaries of the 100 employees of the company (including directors). Thirty employees (including three directors) are categorized as administration, the remainder being in the distribution area. The remuneration of senior management and the directors (including fees of £5,000) was:

	£
Senior management:	
General Manager	23,800

	Excluding pension contributions
Directors	£
Chairman	12,700
Managing	47,600
Finance	40,450
Distribution	35,000
Sales	40,450

(*iii*) £87,290 for social security costs and £72,160 for pension costs. As the result of an actuarial valuation of the pension fund during the year, the latter figure includes a sum of £30,000 which the directors have been advised is necessary to provide the benefits specified in the pension fund rules. The pension contributions of the directors were £13,355, viz:

Chairman	960
Managing	3,610
Finance	3,066
Distribution	2,653
Sales	3,066

(*h*) It is the company's practice to produce its financial statements within the historical cost convention and to follow the requirements of the Companies Act 1985 together with those Statements of Standard Practice which are currently in force.

You are required to prepare:

(*a*) The profit and loss account for the year ended 31 December 19X5.   (*20 marks*)

(*b*) A balance sheet as at that date, and notes thereto.   (*30 marks*)

In view of note (*h*), you are *not* required to show the accounting

policies note to the accounts, but the other notes required should be shown in so far as the information available allows this to be done.
A directors' report and comparative figures are *not* required.
Advance corporation tax is to be taken as 3/7ths where required.
All working should be shown. (*Total 50 marks*)

Chartered Institute of Management Accountants, Financial Accounting 2

3   XYZ plc is a listed company which manufactures in the United Kingdom. It is primarily involved in the production and marketing of crystal glassware, and in the manufacture and installation of kitchen and bedroom furniture.

Crystal glassware accounts for 60 per cent of the company's sales turnover and contributes 45 per cent of the trading profits. 70 per cent of glassware sales is exported, and provides 50 per cent of the glassware trading profits.

For the year ended 31 March 19X5 trading profits, before interest charges and taxation, amounted to £1.6 million on a sales turnover of £28 million.

Details of the company's directors and of their shareholdings are as follows:

(a)   The number of ordinary shares held in XYZ plc at 31 March 19X5, were Director A (Chairman) 30,720, director B 21,200, Director C nil, Director D 800, Director E 750 and Director F 4,200. Directors A and F acquired 1,800 and 2,300 shares respectively during the year ended 31 March, 19X5, but no change had occurred in the holdings of the other Directors.

(b)   During the year fees received by Directors A and E amounted to £15,000 and £8,000 respectively. Other emoluments received by Directors B, C, D and F amounted to £47,000, £28,400, £22,300 and £21,500 respectively. The company paid £37,600 during the year in respect of directors' pension contributions.

Requirement: From the above narrative and information, state which of the items you would expect to find in the Annual Report and Accounts of the company, prepared in accordance with the Companies Acts; indicate where each item would appear, and show, by computation where necessary, how the information for each item would be presented. (*15 marks*)

Chartered Institute of Management Accountants, Financial Accounting 2

4   The Chairman of Goodstart Ltd, a private company has asked for information concerning the definition of small and medium-sized companies as set out in the Companies Act 1981.

Goodstart Ltd, was incorporated and commenced to trade on 1 February 19X3. The first accounts are to be prepared to 29 February 19X4.

The unaudited balance sheet prepared by Goodstart Ltd, as on 29 February 19X4, sets out the figures as follows:

	£	£
Fixed assets	198,722	
Less	55,636	
		143,086
Investment at cost		15,000
Current assets		
Stock	211,518	
Debtors and prepayments	307,419	
Cash	1,731	
	520,668	
Current liabilities		
Creditors and accruals	229,813	
Bank overdraft	85,537	
	315,350	
Net current assets		205,318
		363,404
Less bank loan		200,000
		163,404
Share capital		125,000
Profit and loss account		38,404
		163,404

In addition, Goodstart Ltd has provided the following information about the numbers employed during the period covered by the first accounts:

(a)   Weeks   1–12 inclusive: 4 part time and 28 full time
13–30 inclusive: 6 part time and 43 full time
31–56 inclusive: 6 part time and 56 full time
(b)   All employees, whether part time or full time, were employed under a contract of service.
(c)   Three of the full time employees who were employed by the company throughout the period worked wholly overseas.

Turnover, including exports of £315,812, totalled £1,472,685.

You are required to write a memorandum for the Chairman of Goodstart Ltd:

(a)   Setting out the criteria for deciding whether a company qualifies as a small or medium-sized company.
(b)   Indicating, on the basis of the information provided, into which category Goodstart Ltd falls. Give your reasons with appropriate calculations.   (*12 marks*)

Institute of Chartered Accountants in England and Wales, Professional Examination I.

3 Statements of Standard Accounting Practice

In this chapter we examine an increasingly important aspect of financial disclosure, namely Statements of Standard Accounting Practice (SSAP). As we saw in Chapter 1, accounting standards in the UK are established and enforced by the accountancy profession, through the agency of the Accounting Standards Committee (ASC) and by the professional accountancy bodies themselves.

As Table 3.1 indicates, since its founding, the ASC has prepared accounting standards on twenty-three topics and twenty-two of those standards remain in issue today.

The original intention behind the establishment of an accounting standards body in the UK was to reduce the areas of difference between the financial statements of enterprises and to make the information in financial statements more comparable, reliable and informative to users. Whilst this intention still holds good we noted in Chapter one that accounting standards have come to serve another, perhaps more important, purpose namely the provision of authoritative support for the accounting principles and procedures necessary to ensure that financial statements fulfil their legal requirement to present a true and fair view. This informal role of providing (to use the American phrase), generally accepted accounting principles, was given more formal recognition by the apparent incorporation in the Companies Act of 1981 of a number of the requirements of some SSAPs. However, there remain SSAPs which contain more detailed or specific accounting and disclosure requirements than required by company law.

Nine accounting standards will be considered in this chapter. Some of the remaining standards are considered in later chapters.

SSAP2 – Disclosure of accounting policies

SSAP2 was issued in 1971 and was an attempt to improve the quality of information disclosed in financial statements by establishing as stan-

Table 3.1   *Accounting Standards issued by the ASC*

SSAP1	Accounting for the results of associated companies (amended 1974, revised 1982)	1971
SSAP2	Disclosure of accounting policies	1971
SSAP3	Earnings per share (revised 1974)	1972
SSAP4	The accounting treatment of government grants	1974
SSAP5	Accounting for value added tax	1974
SSAP6	Extraordinary items and prior year adjustments (revised 1978)	1974
SSAP8	The treatment of taxation under the imputation system in the accounts of companies (revised 1977)	1974
SSAP9	Stocks and work in progress	1975
SSAP10	Statements of source and application of funds	1975
SSAP12	Accounting for depreciation	1977
SSAP13	Accounting for research and development	1977
SSAP14	Group accounts	1978
SSAP15	Accounting for deferred taxation (revised 1985)	1978
SSAP16	Current cost accounting (made non-mandatory 1985)	1980
SSAP17	Accounting for post balance sheet events	1980
SSAP18	Accounting for contingencies	1980
SSAP19	Accounting for investment properties	1981
SSAP20	Foreign currency translation	1983
SSAP21	Accounting for leases and hire purchase contracts	1984
SSAP22	Accounting for goodwill	1984
SSAP23	Accounting for acquisitions and mergers	1984

dard accounting practice the disclosure of clear explanations of the accounting policies followed by companies in so far as they are significant for the purpose of giving a true and fair view. The ASC regarded the disclosure of such explanations as fundamental to the understanding and interpretation of financial accounts.

Whilst SSAP2 did not seek to set standards for individual accounting items, it did go some way towards providing a framework which the ASC might use in setting subsequent standards. The standard addresses the relationship between accounting concepts, accounting bases, and accounting policies and defines these three terms as follows:

Fundamental accounting concepts are broad general assumptions which underlie the periodic financial accounts of business enterprises.

Accounting bases are the methods which have been developed for expressing or applying fundamental accounting concepts to financial transactions and items. By their nature, accounting bases are more diverse and numerous than fundamental concepts since they have evolved in response to the variety and complexity of types of business and business transactions and, for this reason, there may justifiably exist more than one recognized accounting basis for dealing with particular items.

Accounting policies are the specific accounting bases judged by business enterprises to be most appropriate to their circumstances and adopted by them for the purpose of preparing their financial accounts.

SSAP2 states that there are four fundamental accounting concepts which should be regarded as established standard concepts. They are as follows:

(a) The going concern concept implies that the enterprise will continue in operational existence for the foreseeable future. This means, in particular, that the profit and loss account and balance sheet assume no intention or necessity to liquidate or reduce significantly the scale of operation.

(b) The accruals concept, which requires that revenue and costs are accrued (that is, recognized as they are earned or incurred, not as money is paid or received), matched with one another so far as their relationship can be established or justifiably assumed, and dealt with in the profit and loss account of the period to which they relate, provided, generally, that where the accrual concept is inconsistent with the prudence concept the latter prevails. The accruals concept implies that the profit and loss account reflects changes in the amount of net assets that arise out of the transactions of the relevant period, other than distributions or subscriptions of capital. Revenue and profits dealt with in the profit and loss account are matched with associated costs by including, in the same account, the costs incurred in earning them, so far as these are material and identifiable.

(c) The consistency concept, which requires that there should be consistency of accounting treatment of like items within each accounting period and from one period to the next.

(d) The prudence concept, which requires that revenue and profits are not anticipated, but recognized by inclusion in the profit and loss account only when realized in the form either of cash or of assets (usually legally enforceable debts), the ultimate cash realization of which can be assessed with reasonable certainty; provision be made for all known liabilities (expenses and losses), whether the amount of these is known with certainty or is a best estimate in the light of the information available.

SSAP2 is concerned with ensuring that accounting bases are disclosed in financial reports, whenever significant items are shown which have their significance in value judgements, estimated outcome of future events or uncompleted transactions, rather than ascertained amounts. In the words of SSAP2:

> In circumstances where more than one accounting basis is acceptable in principle, the accounting policy followed can significantly affect a company's reported results and financial position, and the view presented can be properly appreciated only if the principal policies followed are also described. For this reason, adequate disclosure of the accounting policies should be regarded as essential to the fair presentation of financial accounts.

SSAP2 establishes as standard accounting practice the following:

(a) The disclosure of explanations of circumstances where accounts are prepared on the basis of fundamental accounting concepts other than those set out in the standard. In the absence of disclosures containing such information it is to be presumed that the four fundamental accounting concepts have been observed.
(b) The accounting policies adopted for dealing with items which are judged critical or material in determining profit or loss for the year and in stating financial position should be disclosed in a note to the accounts. Such explanations should be clear, fair and as brief as possible.

A project to review SSAP2 was begun by the ASC in 1986. The project includes a consideration of the nature of realized profit and an examination of the question of the basing of accounting choices on the economic substance of transactions rather than their legal form. An exposure draft is expected to be published and a revised standard should be published in 1987.

SSAP6 – Extraordinary items and prior year adjustments

The widespread use of accounting profit or loss as an indicator of business performance means that the way in which accounting income is measured is important for decision making. For example, decisions with a long run character, such as share purchase decisions or takeover decisions will be best based on a long run view of accounting income. This may involve the extrapolation of a trend of income from current and past period accounting income. Such data will be unrepresentative as the basis of a trend if it contains items whose effects are unlikely to recur or which are unusual in some way. Also, accounting income would be unreliable as the basis for business decisions, if it were subject to manipulation by management by the inclusion of unusual items of income or expenditure, or by other means. Specifically, accounting income is used in the calculation of key stock market ratios such as earnings per share and the price earnings ratio. Concern that companies may be manipulating their earnings per share (EPS) figure through the use of unusual items of income or expenditure prompted a review of accounting policy requirements towards the calculation of ratios such as earnings per share and the determination of accounting earnings themselves. As we shall see in Chapter 13, SSAP3 *Earnings Per Share*, requires that EPS be calculated from profit after tax and before extraordinary items. Here we examine the content and requirements of SSAP6.

As its title suggests SSAP6 is devoted to two categories of accounting items, extraordinary items, and prior year adjustments. Extraordinary items are defined by the standard as 'those items which derive from events and transactions outside the ordinary activities of the business and which are both material and expected not to recur frequently or regularly. They do not include items which, though exceptional on account of size and incidence, derive from the ordinary activities of the business.' (ASC 1974, Paragraph 11.) Prior year adjustments are defined as 'those material adjustments applicable to prior years arising from changes in accounting policies and the correction of fundamental errors. They do not include the normal recurring corrections and adjustments of accounting estimates made in prior years.' (ASC 1974 Paragraph 12.)

Broadly, two accounting treatments might be adopted for extraordinary items and prior year adjustments. One is to exclude them from the profit and loss account for the period and take them directly to reserves or adjust the opening balance of retained profit for their effects. The other is to include extraordinary items which are recognized in a period in the profit and loss account for that period but disclose them separately, together with, subject to certain exceptions, prior year adjustments. The former treatment is termed the current operating approach, and the latter the all-inclusive approach.

The proponents of the current operating approach would include only those transactions in the profit and loss account which result from the ordinary, normal operations of the entity during the current period. Other transactions, those of an unusual, extraordinary nature should be segregated from ordinary transactions and relegated to reserves. Current operating advocates maintain that investors are better served by information that is comparable from year to year. The proponents of the all-inclusive approach maintain the profit and loss account should provide a record of all transactions. Its advocates believe that over the life of an entity the aggregate of net profits should provide a complete history of the earnings of the enterprise. They maintain it is misleading to exclude extraordinary transactions from periodic profit and loss accounts. Furthermore, they argue that the all-inclusive concept avoids the necessity of making highly subjective judgements. These may lead to differences in the treatment of questionable items and create the danger of profit manipulation. For example, losses may be relegated to reserves and gains to profits.

SSAP6 adopts the all-inclusive concept of profit for the following reasons:

(a) Inclusion and disclosure of extraordinary and prior year items will enable the profit and loss account for the year to give a better view of a company's profitability and progress.
(b) Exclusion, being a matter of subjective judgement, could lead to variations and to a loss of comparability between the reported results of companies.
(c) Exclusion could result in extraordinary and prior year items being overlooked in any consideration of results over a series of years.

Treatment of extraordinary items

The all-inclusive concept of profit has also been incorporated in legal requirements. As we saw in Chapter 2, the required formats for presentation of the profit and loss account under the Companies Acts provide headings for 'extraordinary income', 'extraordinary charges' and 'tax on extraordinary profit or loss'. The Acts do not define extraordinary items. These may be interpreted in the light of the definition given above and taken from SSAP6, according to which the classification of items as extraordinary will depend on the particular circumstances of the business: what is extraordinary in one business may not necessarily be extraordinary in other businesses. Subject to this qualification, SSAP6 contains the following examples of how extraordinary items may arise:

(a)   The discontinuance of a significant part of a business.
(b)   The sale of an investment not acquired with the intention of resale.
(c)   Writing off intangibles, including goodwill, because of unusual events or developments during the period.
(d)   The appropriation of assets.

The standard distinguishes extraordinary items such as the above from others which, though abnormal in size or incidence, none the less derive from the ordinary activities of the business. Such items may be termed *exceptional* and examples include:

(a)   Abnormal charges for bad debts and write offs of stocks and work-in-progress and research and development expenditure.
(b)   Abnormal provisions for losses on long-term contracts.
(c)   Most adjustments of prior year taxation provisions.

The accounting standard requires different treatments for extraordinary and exceptional items:

Extraordinary items
Extraordinary items (less attributable taxation) should be shown *separately* in the profit and loss account for the year *after* the results derived from ordinary activities. Their nature and size should also be disclosed.

Exceptional items
Exceptional items should be reflected in the ascertainment of profit *before* extraordinary items although, because of their size and incidence, they may require disclosure if a true and fair view is to be given.

It must be noted that the definition of exceptional items given on page 8 of the SSAP contains the word 'material' and hence, the above requirements relate only to items considered material either because of their effect on profit or loss, or because of their nature.

The treatment of prior year adjustments

The definition of prior year adjustments given above referred to changes in accounting policies and the correction of fundamental errors, and excluded normal corrections of recurring accounting estimates. As we said in our consideration of SSAP2 above, the accounting policies chosen by a company's management will be important for the measurement of individual accounting items and ultimately accounting profit or loss. If accounting policies are changed, this will affect the current period's profit or loss. Such changes may make comparisons with prior years' profits or losses invalid, and will mean that the components of retained profit have been arrived at in different ways. Similarly, if fundamental accounting errors were made in the past, their affects will be included in past profits and will hence be present in the figure for retained profits in the company's accounts. One would not expect accounting policies to be changed as a normal part of business activity, nor would one expect fundamental errors to be made under normal circumstances. On the other hand, in an uncertain world it is normal to find that estimates do not coincide exactly with outcomes. Hindsight is a much more exact science than accountancy. Hence, the distinction between extraordinary and exceptional items (based on what is normal business activity) is echoed in the definition of prior year adjustments: it is considered standard accounting practice to adjust prior years' profits for changes which cannot reasonably be thought of as part of normal business activity (changes in accounting policy and fundamental errors), whereas normal changes (errors in accounting estimates) call for no adjustment to past profits, but should be dealt with entirely through current year's profits or losses. Specifically, the relevant requirements of the standard are as follows:

Prior year items requiring adjustment
Adjustments for prior year items (less attributable taxation) should be made by restating prior years, with the result that the opening balance of retained profit will be adjusted accordingly. Where practicable the effect of the change should be shown separately in the restatement of the previous year.

Prior year items not requiring adjustment
Prior year items not meeting the criterion for adjustment should be dealt with through the profit and loss account for the year.

As with extraordinary items, adjustment for prior year items will only be necessary for material items meeting the criterion. Similarly, disclosures of the effects of prior year items, where adjusted for or not, should be made only where the effects are material.

Illustration and summary
The distinctions drawn above between extraordinary and exceptional items, and prior year items requiring adjustment and those not requiring adjustment, may appear both pedantic and rather difficult to draw in practice. Certainly, it is necessary to exercise judgement in arriving at the appropriate classification for an item and the corresponding accounting treatment. Figure 3.1 provides a summary of the judgements which need to be made. The application of the decisions included in Figure 3.1 is illustrated by the examples contained in Table 3.2.

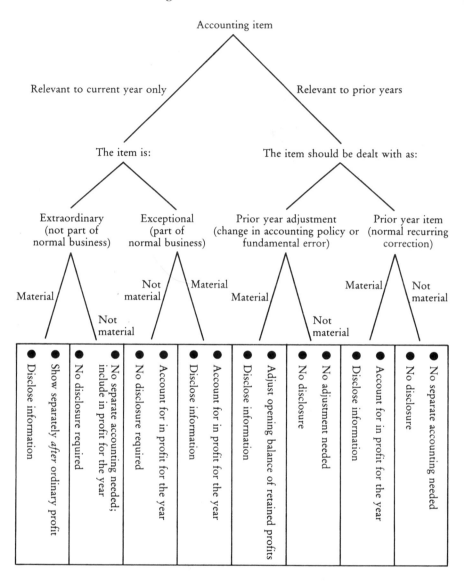

Figure 3.1   *Classification and treatment of accounting items*

Table 3.2 *Examples of treatments of accounting items relating to Miss Fortune Ltd*

	Accounting item	Evaluation	Classification	Accounting treatment
1	Increase in the provision for bad debts in the current year from £25,000 to £100,000 due to bankruptcy of a major customer.	Bad debts are a normal part of business; major customers don't regularly go bankrupt.	Exceptional item.	Through ordinary profits for the year. Disclose information as material due to size in relation to turnover.
2	Miss Fortune's auditors discover the embezzlement of £150,000 by a director in the current year.	Embezzlement is not part of normal business activity.	Extraordinary item.	Through profit after ordinary activities. Disclose information as material due to size and involvement of a director.
3	Miss Fortune's accountants discover the omission of stock valued at £200,000 for last year's closing stock.	Closing stock is a key accounting item and its value is fundamental to profit and should be carefully checked by accountants.	Prior year adjustment.	Material due to size in relation to last year's profit. Adjust reserves by addition of omitted stock. Recalculate last year's profit. Disclose details.
4	Miss Fortune's accountants decide to revise their estimate of the useful life of an asset due to new information being available on changed market conditions.	'Useful life' is always uncertain and market conditions always likely to change. Since the information is new they could not be expected to have used it before, so they are not in error.	Normal reappraisal of accounting information.	Deal with through current year's profit. Not material due to insignificance of asset and market.

Note Miss Fortune Ltd's turnover this year was £1.5 m, net profits were £300,000 against £150,000 last year

In January 1985 the ASC issued ED36, *Extraordinary Items and Prior Year Adjustments*, based on a working party's review of SSAP6. The proposals contained in ED36 do not differ substantially from the principles set out in SSAP6 and discussed above. The changes which are proposed relate chiefly to matters of definition and disclosure, especially in regard to the effect of the issue of SSAPs 20 and 22 on foreign currency translation and goodwill respectively. A noteworthy modification is clarification of the phrase 'ordinary activities of the business' which is central to the definition of extraordinary items.

SSAP12 – Accounting for depreciation

Depreciation is part of the larger subject of income measurement and asset valuation. Differences in views on depreciation reflect differences on these wider issues. For example, if assets are valued on a present value basis depreciation is regarded as the periodic reduction in the value of the assets estimated by discounting their future net services to their present value. If, on the other hand, accounting profit is abandoned in favour of cash flow accounting, or a net realizable asset base, the need to define depreciation disappears.

In an accruals based accounting system the value of a fixed asset is charged to the profit and loss account over a number of accounting periods. The size of the depreciation charge obviously affects accounting profit as well as the written down value of fixed assets in the balance sheet. The computation of the annual depreciation charge is very subjective. Considerable judgement is involved in depreciation calculations (e.g. in estimating useful economic life) and a great deal of variety exists in depreciation methods available to, and practised by, company managements. Because of this subjectivity and variety, and because of the significance of depreciation in financial statements, it is essential that users of financial statements are aware of, and understand the effects of, alternative accounting policies which companies may adopt if they are to be able to compare financial statements of companies using alternative depreciation policies.

SSAP12 was originally published at a time when statutory requirements in the UK for the provision of depreciation were limited. Since that time, the Companies Act 1981 has created a number of new accounting requirements in this area which were summarized in Chapter 2. The standard is not prescriptive as to the choice of method to be applied by companies in determining the annual depreciation charge. The standard merely states that a 'fair proportion' be charged in each accounting period making up the asset's useful life. The standard appears to have three main purposes: the definition (and hence clarification) of important pieces of terminology relating to depreciation, the clarification of accounting bases relating to depreciation, and the prescription of disclosure requirements.

SSAP12 defines depreciation as the measure of the wearing out, consumption or other loss of value of a fixed asset whether arising from use, effluxion of time or obsolescences through technology and market changes. The standard requires that provision be made for depreciation of fixed assets having a finite useful life by allocating the cost (or revalued amount) of the fixed assets less residual values to the periods expected to benefit from their use.

The assessment of depreciation and its allocation to accounting periods initially involves the consideration of:

(*a*) The cost (or, where appropriate, valuation) of an asset.
(*b*) The nature of the asset and the length of its expected useful life.
(*c*) Its estimated residual value.

The standard explains that the need for depreciation does not disappear merely because the market value of the asset at any particular time during its life is higher than the net book amount. Rather, if account is taken of increased value by writing up the net book value of an asset, an increased charge for depreciation becomes necessary.

According to the standard, where there is a revision of the estimated useful life of an asset, the unamortized cost should be charged over the revised remaining useful life. If any part of the unamortized cost becomes irrecoverable, it should be written off immediately and the recoverable amount charged over the remaining useful life. Where fixed assets are revalued in the financial accounts the depreciation provision must be based on the new valuation and on the revised estimate of the remaining useful life.

SSAP12 states that freehold land will not normally require a provision for depreciation, unless subject to depletion or loss of value for other reasons. Buildings have a limited life and should be depreciated using the same criteria applied to other fixed assets. There has been considerable resistance to this provision of SSAP12. In order to avoid making depreciation charges many companies have argued that buildings are really an investments, not a depreciating asset. But where a company uses buildings for its own purposes the treatment proposed in SSAP12 should apply. Where properties are held as investments rather than used in the business, another accounting standard, SSAP19, *Accounting for Investment Properties*, requires that such assets should not be depreciated annually but should be in the balance sheet. According to SSAP19, changes in value should be revalued annually at open market value, the valuation being incorporated taken to an investment revaluation reserve, unless the balance on the reserve is insufficient to cover any deficit arising during the accounting period, in which case the excess amount of the deficit should be taken to the profit and loss account. SSAP19 was developed in response to the criticisms of depreciation charges applied to buildings mentioned above.

SSAP12 requires that the following be disclosed in the financial statements for each major class of depreciable asset:

(*a*) The depreciation methods used.
(*b*) The useful lives or the depreciation rates used.

(c)   Total depreciation allocated for the period.
(d)   The gross amount of depreciable assets and the related accumulated depreciations.

SSAP17 – Accounting for post balance sheet events

For going concerns business activities will take place more or less continually. The practicalities of the need to provide financial reports to those entitled to receive them inevitably mean that continuous streams of transactions must be split into arbitrary time periods. Many of the problems of accruals accounting arise because of this. A particular difficulty may occur if financial statements are firmly 'closed' on the last day of the accounting period to which they relate. One might assume that financial statements prepared in respect of a balance sheet date of, say, 31 December, need only relate to events up to that date. However, financial statements based on that assumption might be misleading to users. Events arising after the balance sheet date need to be reflected in financial statements if they provide additional evidence of conditions that existed at the balance sheet date and materially affect the amounts to be included in the financial statements. Similarly, events arising after the balance sheet date may provide information on conditions not existing at that date and hence ought to be disclosed in order to prevent the financial statements from being misleading. A good example of circumstances where such disclosures would be important is the practice commonly known as 'window dressing' a set of accounts which involves entering into transactions (or postponing them) for the express purpose of making a company's accounts (and hence assessments of the company by users of accounts) appear better than they really are, or would be, if business were conducted normally.

SSAP17 requires disclosures of information concerning certain types of post balance sheet events which is necessary for a proper understanding of a company's financial position. A post balance sheet event is defined for this purpose by SSAP17 as 'an event which occurs between the balance sheet date and the date on which the financial statements are approved by the directors'. The lack of need for approval by directors means that there is no open-ended reporting requirement. As we saw in Chapter 2 the Companies Acts recognize the importance of these items by requiring their disclosure in the directors' report. SSAP17 identifies two classes of post balance sheet event – adjusting and non-adjusting events.

Adjusting events provide more information regarding conditions existing at the balance sheet date and necessitate changes in the amounts reported in financial statements. This category could include, for example, a debtor who became insolvent, new information regarding rates of taxation or the discovery of frauds and errors which show that the financial statements were incorrect. In all these cases the information relates to a time at or before the balance sheet date, although it does not become available until afterwards.

Non-adjusting events arise after the balance sheet date and concern characteristics which did not exist at that time. Consequently, they do not result in changes in amounts in financial statements, but they may be of such materiality that their disclosure is required by way of notes to ensure that financial statements are not misleading. This requirement necessitates the disclosure of 'window dressing' practices. The standard does not require that such transactions should be eliminated from the financial statements but that their nature and effect should be disclosed. Examples could include mergers and acquisitions, reconstructions, issues of shares and debentures, purchases and sales of fixed assets and investments, closing a significant part of trading activity or changes in foreign exchange rates.

In summary, the main requirements of the standard are as follows:

(*a*) Financial statements should be prepared on the basis of conditions existing at the balance sheet date.

(*b*) A material post balance sheet event requires changes in the amounts included in financial statements where:

(*i*) It is an adjusting event.

(*ii*) It indicates that application of the going concern concept to all or a material part of the company is not appropriate.

(*c*) A material post balance sheet event should be disclosed where:

(*i*) It is a non-adjusting event of such materiality that its non-disclosure would affect the ability of users to reach a proper understanding of financial position, or

(*ii*) It is the reversal after the year end of a transaction entered into before the year end whose main purpose was to alter the appearance of the balance sheet.

(*d*) For each post balance sheet event for which disclosure is required, the following should be stated in notes to the accounts:

(*i*) The nature of the event.

(*ii*) An estimate of its financial effect, or a statement of why it is not practicable to give such an estimate.

SSAP18 – Accounting for contingencies

Sometimes companies may not wish to disclose information about contingencies because it would prejudice their position. To overcome this problem the Companies Act 1948 introduced a requirement that 'contingent liabilities are required to be disclosed with particulars of their general nature, together where practicable, with an estimate of the amount involved if material'. Prior to the publication of SSAP18 in 1980 there was little in the way of extension to, or amplification of, these Companies Acts requirements. SSAP18 defined a contingency as a condition which exists at the balance sheet date where the outcome will be confirmed only by the occurrence or non-occurrence of one or more uncertain future events. It is not intended that uncertainties connected with accounting estimates fall within the scope of this standard (e.g. the lives of fixed assets, the amount of bad debts, the net realizable value of stocks, the expected outcome of longer term contracts or the valuation of properties or foreign currency balances). Contingencies to which the standard refers are the existence of unresolved legal cases or insurance claims at the balance sheet date.

According to the standard, the treatment of a contingency existing at balance sheet date is determined by its expected outcome:

(*a*)   Some contingent losses should be accrued in the financial statements although there are no particular disclosure requirements relating to them. This applies if:

   (*i*)   the amounts are material and,
   (*ii*)   it is probable that a future event will confirm a loss and,
   (*iii*)   the amount of the loss can be estimated with reasonable certainty.

(*b*)   Some contingent losses should not be accrued but they necessitate disclosure. This applies to any material contingent loss that is not 'probable' enough to be accrued, unless the possibility is remote. Disclosure requirements comprise the nature of the contingency, the uncertainties expected to affect the outcome and a prudent estimate of the potential financial effect (or a statement that it is impracticable to make such estimate).

The standard follows conventional principles in concluding that contingent gains should not be accrued. A material contingent gain should be disclosed in financial statements only if it is probable that the gain will be realized.

SSAP4 – The accounting treatment of government grants

SSAP4 lays down the acceptable methods of dealing with money given to a business to encourage certain activities. SSAP4 divides government grants into two categories:

Revenue-based grants are grants made by reference to specified categories of revenue expenditure. Revenue should be credited in the same period to which the related expenditure is incurred.

Capital-based grants are grants made by reference to certain types of capital expenditure. There are three possible accounting treatments for these:

(*a*)   Credit the profit and loss account immediately with the total amount of the grant.
(*b*)   Credit the amount of the grant to a non-distributable reserve.
(*c*)   Credit the amount to revenue over the estimated useful life of the asset by:

   (*i*)   reducing the cost of the acquisition of the fixed asset by the amount of the grant, or (*ii*) treating the amount of the grant as a deferred credit, a portion of which is transferred to revenue annually.

SSAP4 rejects methods (*a*) and (*b*) on the grounds that they are inconsistent with the matching concept. On the other hand, method (*c*) matches the application of the grant with the amortization of the capital expenditure to which it relates and is therefore considered to be the most appropriate treatment.

In deciding between method (*ci*) or (*cii*) the main argument in favour of the first alternative (reducing the cost of the asset) is its simplicity. By crediting the grant to the cost of the asset the resulting reduced depreciation charge automatically credits the amount of the grant to revenue over the life of the asset.

The arguments in favour of the second (deferred credit) method are:

(*a*) Assets acquired at different times and locations are recorded on the same basis, irrespective of government policy.

(*b*) Control over the ordering, construction and maintenance of assets is based on the gross value.

(*c*) As capital allowances for tax purposes are normally calculated on the cost of an asset before deduction of the grant, adjustments of the depreciation charge shown in the accounts are avoided when computing the amount of deferred taxation.

SSAP9 – Stocks and work-in-progress

SSAP9 states that stocks and work-in-progress include goods for resale, consumable stores, raw materials, products partly completed and finished goods. The standard requires that stocks and work-in-progress, other than long-term contract work-in-progress, should be valued at the lower of cost or net realizable value. Cost is defined as the cost of purchase plus costs of conversion incurred in bringing the product or service to its present location and condition. The cost of conversion includes direct expenditure, production and overheads and any other attributable overheads. Production overheads should be based on the normal level of activity. All overhead expenditure which relates to production should be included in stock, even though some of this may accrue on a time basis. All abnormal conversion costs such as exceptional spoilage and idle capacity, which are avoidable under normal operating conditions, should be excluded. Because the costs of general management are not directly related to current production, they are therefore excluded from costs of conversion.

In selecting the methods for ascertaining costs management must ensure they provide the fairest practical approximation to 'actual cost'. Methods such as LIFO and base stock are usually inappropriate for this purpose. However, as we saw in Chapter 2 the Companies Acts permit companies to use the LIFO method of stock valuation.

Net realizable value is defined as the actual or estimated selling price (net of trade but before settlement discounts), less:

(*a*)   All further costs of completion, and
(*b*)   All costs to be incurred in marketing, selling and distribution.

The comparison of cost and net realizable value needs to be made in respect of each item of stock separately. Where this is impracticable, groups or categories of stock items which are similar will need to be taken together.

SSAP13 – Accounting for research and development

SSAP13 distinguishes clearly between research and development as follows:

SSAP13 requires that all research expenditure be written off as it is incurred. It takes the view that expenditure incurred on pure and applied research may be regarded as part of a continuing operation to maintain a company's business and its competitive position. In general, it is not to be expected that one period rather than another will benefit from such expenditure. Therefore, it is appropriate that such expenditure should be written off as incurred.

Development costs may only be included as an asset in special circumstances, the criteria for which are provided by the standard. These include the clear identification of a project and the clear identification of specific related expenditure.

SSAP22 – Accounting for goodwill

Goodwill is an intangible asset value attached to an entity as a consequence of such factors as the skill of its management, product reputation, technical know-how and marketing organization. The value of goodwill is often defined as the excess of the value of the entity as a whole over the sum of the fair value of its accountable net identifiable assets.

A firm may be creating goodwill continuously, but it is recorded in the accounts only when an existing enterprise is purchased. As a result, in accounting, goodwill is acquired at a particular time and through a market transaction. The goodwill debited to the goodwill account will be equal to the difference between the total price paid for the enterprise and the fair market value assigned to the net assets (assets less liabilities).

SSAP22 requires that goodwill be eliminated either by immediate write off on acquisition against reserves, or by amortization through the profit and loss account over its useful economic life.

Questions

1 Statement of Standard Accounting Practice Number 2 *Disclosure of accounting policies* issued in June 1973, introduced important terminology, viz:

(*a*) Fundamental accounting concepts
(*b*) Accounting bases
(*c*) Accounting policies

You are required to:

(*a*) Distinguish, briefly, between these three terms. (*6 marks*)
(*b*) State and explain briefly the fundamental accounting concepts. (*9 marks*)
(*Total: 15 marks*)

Chartered Institute of Management Accountants Financial Accounting 2

2 You are required to:
(*a*) State possible alternative approaches to accounting for government grants which may be received by a company. (*5 marks*)
(*b*) Discuss the reasons given for the rejection of certain of these approaches by the Statement of Standard Accounting Practice (SSAP4) on this topic, and indicate what was recommended and why. (*10 marks*)
(*Total: 15 marks*)

Chartered Institute of Management Accountants, Stage 2 Financial Accounting, Specimen Examination Paper, New Syllabus

3 In dealing with the annual accounts of three companies, the following information is available:

(*a*) At the balance sheet date Builditt Ltd has an overseas contract at cost, net of progress payments, of £2.6 million. Total work-in-progress is £13.7 million. Progress payments on the overseas contract are £1 million in arrears. Before the accounts are finalized there is a change of regime in the foreign country and the company suspended work on the contract. There is no export credit guarantee in force.

(*b*) Weldilt Ltd has a contract to build an oil pipeline in the Middle East for a North American company. Part of the pipeline has been handed over. During unusual weather conditions, the pipeline has been damaged and this has resulted in considerable financial loss to the North American company. The latter company has indicated that it will take out civil actions in both the British and American courts claiming $16 million. Weldilt Ltd has obtained counsel's opinion that any case to be heard in the British courts will fail. Counsel is unable to give an opinion on the outcome of the case if heard in America until he has sight of the claimant's case. At the date the accounts were approved by the directors no case had been filed or legal proceedings commenced in either country.

(c)   Clampitt Ltd specializes in design and construction of roller coasters. During 19X3 it completed eight roller coasters and commenced work on a further seven. During the final commissioning checks on the first completed roller coaster, a stress fracture was discovered in a major structural girder. The cost of replacing the girders in all roller coasters is estimated to be £1.9 million. All fifteen customers have been advised that the replacements will be carried out immediately at no cost to themselves and they have accepted that satisfactory completion of the work is the only redress they will seek. The manufacturer of the girders, a substantial quoted company, has accepted liability and agreed to meet all costs incurred by Clampitt Ltd.

You are required to:

(a)   Define a contingency and explain the principles of accounting for contingencies.   (*10 marks*)
(b)   Discuss how Builditt Ltd, Welditt Ltd and Clampitt Ltd should deal with the above matters in their accounts.   (*10 marks*)
                                                           (*Total: 20 marks*)

Institute of Chartered Accountants in England and Wales, Professional Examination 1

4   On 1 January 19X4, Hideehigh Ltd was incorporated to acquire from a property development company a ready made holiday complex on the North Wales coast.

The complex is divisible into three distinct areas: a freehold site and two leasehold sites. The leases expire on 25 December 2000, and 25 December 2080. The developer designated these sites Meg I, II and III, respectively.

A schedule of the properties acquired describes the properties as:

Property description	Meg I	Meg II	Meg III	Total
6-room timber construction chalets	38	48	66	152
3-storey brick built 'town houses'	64	32	–	96

Hideehigh Ltd intend to lease the chalets and town houses. They have been advised that the chalets, which have a life of 25 years, and the town houses, which have a life of 50 years, should be let on 15 year leases.

You are required to discuss how Hideehigh Ltd should treat the properties in their annual accounts.   (*13 marks*)

Institute of Chartered Accountants in England and Wales, Professional Examination 1

5   An extract from the asset schedule of A Manufacturing Limited to 31 December 19X4 discloses the following:

		Date acquired	Cost £	Estimated scrap value
(a)	*Equipment:*			
	Machine A	1 Jan. 19W9	240,000	Nil
	Machine B	1 Jan. 19X0	400,000	Nil
	Machine C	1 July 19X4	100,000	Nil
(b)	*Premises:*			
	Freehold factory:			
	Land	1 Jan. 19W8	80,000	
	Building cost	1 Jan. 19W8	400,000	
	Leasehold offices	1 Jan. 19W9	120,000	

The accounting policy of the company in respect of depreciation is stated to be the straight-line basis of depreciation used at the following rates

Equipment   10% per annum
Leasehold premises 2.5% per annum

Depreciation during the year of acquisition or disposal is provided in proportion to the use in that year. No depreciation is provided on freehold land and buildings.

The following factors are to be taken into consideration in preparing the accounts for the year ended 31 December 19X4:

(a)   Machine A has a remaining estimated useful life of six years.
(b)   On 1 January 19X4, it was decided that Machine B should be revalued at £150,000. This machine had not been revalued since its purchase.
(c)   On 1 January 19X4, the freehold factory was revalued by a professional firm at £575,000 (site £2,000,000 and buildings £375,000). At that date, it was further estimated that the buildings had a remaining useful life of 42 years.

You are required, adopting the provision of SSAP12 (accounting for depreciation) to:

(a)   Calculate the depreciation charge, and the adjustments arising from the revaluations, for the year ended 31 December 19X4; indicating how these items would appear in the financial statements.   (*10 marks*)
(b)   Explain briefly the provisions of SSAP12 where:
       (i)   an asset is disposed of; and
      (ii) the method of depreciating assets is changed.   (*5 marks*)
                                            (*Total: 15 marks*)

Chartered Institute Management Accountants Professional Stage, Part 1, Financial Accounting 2

4 Capital, reserves and distributable profits

This chapter has two objectives:

(a) To examine the legal requirements related to the headings appearing under 'capital and reserves' in the balance sheet formats. Chapter 5 deals with the issue and redemption of shares and, therefore, extends further the discussion of these topics,

(b) To examine the definition of distributable profit introduced by the Companies Act 1980 (CA 80).

In both cases the purpose of the law is to protect the rights of shareholders and creditors. A shareholder in a limited company is not a part owner of that company, since the company is a legal entity in itself. Rather, a member of a company is the holder of an interest and it is the purpose of a share to delineate that interest in order to measure the member's liability to the company and the member's rights in the company in respect of receipts of dividends and rights to vote at company meetings.

The rights of creditors are not prejudiced by a decision of a sole trader or partner to withdraw part of his capital account balance since sole traders and partners are liable for all their business debts. With a limited liability company, on the other hand, repayment of capital to shareholders would seriously affect the rights of creditors. Consequently, the Companies Acts lay down strict rules which limit the circumstances in which capital may be repaid.

Share capital

We noted in Chapter 2 that the total amount of share capital the company is allowed to issue is stated in the memorandum of association. This is known as the *authorized capital* as distinct from the *issued*

74

capital, the latter being the portion of authorized capital actually issued to shareholders. The amount of issued capital called up for payment is the *called up capital*, while *paid up capital* is the portion of called up capital actually paid for by shareholders.

Types of shares

Share capital is divided into different classes of which the most usual are ordinary shares and preference shares. In the UK, shares of whatever class must be stated in terms of a fixed amount which is called the 'nominal' or 'par' value. For example, the memorandum of a company having an authorized capital of £70,000 may state that this is divided as follows:

£50,000 ordinary shares of £1 each	£50,000
£10,000 preference shares of £2 each	£20,000
	£70,000

The quoted stock market value of shares often bears little resemblance to their nominal value.

Preference shares

Preference shares give preference shareholders certain priorities over the rights attached to ordinary shares. Normally, preference shares carry a prior right to dividend provided sufficient profits are available, and, in the case where a company is being wound up, preference shareholders are usually entitled to be repaid out of assets before ordinary shareholders. Preference shares carry a fixed rate of dividend. Thus, the holders of a 10 per cent preference share would receive a dividend of 10 per cent of the nominal value of the share owned. It is usual that preference shareholders do not have the right to vote at company meetings unless their dividend is in arrear.

Preference shares are divided into the following classes:

(a) Cumulative preference shares carry the right to receive arrears of preference dividend for previous years before any dividend is paid to ordinary shareholders.

(b) Participating preference shares are entitled to a prior dividend at a fixed rate and in addition, participation in surplus profits, usually a proportion of any ordinary dividend declared.

(c) Redeemable preference shares are repayable normally at a given future date or within a given period.

Ordinary or equity shares

Ordinary, or equity, shares are the most commonly issued class of share, dividends on which are paid out of the profits available for distribution after tax and preference dividends have been deducted. In the event of a company being wound up, ordinary shareholders are entitled to the remaining assets of the company after preference shareholders have been paid out. Ordinary shareholders have voting rights at general meetings, giving them control over the election of directors. Until recently, companies were not permitted to issue redeemable ordinary shares or to purchase their own shares.

The Companies Act 1981 altered this position. Companies are now allowed to issue redeemable ordinary shares provided they have some non-redeemable shares already in issue. A company may now also purchase its own shares, subject to a number of conditions, including the prior approval of shareholders.

Deferred shares
Deferred shares, sometimes termed 'founders' or 'management' shares rank for dividend after all other classes. Moreover, in the event of liquidation, ordinary shareholders usually have a priority over deferred shares as regards the return of capital. Deferred shares are seldom issued.

Reserves

Reserves represent the excess of assets over liabilities after deducting a company's called up share capital. In the case of a sole trader profit not withdrawn from the business is added to capital but in the case of a limited company such profits would be contained within reserves. The reserves of a limited company however, extend beyond retained profits. It is important that reserves are distinguished from provisions. The expressions 'reserves' and 'provisions' are defined in the Companies Acts as follows:

1 (a)   The expression 'provision' shall, subject to 2 below, mean any amount written off or retained by way of providing for depreciation, renewals or diminution in the value of assets, or retained by way of providing for any known liability of which the amount cannot be determined with substantial accuracy.
   (b)   The expression 'reserve' shall not, subject to 2 below, include any amount written off or retained by way of providing for depreciation, renewals or diminution in the value of the assets or retained by way of providing for any known liability, or any sum set aside for the purpose of its being used to prevent undue fluctuations in charges for taxation.

Where:

2 (a)   Any amount written off or retained by way of providing for depreciation, renewals or diminution in value of assets, not being an amount written off in relation to fixed assets before 1 July 1984, or
   (b)   Any amount retained by way of providing for any known liability is in excess of that which, in the opinion of the directors, is reasonably necessary for the purpose, the excess shall be treated as a reserve and not as a provision.

It should be noted that the word 'provision' must only be employed to indicate known depreciation or diminution in the value of assets and known liabilities, the amount of which, however, cannot be estimated with reasonable accuracy. If the amount of a known liability can be estimated with substantial precision, it must be classified as a liability, and not as a provision.

Types of reserves

Prior to the Companies Act 1967 companies were required to distinguish between reserves available for distribution as dividend (revenue reserves) and those not available (capital reserves), and although the 1980 Companies Act defines profits which are distributable and the circumstances in which they may be distributed, the Act does not require the disclosure of the amount of distributable reserves. However, some companies do still distinguish between capital and revenue (or distributable and non-distributable reserves) in their accounts, and such a distinction will undoubtedly provide useful information to users of financial statements.

The nature of the legal requirements which govern the disclosure of various types of reserves were examined in Chapter 2. Here we consider some of the characteristics of the most important categories of reserve.

Share premium account

Following the Companies Act 1948, when a company issues shares whether for cash or otherwise, for a consideration in excess of their par value, the excess is to be placed in a share premium account. There are certain exceptions to this rule arising under merger accounting which are considered in Chapter 8.

According to the 1948 Act the share premium account can be used for the following purposes:

(*a*) Issuing fully paid up bonus shares to members.
(*b*) Writing off preliminary expenses of forming the company.
(*c*) Writing off the expenses and commissions incurred in any issue of shares or debentures.
(*d*) Writing off any discount on the issue of shares or debentures.
(*e*) Providing for the premium payable on redemption of redeemable preference shares or debentures.

In addition, private limited companies may write off the excess of the permissible capital payment over the nominal value of shares redeemed or purchased to share premium account. Also, where shares issued at a premium are redeemed or purchased, any premium payable on redemption or purchase may be paid out of the proceeds of a new issue up to an amount equal to the lesser of the premium received on the original issue of the shares or the balance on share premium account. The practical result of these provisions is to allow the reduction of the share premium account.

The role of the *capital redemption reserve* will be discussed at length in

Chapter 5. The Companies Acts do not allow this reserve to be used for any other purpose than to pay up fully paid bonus shares.

Revaluation reserve
The Companies Acts require that the amount of any profit or loss due to the valuation of any asset by any of the alternative valuation methods prescribed by company law (discussed in Chapter 2), be credited or debited to the revaluation reserve. Hence, this reserve contains gains and losses on asset revaluation.

Further, the revaluation reserve is required to be reduced by any amounts which, in the opinion of the directors, are no longer required for the purposes of the accounting policies adopted. However, an amount may only be transferred from revaluation reserve to profit and loss account if either:

(a)   It represents a realized profit, or
(b)   It is in respect of an account previously charged to the profit and loss account.

Any surplus on revaluation of an asset which is realized by sale may be transferred to the profit and loss account, but must be disclosed separately. The problem of the extent to which revaluation reserves may be distributed is part of the broader question of distributable profit and is considered below.

The Companies Acts enable investment companies (defined in the section on distributable profits below) to depart from some of the accounting requirements applicable to companies generally. One such departure concerns the treatment of investments held by such companies, namely:

(a)   Profits or losses on revaluation of any investments need not be taken to revaluation reserve.
(b)   Provisions for diminution of value of investments may be charged against any reserve account to which previous revaluations have been credited or shown in a separate balance sheet item 'other reserves' as an alternative to writing off the amount to profit and loss account.

Profit and loss account
The accumulated balance of undistributed profits of the company are shown on the face of the balance sheet as this reserve item. Amounts set aside to, or withdrawn from reserves, and dividends paid and proposed are required to be shown as separate items in the profit and loss account. This can be achieved in two ways. First, by showing the opening balance on the face of the profit and loss account after profit or loss for the year, then dividends and transfers followed by the closing balance. Alternatively, profit and loss retained after dividends and transfers may be shown as the last item in the profit and loss account

and the opening balance, profit retained and the closing balance may be shown in a note to the financial statements.

Dividend payments

Dividends are the payments made by a company to its members out of profits and provide one part of the return to investment in a company. The rules governing the procedure for the payment of dividends will be laid down in the company's articles. These usually follow the same lines as the provisions of the Companies Acts. These allow directors to make interim payments and most companies pay one interim dividend per year. The final dividend may be recommended by the directors but must be sanctioned by the company at the annual general meeting, where members can reduce the proposed amount of the final dividend but cannot increase it. The fact that the final dividend is declared at the annual general meeting is the reason why published accounts contain the phrase 'proposed dividend', the accounts being sent to members prior to the meeting. Dividends are expressed in terms of so many pence per share.

The proportion of a company's annual profits which are appropriated for dividend payments is a decision of the company's directors and is part of the financial management of the company. It may be said to depend upon the company's dividend policy. A number of factors help determine dividend policy, important amongst which are:

(a) Cash flow considerations, notably the availability of cash with which to pay dividends and the company's other demands on cash resources, notably for financing operations and investment.
(b) Stock market considerations, such as directors' perceptions of the expectations of the market for dividends.
(c) Accounting principles applied in calculating profit.
(d) Legal restrictions on dividend distribution.

Legal restrictions

There are two main legal restrictions on dividend distributions. One derives from periodic legislation enacted as part of government economic policies directed towards the control of inflation. Such policies frequently involve prices and incomes policies, part of which involves control of dividends. The second source of restriction derives from company law, both statute and case law and it is this type of restriction which we consider here.

A long-standing problem in both company law and accounting has been the determination of the portion of a company's resources which is capital and that which might legitimately be termed 'profits' and be available for distribution. This is an important distinction, particularly for creditors, since an unscrupulous management might gradually return shareholders' capital to them by paying dividends in excess of profits and thereby leave creditors unprotected. Prior to 1980 restrictions on the distribution of capital were more implicit than explicit in company law although the Companies Act 1948 provided that dividends should only be paid from profits. The law governing the computation of profits and the valuation of capital developed through a series of cases. As a consequence it became permissible to pay dividends from revenue profits without first having made good a loss of fixed assets. Also, it became accepted that distributable revenue profit might arise in an accounting period without any necessity to make good previous periods' losses against it, and further that an increase in the overall value of fixed assets might be distributed as dividends subject to the maintenance of paid up capital. These examples of case law suggest quite a liberal approach to the maintenance of capital and determination of distributable profits.

From the early 1960s pressure began to accumulate for a tightening and formalization of the law governing distributable profit. In 1963 the Jenkins Committee on Company Law recommended that statutory rules should govern distribution of profits. These rules were echoed in the Second and Fourth Directives of the EEC and were incorporated into UK company law by the Companies Acts 1980 and 1981.

Companies Act 1980

The Companies Act 1980 had as its main purpose the clarification of the definition of distributable profits. According to Section 39 of CA 80 a company must not make a distribution except out of profits lawfully available. For that purpose a 'distribution' is any distribution of the company's assets to its members, including preference shareholders, whether in cash or otherwise. Exceptions to this are: the issue of fully or partly paid bonus shares, the redemption of redeemable preference shares out of a new issue, an authorized reduction of capital, and the return of assets on winding up. Under the Act, companies are only allowed to distribute the aggregate of accumulated realized profits that have not previously been either distributed or capitalized, less any accumulated realized losses not previously written off in a reduction or reorganization of capital. The Act states that realization is to be determined by reference to normal accounting principles. In Chapter 3 we examined the importance of the prudence concept which, under SSAP2, states: 'revenues and profits are not anticipated, but are recognized by inclusion in the profit and loss account only when realized in the form either of cash or of other assets, the ultimate cash realization of which can be assessed with reasonable certainty'.

In order to compute profits available for distribution it is necessary to:

(*a*)   Determine the amount of accumulated profits.
(*b*)   Deduct accumulated realized profits previously utilized by dis-

tribution or by capitalization into a capital redemption reserve or into fully or partly-paid bonus shares.

(c)   Deduct the amount of accumulated realized losses

(d)   Add back any accumulated, realized losses previously written off in a reduction or reorganization of capital.

Example 4.1

Alfa Limited has accumulated realized profits/losses as follows:

	£000
Realized profits	200
Realized losses	30

Distributable profits:

	£000	£000
(a) Accumulated realized profits, *less*	200	
(b) Previous distributions and capitalizations	nil	
Net accumulated, realized profits		200

Less

	£000	£000
(c) Accumulated realized losses, *less*	30	
(d) Any sums written off in capital reductions or reorganization	nil	
Net accumulated, realized losses		30
Distributable profits		170

In addition, a public company must satisfy two further conditions before paying a dividend. First, the amount of its net assets at the time of distribution must exceed the aggregate of its called up share capital plus its undistributable reserves. Second, the amount of the distribution must not reduce the amount of its net assets below the aggregate of its called up share capital plus its undistributed reserves. Undistributable reserves are defined as the sum of share premium account, capital redemption reserve, accumulated unrealized profits not capitalized, less accumulated, unrealized losses not previously written off in a capital reduction or reorganization, and any reserve which the company's memorandum or articles prohibit being distributed. This definition excludes a previous distribution and as a consequence a public company (unlike a private one) which had made a distribution out of unrealized profits will be unable to make a distribution until it has made sufficient realized profits to cover such a distribution.

Example 4.2

Assume the information given in Example 4.1 refers to a public company and, in addition, the following details apply:

	£000
Unrealized profits	60
Unrealized losses	80
Share capital	1,000

(a) Net assets must exceed	£000	£000
Share capital		1,000
Realized profits	200	
Less: realized losses	30	170
Unrealized profits	60	
Less: unrealized losses	80	(20)
		1,150

(b)   Distribution must not reduce net assets below:

Share capital	1,000
Excess of unrealized profits over losses	nil
	1,000
Distributable profits	150

Additional restrictions are applied to investment and insurance companies.

An investment company is defined by CA 80 as a public company listed on the Stock Exchange whose business consists of investing its funds mainly in securities with the aim of spreading investment risk and whose constitution bars the payment of capital profits. Such a company has an alternative basis of distribution, thus:

Accumulated, realized profits (so far as undistributed or capitalized) *Less* accumulated revenue losses (both realized or unrealized, so far as not written off).

Provided that before and after the distribution, the company's assets are equal to at least one and a half times the total its liabilities.

In general, provisions relating to distributable profits of companies other than investment companies apply also to insurance companies with long-term business. However, those which have properly transferred to its profit and loss account from a surplus or deficit on its long-term business funds are to be treated as a realized profit or loss as appropriate.

The accounts from which it is necessary to compute distributable profits are:

(a)   The last annual accounts prepared under the Companies Acts, or if they are not available or cannot sustain a distribution.
(b)   The initial accounts of a new company which has yet to file its annual accounts.
(c)   Interim accounts such as will provide a reasonable judgement to be made concerning distributable profits.

Questions

1   Distinguish between ordinary, preference and deferred shares.
2   Distinguish between a reserve and a provision.

3 Describe the nature of a share premium account and a revaluation reserve.
4 The following are details of three separate companies' summarized balance sheets at 31 March 19X2:

	Angie plc £000	*Betty plc* £000	*Cathy plc* £000
Fixed assets	2,500	380	500
Current assets	900	180	(300)
Current liabilities	(700)	(160)	(200)
	2,700	400	600
Share capital	200	300	2,000
Reserves:			
Revaluation	1,100	(200)	–
Realized capital profit	800	–	–
Brought forward realized revenue profit (loss)	400	500	(1,600)
Current year realized revenue profit (loss)	200	(200)	200
	2,700	400	600

Angie and Betty are public companies and Cathy a private company under the Companies Act 1980. Angie's property, previously included in the financial statements at original cost of £900,000 was revalued on 1 April 19X1 at £2 million. This revalued amount is included in the figures above, subject to the full amount being written off equally over the next 50 years from 1 April 19X1. Prior to this date, no depreciation had been provided on property. At 31 March 19X2, no transfer had been made between revaluation reserve and realized revenue profit.

You are required to:

(a) Compare briefly the bases for calculating the maximum distribution under the provisions of the Companies Act 1980 in respect of public, private and investment companies.
(b) Calculate the maximum distribution that Angie, Betty and Cathy could each make under the Companies Act 1980.
(c) Calculate the maximum distribution if Betty plc is an investment company and its dividend is to be paid from bank overdraft.

Institute of Chartered Accountants in England and Wales

5 Accounting for share and loan capital

Share issues

A private company may not invite the public to subscribe for its shares. Hence, if new shares are to be issued by a private company it is not allowed to advertise for new shareholders, but must instead approach specific individuals or institutions and invite them to subscribe. Public companies, on the other hand, are permitted to advertise, and the mechanics of such a public issue are set out below.

Shares may be offered to the public on three bases as follows:

(a) At par, or nominal value. If a share with a nominal value of £1 is issued at par the company receives £1.

(b) At a premium, where shares are issued at a price higher than their nominal value. Shares will be issued at a premium if the promoter considers that the company will attract considerable applicants and the market price is likely to commence above the nominal value. In the case of an existing company, where the market value is already higher than the nominal value the issue price will be commensurate with market price to eliminate excessive dealings. The excess of the issue price over the nominal value (the premium) is required to be transferred to a special reserve, the share premium account, which was considered in Chapter 4.

(c) At a discount. Prior to the Companies Act 1980 it was permitted, subject to Court approval, to issue shares at less than nominal value. However, the Act revoked this practice.

To understand the book-keeping entries for public issues of shares it is first necessary to examine the events involved. Six stages may be identified.

First, an advertisement in the form of a prospectus is published inviting applications to subscribe to the share issue. Application forms

84

are distributed to the public. Second, completed application forms, together with any money which may be due on application, are received. Third, shares are allotted to successful applicants. Where an issue is oversubscribed the surplus application money may be carried forward to reduce the amount due on allotment from successful applicants. Where any applications are unsuccessful, and the applicants are not allotted any shares, the application money is refunded. The company may insure against the possibility of an undersubscription of shares by entering into an agreement with underwriters who, for a commission, will agree to buy all the shares which are not taken up by the public. As a result, all the shares are sold, whether or not they are over or undersubscribed. Fourth, allotment money is received. Fifth, in the event of shares being issued with payment by instalments, the company will make calls on the holders of shares for instalments usually on dates specified at the time the shares are advertised for sale. Sixth, call money is received. 'Calls in arrear' arise if a shareholder fails to pay calls made on the shares he holds.

Accounting for share issues

The company will open a separate bank account for the purpose of receiving money subscribed for the shares offered. An application and allotment account is credited with cash received with applications and debited where refunds of application money are made. A share capital account records the amount of called up share capital and a share premium account records the difference between the nominal value of shares and the issue price. Corresponding debits are made to application and allotment account. Separate call accounts are opened for each call made. A debit balance would represent calls in arrear.

Where shares are payable by instalments the following accounting entries are made:

Bank account	Debit	
Application and allotment account		Credit
Receipt of application money, including premium		
Application and allotment account	Debit	
Share capital account		Credit
Share premium account		Credit
Allotment of new shares issued		
Application and allotment account	Debit	
Bank account		Credit
Money returned to unsuccessful applicants		
Bank account	Debit	
Application and allotment account		Credit
Money received on allotment		
Call account	Debit	

Share capital account   Credit
Amount due on call

Bank account   Debit
  Call account   Credit
Receipt of call money

Example 5.1
Rain plc decided to increase the issued share capital of the company by
offering for subscription a further 100,000 ordinary shares of £1 each at
a price of £1.50 payable as follows:

80 pence on application, including premium
40 pence on allotment
30 pence on call

Applications for 125,000 shares were received. The board decided to
reject applications for 5000 shares and to allot the remainder pro rata
on a five for six basis. The surplus application money was carried
forward to reduce the amount due on allotment. The calls were duly
made and the sums received except for one applicant for 1000 shares
who failed to pay the money due on call.

Application and allotment

	£		£
Share capital	70,000	Bank – application money	
Share premium	50,000	received	100,000
Bank – refund	4,000	Bank – balance due on	
	124,000	allotment	24,000
			124,000

Share capital

	£		£
Balance c/d	100,000	Application and allotment	70,000
		Call – balance due	30,000
	100,000		100,000
		Balance b/d	100,000

Share premium

	£		£
Balance c/d	50,000	Application and allotment	50,000
		Balance b/d	50,000

Call

	£		£
Share capital	30,000	Bank	29,700
		Balance c/d calls in arrear	300
	30,000		30,000
Balance b/d	300		

Forfeiture of shares

Where a shareholder fails to pay the amount due by him for a call on the shares the directors are usually given powers by the company's articles of association to forfeit the shares provided that proper notice (usually fourteen days) has been given. Forfeited shares may be reissued at any price provided that the amount received on reissue plus the amount received from the original shareholder is not less than their nominal value. The accounting entries to record the forfeiture of shares are as follows:

Share capital account	Debit	
Forfeited shares account		Credit
Called up value of the forfeited shares		
Forfeited shares account	Debit	
Call accounts		Credit
Amounts unpaid on shares		

The following entries record the reissue of the forfeited shares:

Forfeited shares account	Debit	
Share capital		Credit
Called up value of the reissued shares		
Bank account	Debit	
Forfeited shares account		Credit
Cash received on reissue		
Forfeited shares account	Debit	
Share premium account		Credit
To record the treatment of any balance		
remaining on forfeited shares account		

Example 5.2
Using the data given in Example 5.1, assume that the 1000 shares shown as calls in arrear were forfeited and subsequently reissued for £1.30 per share.

Share capital

	£		£
Forfeited shares	1,200	Balance b/d	100,000
Balance c/d	100,000	Forfeited shares	1,200
	101,200		101,200
		Balance b/d	100,000

Forfeited shares

	£		£
Call	300	Share capital	1,200
Share capital	1,200	Bank	1,300
Share premium	1,000		
	2,500		2,500

Rights issue

A rights issue is an issue of new shares to raise additional capital. The new shares are offered to shareholders in proportion to their existing holdings at a favourable price. The shareholder may accept the offer or renounce all or part in favour of someone else. A great advantage of such issues is that costs are kept at a minimum. The accounting entries to record a rights issue are the same as those to record a new issue. Because applicants will know in advance the number of shares to which they are entitled, they will subscribe the correct amount. An alternative to a rights issue is to issue a smaller number of shares at full market price, followed by a bonus issue of shares.

Bonus issues

A bonus issue is a free issue of additional new shares to existing share-holders on the basis of existing holdings, made by capitalizing reserves. The objective is merely to bring the issued capital figure in the balance sheet nearer to the true amount of capital which the shareholders have in the company, namely, the net worth of the business. An issue of bonus shares may follow a revaluation of fixed assets. The distribution of profits over a larger number of shares will reduce the amount of dividend paid per share and bring it more into line with the capital employed in the business. Because the transaction is merely a paper one, it is sometimes referred to as a 'scrip issue'.

Example 5.3
The summary balance sheet of Paul plc as at 31 December 19X7 is as follows:

	£		£	£
Ordinary share capital	10,000	Fixed assets		35,000
Retained profits	30,000	Current assets	8,000	
		Less: current liabilities	3,000	5,000
	40,000			40,000

Technically, the retained profits of £30,000 could be distributed as dividends but this appears to be unpractical since the current assets cannot contain sufficient cash for this to occur. It is more likely that the funds retained have been used for asset acquisition and the company may decide to bring its 'permanent' capital more into line with its net assets by capitalizing (or 'freezing') some or all the retained profit. Thus, the company proposes to convert all the retained profits into share capital by issuing three bonus shares of £1 each for each £1 share already held by shareholders. The accounting entries to record this decision are as follows:

	£	£
	Debit	*Credit*
Retained profits account	30,000	
Bonus account		30,000
Bonus account	30,000	
Share capital account		30,000

After the issue of the bonus shares, the balance sheet would show ordinary share capital as £40,000 and the asset structure unchanged. Bonus issues must be in the form of fully paid up shares and the company could not issue £1 shares and deem that, say, 40p is a bonus element. Bonus issues may also be made from share premium account.

Loan capital

Although long-term borrowings may be obtained from financial institutions such as banks, the conventional method of obtaining long-term loan capital is by the issue of debentures. A debenture is a document acknowledging a company's indebtedness. Debentures, like shares, have a nominal value, are normally issued to provide the company with long-term capital, and the holders of them have the right of transfer, by sale or otherwise, to another person. Unlike shares, they are issued in large monetary units, usually with a nominal value of £100.

A company should obtain long-term capital with the objective of investing in assets whose expected return exceeds the cost of capital. Two important disadvantages attach to long-term borrowing in this regard. First, because the holders of debentures are not members of the company but are creditors, interest on debentures must be paid as a contractual obligation whether profits are made or not. Unlike dividends, interest is a charge against profits, which must be treated, as an expense, rather than an appropriation. This introduces the problem of gearing and with it risks to both the issuing company's shareholders and the purchasers of the debentures. Second, most borrowings have to be repaid by a certain date and on pre-determined terms, unlike most share capital which is repayable on liquidation. Debentures which are to be repaid are termed redeemable. Irredeemable debentures may be issued but are very rare.

Debentures are either secured or unsecured. They are secured by means of either a fixed charge on specific assets of the company or by creating a floating charge over all its assets. Both charges are the result of a legal process, usually associated with drawing up a trust deed on behalf of the debenture holders. Securing debentures is a way of reducing the risks faced by debenture holders. Convertible debentures carry the right to convert into equity share capital on or after a specific date, possibly at a given conversion price per share.

Issue of debentures

Debentures, like shares, may be issued at par, or at a premium, or at a discount. The accounting procedures are similar to those for a share issue, the proceeds of the issue being credited to a debenture account instead of to share capital. When debentures are issued at a premium the amount of the premium is placed to the credit of a debenture premium account. Unlike shares, the Companies Acts do not specify how the balance on this account should be treated, but it would normally be classified as a non-distributable reserve to be used for example, in writing off debenture issue expenses. When debentures are issued at a discount, a discount on debentures account is debited. This balance may be written off immediately to share premium account or to profit and loss account. Alternatively, it may be capitalized and written off over a period.

Purchase or redemption of shares

The Companies Act 1948 permitted the redemption of preference shares by companies whose articles included provision for it. The Companies Act 1981 extended this permission to ordinary shares. The current position may be summarized in the following points:

(a)   A company may purchase or redeem its own shares only if it is authorized to do so by its articles of association. If this is done by an off-market purchase, it must be authorized by a special resolution of the company, whilst a market purchase must be authorized in general meeting.

(b)   The power to issue redeemable shares or to purchase a company's own shares is limited by the requirement that there must always be in issue shares that are non-redeemable, thus providing an irredeemable foundation for the company's capital structure.

(c)   Shares may not be redeemed or purchased unless they are fully paid.

(*d*) Shares which are redeemed or purchased must be cancelled, but such cancellation does not reduce the company's authorized share capital.
(*e*) Except in the case of private companies shares may only be redeemed or purchased out of distributable profits or out of the proceeds of a new issue made for that purpose.
(*f*) Company law places restrictions upon:
    (*i*) How a premium on redemption or purchase may be met.
    (*ii*) The use which may be made of balances on share premium accounts.
(*g*) In the case of a redemption wholly or partly financed out of profits a transfer shall be made to a capital redemption reserve. This is discussed further below.
(*h*) Where redeemable preference shares have been issued with an obligation on the company to redeem them at a premium, the premium must be paid out of distributable profits.

Capital redemption reserve

The Companies Acts stipulate that where the shares of a company are redeemed:

(*a*) Wholly out of the profits of the company, the amount by which the company's issued share capital is diminished shall be transferred to a reserve called 'the capital redemption reserve'.
(*b*) Wholly or partly out of the proceeds of a fresh issue and the aggregate amount of those proceeds is less than the aggregate nominal value of the shares redeemed or purchased, the amount of the difference shall be transferred to the capital redemption reserve.

Transfers to capital redemption reserve are 'frozen' except for the purpose of financing an issue of fully paid bonus shares. Hence the reserve is non-distributable. The above requirements prevent a company's overall share capital plus non-distributable reserves from being reduced when share capital is redeemed. The objective is to protect the company's creditors from the effects of a reduction in capital.

Accounting for the purchase or redemption of shares

As we stated above the purchase or redemption of shares may, in the case of a public company, be financed from profits otherwise available for distribution or out of the proceeds of a new issue of shares made for the purpose of redeeming the shares in question. We shall next consider how one accounts for the purchase or redemption of shares under various financing arrangements.

1 *Financing purchase or redemption with the proceeds of a new issue*

  (*a*) *Redemption or purchase at less than nominal value*

Example 5.4
A company decides to redeem or purchase shares with a nominal value
of £80,000 of £1 shares for £60,000 and makes a new issue of 60,000
shares at a nominal value of £1 each to finance the transaction. Since
the aggregate proceeds of the new issue (£60,000) is less than the nominal value of the shares redeemed or purchased (£80,000), the difference is
transferred to the capital redemption reserve. The accounting entries
are as follows:

	£ Debit	£ Credit
Cash	60,000	
Called up share capital		60,000

(*i*)   To record the allotment of 60,000 shares of £1 each nominal value

	£ Debit	£ Credit
Called up share capital	80,000	
Cash		60,000
Capital redemption reserve		20,000

(*ii*)   To record the redemption or purchase of 80,000 £1 shares for
£60,000

Assuming profit and loss account to be £100,000 the portion of the
company's balance sheet showing shareholders' funds before and after
the redemption or purchase is as follows:

Before	£	*After*	£
Share capital		Share capital issued:	
authorized and issued:		60,000 at £1	60,000
80,000 at £1	80,000	Capital redemption reserve	20,000
Profit and loss account	100,000	Profit and loss account	100,000
	180,000		180,000

(*b*)   *Redemption or purchase at a premium of shares issued at par*
In such a case, the premium must be paid out of distributable profits
even though the proceeds of a new issue might be sufficient to cover
the full purchase price.

Example 5.5
Assume that shares of nominal value £75,000 which had initially been
issued at par are redeemed at £90,000 using the proceeds of an issue of
90,000 £1 shares at par. The accounting entries are:

	£ Debit	£ Credit
Cash	90,000	
Called up share capital		90,000

(*i*)   To record the allotment of £90,000 shares of £1 each nominal value.

	£ Debit	£ Credit
Called up share capital	75,000	
Profit and loss account	15,000	
Cash		90,000

(*ii*) To record the redemption of £90,000 shares of £1 each nominal value.

The portion of the company's balance sheet showing shareholders funds before and after the redemption or purchase is as follows:

Before	£	*After*	£
Share capital	75,000	Share capital	90,000
Profit and loss account	100,000	Profit and loss account	85,000
	175,000		175,000

2   *Financing purchase or redemption wholly out of distributable profits*
When the shares which are purchased or redeemed are cancelled, the company's issued share capital must be reduced by the nominal value of the shares in question and that amount should be transferred to the capital redemption reserve. Using the data in Example 5.5 above, but with the purchase or redemption being financed wholly from distributable profits, the accounting entries are as follows:

	£ Debit	£ Credit
Profit and loss account (distributable reserves)	90,000	
Called up share capital	75,000	
Cash		90,000
Capital redemption reserve		75,000

To record the redemption or purchase of 75,000 £1 shares at £1.20 per share and to transfer the nominal value of such shares to capital redemption reserve. If the shares were purchased at a discount from nominal value, say at £60,000, the debit to profit and loss account would be £60,000 with the transfer to capital redemption reserve being £75,000 as above.

3   *Financing purchase or redemption of shares partly from a new issue and partly from distributable profits*
In such cases the above procedures apply. Using the data in Example 5.5, but with the purchase or redemption being financed partly by £60,000 received from the proceeds of a new issue of 60,000 £1 shares, and £30,000 from distributable profits, the accounting entries are as follows:

	£ Debit	£ Credit
Cash	60,000	
Called up share capital		60,000

(*i*)   To record the issue of 60,000 shares of £1 each nominal value

Called up share capital	75,000	
Profit and loss account	30,000	
Cash		90,000
Capital redemption reserve		15,000

(*ii*)   To record the redemption or purchase of £75,000 shares of £1 each nominal value for £90,000 and to transfer to capital redemption reserve the difference between the nominal value of the shares issued and redeemed.

If the shares are redeemed at a discount, say at £70,000, the balance to be met from distributable profit is £5,000, and the accounting entries equivalent to those in (*ii*) above are:

	£	£
	Debit	*Credit*
Called up share capital	75,000	
Profit and loss account	£5,000	
Cash		70,000
Capital redemption reserve		£10,000

4   *Financing redemption or purchase of shares out of capital*
If authorized to do so by its articles, a private company may redeem or purchase its own shares out of capital. The portion of redemption or purchase made from capital (defined as the permissible capital payment) is:

the price of redemption or purchase
Less the sum of:
distributable profits and
the proceeds of a new issue of shares made for that purpose.

In addition, before a payment out of capital can be made certain safeguards must be satisfied. These are as follows:

(*a*)   The payment must be approved by special resolution.
(*b*)   The directors of the company must make a statutory declaration stating the amount of the permissible capital payment and their opinion that there will be no grounds upon which the company will be unable to meet its debts after such a payment and that the company will continue as a going concern during the year following the payment out of capital.
(*c*)   An auditor's report must be attached to the directors' declaration stating that the auditor has enquired into the company's affairs and that in his opinion the permissible capital payment has been properly determined and that he/she is not aware of anything indicating that the directors' opinion is unreasonable.
(*d*)   Details of the capital payment must be published in the London Gazette and a national newspaper, or be notified to each creditor

individually. Creditors and members of the company may apply to the court for cancellation of the resolution.

(e) If the company is wound up within one year of the capital payment date, the directors who signed the declaration and the shareholders whose shares were redeemed or purchased shall be liable to contribute to any deficiency in net assets and the cost of winding up the company.

Additionally, the capital redemption reserve is relevant to accounting for redemptions or purchases out of capital. Two cases may be recognized:

(a) Where the total of the permissible capital payment plus the proceeds of a new issue is less than the nominal value of the shares redeemed or purchased the difference is to be transferred to capital redemption reserve.

(b) Where the total of the permissible capital payment and the proceeds of a new issue is greater than the nominal amount of the shares redeemed or purchased, the excess may be applied to reduce the amount of capital redemption reserve, share premium account, the company's full paid share capital, or revaluation reserve. Aspects of these two circumstances are illustrated in the following examples.

(a) *Redemption or purchase requiring transfers to capital redemption reserve*

(1) *Purchase or redemption of shares at a premium*

Example 5.6
A company with distributable profits of £48,000 wishes to purchase or redeem 120,000 £1 shares for £140,000. This is to be funded partly from the proceeds of a new issue of shares which raises £60,000. According to the rule noted above, the company's permissible capital repayment is given by:

	£	£
price of purchase		140,000
Less the aggregate of distributable profits	48,000	
proceeds of new issue	60,000	(108,000)
permissible capital payment		32,000

The relevant accounting entries are as follows:

	£ Debit	£ Credit
Cash	60,000	
Called up share capital		60,000

(i) To record the issue of 60,000 shares of £1 each at nominal value

Called up share capital	120,000	
Profit and loss account	48,000	
Cash		140,000
Capital redemption reserve		28,000

(*ii*)   To record the purchase or redemption of 120,000 shares of £1 each for £140,000 and to transfer to capital redemption reserve the shortfall between the nominal amount of such shares and the sum of the permissible capital payment of £32,000 and the proceeds of the new issue of £60,000. Thus, the transfer to capital redemption reserve is £(120,000 − (32,000 + 60,000)) or £28,000.

(2)   Purchase or redemption of shares at a discount
Assuming the data in Example 5.6 above except that the nominal value of shares redeemed or purchased is £160,000, the accounting entries are as follows:

	£	£
	Debit	*Credit*
(*i*) As above		
Called up share capital	160,000	
Profit and loss account	48,000	
Cash		140,000
Capital redemption reserve		68,000

(*ii*)   The transfer to capital redemption reserve is again the shortfall of the total of permissible capital repayment and new issue proceeds below nominal value of shares redeemed or purchased, thus:

	£	£
Nominal value of shares redeemed or purchased		160,000
Permissible capital payment	32,000	
Proceeds of new issue	60,000	(92,000)
Transfer to capital redemption reserve		68,000

(b)   Redemptions or purchases where various adjustments to capital and reserves are permitted
As we noted above, where the total of the permissible capital payment and the proceeds of a new issue are in excess of the nominal value of shares redeemed or purchased the excess may be applied to reduce various reserves or share capital.

Example 5.7
A company redeems or purchases 100,000 shares of £1 each for £110,000. The transaction is partly funded by £75,000 obtained from a new issue of £1 shares at nominal value. The company has a deficit on profit and loss account of £5,000. The permissible capital payment is hence:

	£	£
Price of purchase or redemption		110,000
Distributable profit	–	
Proceeds of new issue	75,000	(75,000)
Permissible capital payment		35,000

We shall further assume that the company has a share premium account of £25,000 and a revaluation reserve of £50,000. The accounting entries are:

	£ Debit	£ Credit
Cash	75,000	
Called up share capital		75,000

(*i*) To record the issue of 75,000 shares of £1 each nominal value

Called up share capital	100,000	
Share premium account	10,000	
Cash		110,000

(*ii*) To record the redemption or purchase of 100,000 £1 shares for £110,000 and to reduce the balance on share premium account by the difference between the nominal value of the shares redeemed or purchased (£100,000) and the total of the permissible capital repayment (£35,000) and the proceeds of the new issue (£75,000).

The above assumes that the company has chosen to reduce share premium account. It could also have chosen called up share capital, capital redemption reserve, or revaluation reserve.

Use of the share premium account

We noted in Chapter 4 that company law places restrictions on how premiums on redemption or purchase may be met and how the share premium account may be used in redeeming or purchasing shares. In this section we examine these restrictions in more detail.

If redemption or purchase is not financed from a new issue of shares any premium payable must be charged to distributable profits. A debit to share premium account is not permitted for this purpose. If a new issue of shares is used to finance redemption or purchase, it may also be used to finance the payment of a premium if the original shares themselves were issued at a premium. The extent to which this provision may be used is restricted by the Companies Acts to the proportion which is the lower of (*a*) the premium received at the time when the shares now redeemed were issued and, (*b*) the balance on the company's share premium account after the fresh issue. The effect of this rule is to place a restriction on the use of the share premium account for the purpose of paying premiums on the redemption of shares and ensures that the original capital sum is preserved by the fresh resources raised to replace it. Where the premium payable on redemption is greater than the proportion which may be debited to the share premium account, the balance must be found from the profit and loss account. This new rule does not apply to the redemption of redeemable shares issued prior to the Companies Act 1981. These cases are subject to the provisions of the 1948 Act which made it possible for any premium payable on the redemption of preference shares to be paid out of the share premium account.

Example 5.8
On 1 January 19X1, in addition to having an issue of 100,000 non-redeemable shares of £1 each, Wade plc issued 50,000 redeemable ordinary £1 shares at a premium of 50p per share. These shares are redeemable on 1 January 19X5 at £1.70 per share. To finance the cost of redeeming the shares Wade plc issued 50,000 £1 ordinary shares at £1.40. Since a new issue has been made, a proportion of that issue may be used to finance the premium on purchase or redemption. From the rules set out above, the proportion of the proceeds of the new issue of shares which may be so used may be calculated as the lower of:

(*a*)   Premium received by the company on the issue of the shares now to be redeemed, £25,000.
(*b*)   The balance of share premium account after the inclusion of the premium received on the new share issue, £45,000 (£25,000 plus £20,000).

Applying the rule provided in the Companies Act 1981, since (*a*) is less than (*b*), the proportion of the proceeds of the new issue which may be used to pay the premium on redemption is £25,000. It follows that the sum of £10,000 (£35,000−£25,000), representing the proportion of the premium on redemption which may not be paid out of the share premium account, must be paid out of profits available for distribution and charged, therefore, against the balance of undistributed profits.

Redemption of preference shares

The above examples refer to the redemption or purchase of ordinary shares. As we noted above, preference shares may also be redeemed or purchased and broadly the same procedures apply in that the transactions may be financed (*a*) out of profits otherwise available for distribution, transferred for that purpose to a capital redemption reserve account or, (*b*) out of the proceeds of a new share issue effected for redeeming the shares in question.

When a declaration of redemption is made, the nominal value of the shares to be redeemed, plus the premium payable on redemption, is transferred to a preference share redemption account. The accounting entries for recording shares redeemed out of profits are as follows:

	Debit	Credit
Preference share capital account	Debit	
Preference share redemption account		Credit

The nominal value of the shares to be redeemed

Profit and loss account	Debit	
Preference share redemption account		Credit

The premium payable on redemption

Preference share redemption account	Debit	
Bank account		Credit

The amount payable on redemption

Profit and loss account	Debit	
Capital redemption reserve		Credit

The nominal value of the shares redeemed

Where shares are redeemed partly out of the proceeds of a new share issue, the accounts illustrated previously in this chapter for recording share issues are used in addition to those listed above.

Example 5.9
Beadle plc has a share capital of £20,000 ordinary shares of £1 each fully paid and £10,000 redeemable preference shares of £1 each, fully paid and redeemable at a premium of 5p per share. The company has a credit balance of £8,000 on its profit and loss account. It has decided to redeem the preference shares:

(a) By issuing 6000 ordinary shares at a premium of 10p per share payable in full on application.
(b) By utilizing the profit and loss account to finance the balance.

The accounting entries to record the redemption are as follows:

	£ Debit	£ Credit
Preference share capital account	10,000	
Preference share redemption account		10,000
The nominal value of the shares to be redeemed		
Profit and loss account	500	
Preference share redemption account		500
The premium payable on redemption		
Bank account	6,600	
Application account		6,600
Amount received on the issue of new shares		
Application account	6,600	
Ordinary share capital account		6,000
Share premium account		600
The allotment of new shares issued		

	£ Debit	£ Credit
Preference share redemption account	10,500	
Bank account		10,500

The amount payable on redemption

	£ Debit	£ Credit
Profit and loss account	4,000	
Capital redemption reserve		4,000

The nominal value of the shares redeemed otherwise than out of the proceeds of the new issue

The company's capital and reserves after redemption appear as follows:

	£
Ordinary share capital	26,000
Capital redemption reserve	4,000
Profit and loss account	3,500
	33,500

Repayment of loan capital

Debentures are normally issued in the expectation that the loan will be repaid at some future date. The Companies Acts do not lay down any regulations regarding debenture repayment as they do for the redemption of share capital. Redeemable debentures are redeemed according to the terms of issue which are usually:

(a) Redemption by annual instalments over a number of years; or
(b) Redemption in a lump sum at a fixed date; or
(c) Redemption by purchase in the open market.

Since the redemption of debentures could place a burden on a company's liquidity position and hence its financial stability, it is financially prudent to transfer a part of profits each year to a debenture redemption reserve, although there is no legal requirement for this, unless the debenture deed contains this particular requirement. It is also necessary to ensure that the funds appropriated by this process are available at the repayment date and have not been employed in other ways such as financing the purchases of long-term assets. There are two forms of debenture redemption reserve:

(a) A sum equal to that required for redemption is transferred by annual instalments from profit and loss account to a debenture redemption reserve.
(b) By the use of a debenture redemption reserve fund (or sinking fund). A sinking fund is a fund devoted to the redemption of a debt and whose value is built up to that required for redemption at the time of redemption.

Redemption without a sinking fund

In the absence of a sinking fund, and employing instead a debenture redemption reserve, the accounting entries to record the redemption of debentures are similar to those to record the redemption of preference shares, discussed previously, viz:

Profit and loss account	Debit	
Debenture redemption reserve		Credit
To record the annual transfer to debenture		
redemption reserve		
Debentures account	Debit	
Debenture redemption account		Credit
The nominal value of the debentures to		
be redeemed		
Share premium account	Debit	
Debenture redemption account		Credit
Any premium payable on redemption		
Debenture redemption account	Debit	
Bank		Credit
The total amount paid on redemption		

Example 5.10
Leary plc issued 50,000 10% debentures on 1 January 19X0 with redemption to be made by the open market purchase of ten equal tranches on 31 December each year, commencing on 31 December 19X1. The redemption occurring on 31 December 19X6 was at a price of £102 per cent. The accounting entries recording the 19X6 redemption were:

Debenture redemption

	£		£
Bank	5,100	10% Debentures	5,000
		Share premium	100
	5,100		5,100

The item 'share premium' arises as a result of the premium of £2 per £100 of debentures redeemed in 19X6. Such premiums (or losses) on redemption is written off against share premium account, or if none exists, against profit and loss account.

The debenture redemption reserve is adjusted from its opening balance of £25,000 (representing the five redemptions up to and including 31 December 19X5) by the 19X6 redemption, valued at par. The accounting entries are:

Debenture redemption reserve

	£		£
Balance c/d	30,000	Balance b/d	25,000
		Profit and loss	5,000
	30,000		30,000

Thus, the debenture redemption reserve is built up each year by the nominal value of the debentures redeemed. When the entire issue has been redeemed the balance on this account will equal that of the redeemed debentures and should be transferred to the credit of a general reserve account. Finally, the value of the balance of the unredeemed debentures is determined as:

10% debentures

	£		£
Debenture redemption	5,000	Balance b/d	25,000
Balance c/d	20,000		
	25,000		25,000
		Balance b/d	20,000

Redemption with sinking fund

Using a sinking fund approach an equal sum is set aside annually out of profits which, with compound interest at a rate decided upon, will amount to the sum required to pay off the debentures at the date fixed for redemption. Simultaneously, a like sum of money is invested in gilt-edged securities together with the interest received therefrom.

In accounting for transactions involving a sinking fund it is convenient to maintain a separate set of accounts. A special cash account, for example, would record all cash items affected by the sinking fund. The following accounts are required:

(a)   A *sinking fund account* is credited with annual transfers from profit and loss account. These transfers, together with interest on investments and profits on the sale of investments provide the funds for the eventual redemption of debentures.

(b)   A *sinking fund cash account* receives annual transfers from the company's general bank account to correspond with transfers in (a). The money accumulated in this account is used to purchase suitable investments, the interest on which is debited to this account and credited to sinking fund account.

(c)   A *sinking fund investment account* records the investments held. Profits relating to the sale of investments are debited to this account and credited to sinking fund account.

The accounting entries at the date of the creation of a fund are:

1	Profit and loss account	Debit	
	Sinking fund account		Credit
	Annual transfers to sinking fund		
2	Sinking fund investment account	Debit	
	Sinking fund cash account		Credit
	The annual sum invested		

This process will be repeated each year. In addition, the annual interest will be dealt with as follows:

3	Sinking fund cash account	Debit
	Sinking fund account	Credit
	Interest received on investments	

4	Sinking fund investment account	Debit
	Sinking fund cash account	Credit
	Reinvestment of interest received	

Upon realization and redemption the entries are:

5	Sinking fund cash account	Debit
	Sinking fund investment account	Credit
	On sale of investments	

6	Debentures account	Debit
	Sinking fund cash account	Credit
	On redemption of debentures	

7	Sinking fund account	Debit
	Capital reserve account	Credit
	With part of the sinking fund no longer required	

Example 5.11
On 1 January 19X1 Pit plc made an issue of £100,000 of 9% debentures at par, repayable three years later. The company expects that a 10% interest rate is available on financial investments which it might make during that period and hence plans to set aside a constant sum x to be invested at 10% per annum compound, commencing on 31 December 19X1 and annually thereafter, to ensure the availability of sufficient funds to ensure redemption. The value of the sum to be set aside can be determined on a per £ basis as:

$$£x (1.1)^2 + £x (1.1) + £x = £1$$
$$£3.31x = £1$$
$$x = £0.3021148$$

Thus, £30,211.48 should be set aside each year to ensure the redemption of £100,000 worth of debentures at 31 December 19X3. Figures entered in the accounts have been rounded to the nearest £.

The development of the sinking fund is shown by the following accounting entries (the figures in brackets refer to the journal entries listed as 1 to 7 above).

Sinking fund

£		£
	19X1	
	31 December	
	Profit and loss (1)	30,211

	£		£
		19X2	
		31 December	
		Profit and loss (1)	30,211
		Cash: interest (3)	3,021*
19X3		19X3	
31 December		31 December	
Transfer to reserve (7)	100,000	Profit and loss (1)	30,211
		Cash: interest (3)	6,346**
	100,000		100,000

Notes:
*   This sum represents interest at 10 per cent on the £30,211.48 invested at 31 December 19X1.
**   This sum represents interest at 10 per cent on £30,211.48 + £3,021.15 + £30,211.48 and has been rounded up to balance.

The sinking fund investments are accounted for as follows:

Sinking fund investments

	£		£
19X1			
31 Dec. Cash (2)	30,211		
19X2			
31 Dec. Cash (2)	30,211		
Interest (4)	30,211		
19X3			
31 Dec. Cash (2)	30,211	19X3	
Interest (4)	6,346	31 Dec. Cash (5)	100,000
	100,000		100,000

The transfer of the cash balance of the sinking fund at 31 December closes the 9% debentures account on their redemption, as below:

9% debentures

	£		£
19X3		19X1	
31 Dec. Cash: debentures		1 Jan. Cash: debentures	
redeemed (6)	100,000	issued at par	100,000

The investments which make up the sinking fund represent an asset of the company, as does the cash on their realization prior to the redemption of the debentures. An extract from Pit's balance sheet after realization of the investments, but before redemption of the debentures would appear:

Balance sheet 31 December 19X3

£100,000 9% debentures	£100,000	Cash	£100,000
Sinking fund	100,000		

Conversion of a firm to a limited company

Transactions involving shares and debentures often arise when an existing non-incorporated business (whether a sole trader or a partnership) is converted into a limited company. It is common practice for the business of the partnership or of the sole trader to be sold as a going concern to a company formed specifically to take over the business. The arrangement in these cases is for the company to take over the assets and liabilities of the business in return for the payment of cash and/or the allotment of shares and/or debentures.

Closing the books of the old firm

The entries to close off the old firm's books are as follows:

(a) Debit realization account with all the balances of accounts representing assets taken over by the limited company. Credit realization account with the liabilities transferred.
(b) Transfer the remaining assets and liabilities taken over (at agreed valuations) by the proprietor to his capital account. Close off the relevant ledger accounts by transferring any profit or loss on the transactions to a revaluation account. Transfer the profit or loss on the revaluation account to the proprietor's capital account.
(c) Debit the limited company's account and credit realization account with the purchase consideration (i.e. the agreed sale price of the assets less liabilities taken over).
(d) Credit the limited company's account and debit proprietor's capital account with all the elements of the purchase consideration.
(e) Credit cash and debit realization account with any expenses borne by the proprietor.
(f) The balance on realization account represents the profit or loss on realization and should be transferred to the proprietor's capital account.

Example 5.12
The balance sheet of Alan Pinner, a sole trader, at 31 December 19X1 was as follows:

	£	£
Fixed assets		
Delivery van		5,000
Current assets		
Stocks	9,000	
Debtors	8,000	
Cash at bank	3,000	
	20,000	
Less: current liabilities		
Creditors	4,000	16,000
		£21,000
Capital		£21,000

Alpin Limited was registered on 1 January 19X1 to take over all the assets and liabilities of the business with the exception of the delivery van which is retained by the proprietor at a valuation of £6,000. The purchase consideration was agreed at £17,600 to be settled by the allotment to A Pinner of 16,000 £1 ordinary shares, valued at £1.10 each. The appropriate ledger accounts required to close off the books of the old firm are as follows:

Realization account

	£		£
Stocks	9,000	Creditors	4,000
Debtors	8,000	Purchase consideration	17,600
Cash	3,000		
Capital account			
Profit on realization	1,600		
	21,600		21,600

Alpin Limited

	£		£
Purchase consideration	£17,600	Capital account	£17,600

Revaluation account

	£		£
Capital account	£1,000	Delivery van	£1,000

Capital account

	£		£
Delivery van	6,000	Balance b/f	21,000
Shares in Alpin Limited	17,600	Profit on realization	1,600
		Revaluation account	1,000
	£23,600		£23,600

The books of the purchasing company

In the books of the purchasing company the assets acquired are debited at acquisition values, which may be very different from the value shown in the selling firm's books. Book debts are usually acquired at book values less an agreed provision for bad or doubtful debts. In addition to the purchase price of the tangible assets a further sum may be payable for goodwill defined as the excess of the purchase consideration payable to the seller over the value of the net tangible assets acquired. The net tangible assets are the assets less the liabilities taken over.

The entries required in the purchasing company's books are as follows:

(a)   Debit each asset account, including goodwill, with the values at which the various assets are acquired and credit purchase of business account with these values.

(b) Debit purchase of business account with the liabilities taken over and credit separate liability accounts.

(c) Credit share capital account, share premium account, debentures account and cash account with payments to the proprietor of the old firm and debit purchase of business account with these values.

The balance remaining on purchase of business account will be goodwill or reserve arising.

Example 5.13
Assume that Alpin Limited valued the stocks and debtors shown in Example 5.12 at £9,300 and £7,500 respectively. The purchase of business account will appear as follows:

Purchase of business account

	£		£
Creditors	4,000	Stock	9,300
Purchase consideration	17,600	Debtors	7,500
		Cash	3,000
		Goodwill	1,800
	£21,600		£21,600

Questions

1   Barlow plc has issued 120,000 ordinary shares of £1 each at a premium of 30 pence per share. According to the terms of the issue the following cash payments were due:

Date		Pence per share
1 May 19X7	On application	50
1 June 19X7	On allotment	50
1 July 19X7	Balance	30

The payment on application includes the 30 pence premium on issue.

The details of applications are:

Number of shares applied for by categories	Number of applicants	Number of shares issued to each applicant
1,500	60	750
15,000	30	1,500
60,000	2	15,000

The conditions of the share issue required that sums overpaid on application would be retained by the company and used to reduce any additional sums due on shares allotted. Surplus contributions were returned on 15 June 19X7. All but one applicant paid the sums due on the given date. The exception was Mr A J Pithey who applied for 1500 shares, subscribed £750, and was allotted 750 shares. Pithey was unable to meet the cash due on allotment and on 2 August 19X7 the shares were forfeited.

On 1 September 19X7 the directors re-issued Pithey's 750 shares as fully paid to Mr R G Currie in return for his cheque in full settlement.

You are required to:

(a)   Prepare a statement showing any overpayment and underpayment in regard to each class of applicants on 1 June 19X7.
(b)   Show how the transactions detailed in the question would appear in Barlow's books.

2   Pollock plc issued £250,000 of 10 per cent redeemable debentures at par on 1 March 19X7. Interest on the debentures is paid twice yearly on 1 September and 28 February.

Redemption is required on the following terms by the debenture trust document. The company is to pay to the debenture trustees annually, commencing on 28 March 19X8, the sum of £25,000 which is to be used for the redemption and cancellation of an equivalent amount of debenture stock. As an alternative, the company is permitted to purchase its own debenture stock on the market but must surrender such purchases to the debenture trustees. If there is any accrued interest on debentures purchased under this scheme, appropriate adjustments must be recorded in the company's books. In any years when Pollock makes such purchases any shortfall of the nominal value of stock purchased below £10,000 must be paid by the company to the debenture trustees by 28 February in that year.

To date Pollock has made the following open market purchases of debenture stock:

			Nominal value of debenture stock (£)	Purchase price per £100 of debentures
30 November	19X8		30,000	98
31 July	19X9		18,750	95
31 July	19Y0		28,750	92

You are required to:

Record the transactions concerning Pollock's debenture issue in the company's books for the period up to 28 February 19Y0.

3   Some years ago M plc had issued £375,000 of 10 per cent debentures 19X6–19Y0 at par. The terms of the issue allow the company the right to re-purchase these debentures for cancellation at or below par, with an option to redeem at a premium of 1 per cent, on 30 September 19X6. To exercise this option the company must give three months' notice which it duly did on 30 June 19X6 indicating its intention to redeem all the debentures outstanding at 30 September 19X6.

M plc had established a sinking fund designed to accumulate the sum of £378,750 by 30 September 19X6 and had appropriated profits annually and invested these, together with the interest from such investments and the profits made on any realizations from time to time. A special No 2 bank account was established specifically to deal with the receipts and payments relating to the debentures and the sinking fund.

By 30 June 19X6 annual contributions amounting to £334,485, together with the interest on the sinking fund investments of £39,480, had all been invested except for £2,475 which remained in the No 2 bank account at that date.

The only investments sold, prior to 30 June 19X6, had cost £144,915 and realized £147,247. This was used to re-purchase debentures with a par value of £150,000.

Transactions occurring between 1 July and 30 September 19X6 were:

(a)   Interest received on the sinking fund investments:

7 July – £1,756

13 September – £1,455

(b)   Proceeds from sale of investments:

2 August –   £73,215 (book value was £69,322)

25 September – £160,238 (remaining investments)

(c)   Redemption of all the debentures on 30 September, with the exception of £15,000 held by B Limited. The company had received notice of a garnishee order.*

(d)   M plc deposited with the W Bank plc the sum of £15,150 on 30 September, 19X6.

You are to ignore debenture interest and income tax.

You are required, from the information given above, to prepare the ledger accounts (including the No 2 bank account) in the books of M plc for the period 30 June to 30 September 19X6 showing the transfer of the final balances of the appropriate accounts.   *(25 marks)*

* This order issued by the court, instructs M plc not to release the money owing to B Limited until directed by the court to do so.

Chartered Institute of Management Accountants, Stage 2 Financial Accounting, Specimen Examination Paper (New Syllabus)

6 Taxation in company accounts

In dealing with the treatment of taxation in company accounts, the following topics have to be considered:

(a) Corporation tax payable on the taxable profits of the company.
(b) Advance corporation tax arising on the payment of dividends.
(c) The treatment of franked investment income, i.e. dividends received by one UK company from another.
(d) The impact of income tax on company accounts.
(e) Deferred taxation arising on differences between accounting profit and taxable profit which are of a 'timing' nature.
(f) Value added tax arising on taxable supplies made by the company.

In order to deal with these topics, a knowledge is required of the following statements of standard accounting practice:

* SSAP 5 – *Accounting for value added tax*
* SSAP 8 – *The treatment of taxation under the imputation system in the accounts of companies*
* SSAP 15 – *Accounting for deferred taxation*

In addition, some points of relevance are also contained in the accounting requirements of the Companies Act 1985.

This section of the book gives an outline explanation of the various taxes dealt with, sufficient for an understanding of the impact of the taxes on the company accounts.

Basic corporation tax accounting

Companies which are resident in the United Kingdom pay UK corporation tax on their worldwide profits; other companies generally pay UK corporation tax on their UK profits only.

110

Since in law a company is a separate legal entity, the tax payable on its profits is seen as a charge against the entity's profit and the incurrence of a corresponding liability by the company. Thus, in double entry terms, the company should record the tax arising on the profit of the accounting period as follows:

DR   Taxation expenses (P/L)
CR   Corporation tax payable (B/S)

with an amount computed by applying the rate of corporation tax payable by the company to its profits, as adjusted in accordance with the tax law.

The profit and loss account charge should be disclosed separately in the profit and loss account. Since other items of taxation expense may arise, the full disclosure details are dealt with below, after considering other aspects of tax accounting.

The balance sheet amount will be classified according to payment date, i.e. either under 'creditors – amounts falling due within one year' or under 'creditors – amounts falling due after more than one year'. In each case the Companies Act formats include a heading 'Taxation and social security'.

In this context, the reader should be aware that some companies pay their corporation tax liability nine months after the end of the accounting period to which the liability relates, whereas others may pay their tax anything up to twenty-one months after the end of the period. The payment gap depends on whether the company was in existence when corporation tax was introduced in 1965. The payment date is, where relevant, likely to be given in examination questions. It should be noted that if tax is payable more than twelve months after the end of the period, any balance sheet is likely to contain two years tax liabilities, which must of course be classed under appropriate Companies Act headings.

Example 6.1
X plc, a long established trading company, makes up accounts to 31 December each year and pays its corporation tax fifteen months after the end of each accounting period. The company is preparing its financial statements for the year to 31 December 19X6. It has been established that the corporation tax payable for the year to 31 December 19X5 (due 1 April 19X7) amounts to £50,000 and that for the year to 31 December 19X6 (due 1 April 19X8) is £70,000.

The disclosure based on the above data is as follows (comparative figures ignored).

X plc balance sheet as at 31 December 19X6

Creditors: amounts falling due within one year (includes)
            Corporation tax   £50,000

Creditors: amounts falling due after more than one year (includes)
            Corporation tax   £70,000

Finally, on basic corporation tax accounting, it may happen that a major dispute arises with the Inland Revenue as to the taxation treatment of certain transactions. The outcome of such disputes may well remain uncertain for some time. Any tax which may arise as a result of such disputes would be classified as a 'provision'. As we saw in Chapter 4 the term provision is used by the Companies Acts to refer to a situation where a liability or loss is likely to be incurred, or certain to be incurred but uncertain as to amount or date. The Companies Acts' formats include the heading 'Provisions for liabilities and charges', including the sub-heading 'Taxation, including deferred taxation'.

Accounting for advance corporation tax

Advance corporation tax (ACT) is best thought of as a 'payment on account' of the company's corporation tax liability, such a payment being set in motion by the company paying a dividend. At a basic rate of income tax of 29 per cent ACT amounts to 29/71 of the dividend payments.

The nature of ACT as a payment on account is most important since it indicates that the recording of ACT by the company is primarily a balance sheet transaction which, in normal circumstances, will have no effect on the company's profit and loss account.

Corporation tax law allows the ACT arising on the excess of dividends paid ('franked payments') over UK dividend income received ('franked investment income') to be offset against the company's corporation tax liability for the period, up to a maximum offset amounting to 29 per cent of the company's income (excluding any capital gains).

The recording of ACT is as follows:

(a) When the dividend is paid
     DR ACT recoverable (B/S)

     CR ACT payable   (B/S)

     } with the amount of ACT arising

(b) When ACT is paid (within fourteen days of the end of the calendar quarter in which the dividend is paid)
     DR corporation tax payable

     CR ACT recoverable

     } with the amount of the ACT offset

The following additional points should be noted:

(a) The balance remaining on corporation tax payable, after the ACT offset, is known as 'mainstream corporation tax' and is disclosed as discussed earlier.
(b) If dividends are paid close to the company's year end, the related ACT may not have been paid by the balance sheet date, i.e. entry (a) above has been effected but not entry (b). In such a case, the ACT is still offsettable and ACT payable which is still outstanding

is classified under 'creditors: amounts falling due within one year'. Such an amount would normally be added to any corporation tax payable included under that heading, without separate disclosure, unless material.

(c)   If, because of the maximum 29 per cent restriction referred to above, not all ACT arising is offsettable, further tax and accounting considerations apply. These are dealt with below.

(d)   It is important to appreciate that the above entries all relate to the balance sheet and have no profit and loss account impact. It also follows that dividend payments reported by a company are shown 'net' (i.e. ignoring any ACT) in the company's profit and loss account.

Example 6.2

Alpha plc makes up accounts to 30 September each year. For the year to 30 September 19X6 the company's taxable income amounted to £700,000 and corporation tax was payable at the rate of 40 per cent. The company's dividend details are as follows:

Paid:	final year ending 30 September 19X5 paid 30 November 19X5	£13,000
	interim for year ending 30 September 19X6 paid 31 July 19X6	£7,000
Received:	dividend from Beta Ltd, first and final dividend for year to 31 March 19X6, received 31 May 19X6	£6,000

Note: dividend amounts are exclusive of the related ACT unless referred to as being 'gross'.

The tax accounting is as follows:

(a)   Record the corporation tax liability
    (i.e. £700,000 @ 40% = £280,000)
        DR taxation expense (P/L) £280,000
        CR corporation tax payable (BS)   £280,000

(b)   Calculate the ACT arising

Dividends paid	£20,000
Dividend income	(£6,000)
Excess dividend payments	£14,000
ACT: £14,000 × 29/71 =	£5,718

(c)   The ACT arising can then be recorded as follows:
        DR ACT recoverable   £5,718
        CR ACT payable   £5,718
    and then assuming the ACT arising has been paid by 30 September 19X6
        DR ACT payable   £5,718
        CR cash   £5,718

(d)   Record the ACT setoff
    DR corporation tax payable   £5,718
    CR ACT recoverable   £5,718
    (check: the ACT setoff must not
    exceed 29% × £700,000 = £203,000)

Summary:

(a)   All ACT arising has been paid.
(b)   The mainstream corporation tax liability is £274,282 (i.e. £280,000 − £5,718).
(c)   The taxation expense in the profit and loss account stays at £280,000, i.e. is unaffected by the ACT position.

Proposed dividends

The corporation tax law limits a company's ability to offset ACT against its corporation tax liability to the amount of ACT arising on dividends *paid* in the accounting period. Thus dividends which are *proposed* at the balance sheet date do not, under the tax law, give rise to offsettable ACT (at least, not until the next period, when its proposed dividend is actually paid).

However, SSAP8 takes the view that if a company records a proposed dividend, it should record the full impact of such a dividend, i.e. it should also record its ACT effect, even though under the tax law no ACT is payable until the dividend is paid. This approach can be related to the 'accruals' or 'matching' concept of SSAP2 and the Companies Act. Any ACT arising on proposed dividends is, of course, not offsettable in the accounting period to which the dividend relates, since that dividend has not been paid.

The basic accounting for the ACT on proposed dividends begins with the normal entry, i.e.:

DR ACT recoverable   ⎫   ACT on the
                                ⎬   proposed
CR ACT payable   ⎭   dividend

Since the dividend has not yet been paid, however, additional considerations arise, as follows:

(a)   The ACT payable will appear on the balance sheet under 'creditors – amounts falling due in the one year', as discussed above.
(b)   The ACT recoverable *cannot* be offset against the company's corporation tax liability *for the period*. The company must now decide what is the nature of the debit balance on the ACT recoverable account. The question to be asked is whether this amount really is 'receivable' by the company or should it be treated as a loss and written off in the profit and loss account.

The basic view outlined in SSAP8 is that such ACT should be viewed as being recoverable if it is likely to be offset against the tax on the profit of the previous six accounting periods or of the next one accounting period only. Otherwise, such ACT should be seen as 'irrecoverable' and written off as part of the taxation expense for the year, being disclosed separately if material. Any recoverable ACT is treated as an asset of the company and dealt with on the balance sheet by offset against a deferred tax account (if one is maintained); if no deferred tax account is maintained, SSAP8 requires the ACT recoverable to be shown as a deferred asset. To comply with the Companies Acts, this would normally be included in 'current assets – debtors' and disclosed separately. The same basic principles would apply to the treatment of any ACT paid which is not fully offsettable, because of the 29 per cent restriction referred to above, usually known as 'surplus ACT'.

Example 6.3
Ant plc has a year end of 31 March. The taxable income of the year to 31 March 19X6 was £900,000 and corporation tax is payable at 40 per cent. The following details in respect of dividends are available:

Paid:	final for year ending 31 March 19X5 paid 31 May 19X5	£110.000
	Interim for year ending 31 March 19X6	£30.000
Proposed:	final for year ending 31 March 19X6	£91.000
Received:	none	

The company does not maintain a deferred tax account and has offset ACT to the maximum in each of the previous ten years. Profits and dividends for the year ended 31 March 19X7 are expected to be broadly the same as for the current year.

The tax accounting would be as follows:

(a)	DR taxation expense (P/L)	40% × £900,000
	CR corporation tax payable (B/S)	= £360,000
(b)	DR ACT recoverable	29/71 × £140,000
	CR ACT payable	= £57,183
	being ACT on dividends paid	
(c)	DR ACT payable	
	CR cash	£57,183
(d)	DR ACT recoverable	29/71 × £91,000
	CR ACT payable	= £37,169
(e)	DR corporation tax payable	
	CR ACT recoverable	£57,183

Being ACT on dividends paid offset against the corporation tax liability
(Check: not to exceed 29% × £900,000 = £261,000)

Summary

(a)   Mainstream corporation tax payable – £302,817 (i.e. £360,000 – £57,183) classified as a 'current' or 'long-term' liability as appropriate.
(b)   ACT payable £37,169 classified as 'current' liability.
(c)   ACT recoverable (against corporation tax of the next accounting period) – £37,169 classified under 'debtors'.
(d)   Taxation expense (P/L) – £360,000 unaffected by ACT accounting.
(e)   Dividends proposed (B/S and P/L) – £91,000.

The accounting treatment of dividend income

We have already seen that, under the corporation tax law, ACT is payable on the excess of dividends paid over dividend income received. (See Example 6.2.) Dividend income thus affects the amount of ACT which a company must pay on its dividend payments.

Quite apart from this, SSAP8 stipulates how dividend income from other UK companies (technically known as 'franked investment income') should be presented in the company's published profit and loss account. In order to ensure that income from all sources is shown on a consistent basis (i.e. gross, before any tax thereon), dividends from UK companies should be presented gross in the published profit and loss account, i.e. inclusive of the related ACT credit. This tax credit attributable to franked investment income is then included as part of the company's taxation expenses for the period and disclosed separately where material.

Example 6.4
M plc holds a large number of investments in the form of shares in other UK companies. For the year to 30 September, 19X6 M plc has the following dividend details.

Paid:	final for year ending 30 September 19X5	£200,000
	interim for year ending 30 September 19X6	£150,000
Received	from various UK companies	£280,000

The company has taxable income of £1,000,000 and pays corporation tax at 40 per cent.
The tax accounting effect of the above is as follows:

(a) ACT arising:	dividends paid	£350,000
	dividends received	(280,000)
	excess dividend	
	payment is	£70,000
	ACT: £70,000 × 29/71 =	£28,592

This is accounted for as discussed previously.

(*b*) Franked investment income: dividend income received £280,000
add the related ACT
(£280,000 × 29/71) = £114,366
Franked investment income £394,366

Extract from the published profit and loss account for the year to 30 September 19X6:

	£	£
Income from fixed assets investments		394,366
Taxation on the profit on ordinary activities, UK corporation tax at 40 per cent based on the profit for the year	400,000	
Tax credit on franked investment income	114,366	514,366

It should of course be evident that the profit after tax figure includes the actual cash dividends received of £280,000. However, for profit and loss account presentation purposes the profit before tax figure includes the gross amount of £394,366. The related ACT (£114,366) is then added to the taxation expense figure. The objective of this treatment is to ensure consistency of presentation with other forms of income.

The impact of income tax on company accounts

Although UK companies do not bear income tax, they will frequently be involved in transactions which have an income tax impact. Such transactions have both tax and accounting implications.

The transactions referred to are of two types:

(*a*) Unfranked investment income received (UFII) is income which is received by a company net of basic rate (29 per cent) income tax. Examples include debenture interest received from other companies, some royalty receipts and the receipt of interest on most government securities. The gross amount of UFII is subject to corporation tax. As this income is received net of 29 per cent income tax, the tax system allows some form of relief for this income tax, to avoid a penal rate of tax applying to UFII.

(*b*) Charges on income paid – this comprises payments made by the company net of basic rate (29 per cent) income tax. Examples include debenture and other long-term interest payments, some royalty payments and covenant payments. When making such payments the company must deduct 29 per cent income tax, pay the net sum to the recipient of the charge, and account to the Inland Revenue for the 29 per cent income tax deducted. The gross amount of charges paid is deducted in arriving at the profits subject to corporation tax.

In summary then, the company may receive income (UFII) from which 29 per cent income tax has been deducted at source and may make payments from which it must deduct 29 per cent income tax when the payment is made.

From an accounting point of view, the key point to appreciate is that both types of item must appear gross in the profit and loss account. The income tax is a balance sheet amount, being a debtor from/creditor to the Inland Revenue.

The double entry is as follows:

(*a*)   To record the receipt of UFII:
DR   Cash   – net sum received
DR   Income tax account   – basic rate tax deducted
CR (say) Income from
fixed asset investments   – gross amount
The debit to the income tax account represents an amount due from the Inland Revenue (see below).

(*b*)   To record the payment of charges on income:
DR (say) Interest payable   – gross amount
CR   Cash   – net sum paid
CR   Income tax account   – basic rate tax deducted
The credit to the income tax account represents a liability due to the Inland Revenue (see below).

In order properly to reflect the relevant tax law, the accounting treatment must deal with any balance on the income tax account at the end of the company's accounting period.

Consider the two situations depicted by the income tax accounts shown in Figure 6.1.

	(*a*) *Income tax account*			(*b*) *Income tax account*	
Tax deducted		Tax deducted	Tax deducted		Tax deducted
from UFII	£4,500	from charges paid £6,000	from UFII £10,000		from charges paid £7,100
Cash to Inland Revenue	1,500				Balance 2,900
	£6,000	£6,000	£10,000		£10,000

Figure 6.1   *Income tax accounts*

Situation (a)

It will be noted here that the tax deducted from the UFII received is less than the tax deducted from charges paid by the company, i.e. as a result of the period's income tax transactions, the company owes an amount of tax (£1,500) to the Inland Revenue. Procedures exist under the tax law (not dealt with in detail here) to ensure that this amount is paid to the Inland Revenue either during the accounting period, or possibly within fourteen days of the end of the period. In the latter case, the amount arising is classified as part of the 'taxation and social security' heading under 'short-term creditors'.

Situation (b)

Here, the tax deducted from UFII received exceeds the tax which the company itself deducts from its charges paid. The company has a receivable from the Inland Revenue of £2,900. The tax law here allows for this amount to be recovered by the company as follows:

(a) Primarily by offset against its mainstream corporation tax liability (i.e. after any ACT offset).
(b) If there is no mainstream liability, or if it is insufficient, then the income is recovered by a cash repayment.

From an accounting point of view, the first of these means of recovering tax requires the entry:

DR Corporation tax payable
CR Income tax account

with the amount of income tax recoverable.

The second would require the amount to be recovered by cash settlement to be classified under 'debtors' in the company's balance sheet.

Deferred taxation

This book limits itself to an outline of the general principles of deferred tax accounting and its impact on published accounts of companies.

It is well established that the profit on which corporation tax is payable can be very different from the reported profit of the company in its published profit and loss account. The accounting profit will normally have to be adjusted to produce a taxable profit figure which complies with the tax law. The necessary adjustments fall into two main categories, 'permanent differences' and 'timing differences'.

'Permanent differences' are those adjusting items of income which will never, at any time, be taxable (e.g. dividends from other UK companies – franked investment income) and those items of expenditure which will never, at any time, be tax deductible (e.g. entertaining UK customers, or charitable donations). Deferred taxation is *not* concerned with these types of differences.

'Timing differences' are those items of income or expenditure which are dealt with in different time periods for tax and accounting purposes. It is, however, a basic characteristic of a timing difference that ultimately the accounting and the tax treatments come to the same thing. Thus timing differences 'originate' (i.e. come into being) and subsequently 'reverse' (i.e. disappear). Deferred taxation is concerned only with this type of difference between accounting profit and taxable profits. Examples of timing differences include book depreciation of fixed assets versus tax capital allowances, general provisions, charges on income paid (debenture interest, royalties, covenants) and most forms of investment income.

The following illustration shows the effect of timing differences and deferred taxation on published accounts.

Example 6.5

The corporation tax computation of ABC plc for the year to 31 December 19X6 shows the following:

	£000
Net profit per the accounts	900
Add depreciation	60
entertaining UK customers	5
Less capital allowances	(80)
dividends from UK companies	(15)
Taxable profits	870

The company pays corporation tax at 40 per cent. A dividend of £645,000 was paid during the period; there was an opening balance on deferred taxation account amounting to £16,000 (i.e. timing differences of £40,000 at 40 per cent tax rate).

The company's tax accounting entries are as follows:

(a)   To record the corporation tax payable:

DR taxation expenses (P/L)	£870,000 × 40%
CR corporation tax payable (B/S)	£348,000

(b)   To record the deferred tax arising on the timing differences originating during the period:

Timing difference is: capital allowance	(80)
compared with: depreciation	60
Timing difference	(20)

Deferred taxation: £20,000 × 40%
    = £8,000

DR taxation expense (P/L)

      £8000

CR defered taxation (B/S)

(c)   To record the ACT arising for the year:

Dividends paid	£645,000
Dividend received	(15,000)
Excess dividend payments	£630,000

ACT: £630,000 × 29/71
      = £257,324

DR ACT recoverable

      £257,324

CR ACT payable

Then, on the assumption that the ACT is paid before 31 December, 19X6:

DR ACT payable

£257,324

CR cash

(d) To record the ACT offset:
The maximum offset is 29% × £870,000
= £252,300
ACT paid is £257,324
Thus
DR corporation tax payable

£252,300

CR ACT recoverable

There is surplus ACT of £5,024 which is, in the absence of information to the contrary, offset against the balance on the deferred tax account.

Summary:

Taxation expense (P/L)	£356,000
(of which £8,000 relates to deferred taxation)	
Corporation tax payable (B/S)	£95,700
(£348,000 − £252,300)	
Deferred taxation	
(£16,000 + £8,000)	£24,000
less recoverable ACT	£5,024
	£18,976

Deferred taxation is classified under the balance sheet heading 'provisions for liabilities and charges'.

SSAP15 covers the detail of circumstances in which deferred tax is to be provided under standard UK practice, together with the required methods of computation and provision and disclosure provisions.

Disclosure of taxation expense

We have now seen all the principal items which are likely to affect the taxation expense in the published profit and loss account of a company.

Disclosure of the taxation expense may therefore consist of the following, each item disclosed separately where material:

Taxation on the profit on ordinary activities

	£000
UK corporation tax X%	
based on the profit for the year	
(of which £X represented deferred	
taxation)	XX

Tax credit on franked investment income received	XX
Irrecoverable advance corporation tax written off	XX

Accounting for value added tax

Value added tax (VAT) is a tax charged on 'taxable supplies' of goods and services made by a person (including a company) who is registered as a taxable person with the Customs and Excise authorities.

A company which makes taxable supplies must collect VAT on such supplies from their customers. Such VAT is known as 'output tax' and has to be handed over to the Customs and Excise authorities (normally quarterly). The current standard rate of VAT is 15 per cent. It is important to appreciate that the company is simply acting as a tax collector here, collecting VAT on its supplies on behalf of the tax authorities. This is reflected in the accounting entry to be made for taxable supplies, as follows:

DR Cash/debtors – with the selling price inclusive of VAT (i.e. the full amount collectable from the customers)
CR Sales – with the VAT exclusive amount
CR VAT A/c – with the VAT collected on the sale

The credit entry in the VAT account represents a liability of the company to the Customs and Excise, to be cleared by a cash payment at the end of each quarter. If the liability has not been paid by the balance sheet date, the liability would be dealt with as part of the 'taxation' liability under 'creditors – amounts falling due within one year', not normally disclosed separately.

Companies may also reclaim VAT paid by them on most of their inputs ('input tax'). The double entry involved in recording purchases of goods or expense items which include VAT is thus:

DR Purchase *or* expense – with the VAT exclusive amount
DR VAT A/c – with the VAT on the purchase
CR Cash/creditors – with the VAT inclusive purchase price

The debit entry in the VAT account represents a debtor, i.e. an amount of input tax recovered from the Customs and Excise authorities. Clearly it is appropriate if output tax on sales and input tax on purchases are offset against each other in the same VAT account, with the net liability or debtor being appropriately classified on the company's balance sheet.

There are a limited number of instances in which a company cannot claim back VAT arising on purchases, i.e. the company may suffer 'irrecoverable input tax'. The most common examples of this are input tax on the purchase of motor cars and on the cost of entertaining UK resident customers. In these instances the cost of the item to the company is the full VAT inclusive cost and this should be the debit entry to the motor car or entertaining expense account.

In addition, a second rate of VAT exists, namely zero. Zero-rating applies to most food, gas, electricity for example and means that a trader need not charge VAT on sales of such items but may reclaim a refund of tax on inputs entering into the final product. As well as the zero-rated categories of goods there are goods exempted from VAT. Exempt goods include insurance, letter and parcel post and finance services. Suppliers of exempt services do not have to charge VAT on their outputs but cannot claim refunds of VAT on their inputs.

In conclusion, from the above discussion, based on SSAP5, it will be appreciated that, with the exception of items subject to irrecoverable input tax, all items presented on the balance sheet and profit and loss account of a company registered for VAT will be exclusive of VAT. This includes disclosure items, such as turnover, cost of fixed assets and capital commitments.

Questions

1   Fairweather Sayle Ltd is a boat manufacturing company which has been established for almost fifty years with a 31 March accounting date throughout and still operates from the original rented premises. Some of the original plant and equipment is still in use but, since incorporation, the company's directors have followed a policy of substantial reinvestment of profits in modern equipment and the distribution of only a modest dividend to shareholders; in view of this policy no provision for deferred taxation on the company's balance sheet has been considered necessary. Whilst the intentions of the 19X4 Finance Bill were known at the time the 19X3–X4 accounts were being finalized the directors decided to take no action on the proposals until they were enacted. The draft accounts for the year ended 31 March 19X5 have recently been completed subject to entries relating to taxation. The following information is available:

(a)   The balance sheet at 31 March 19X4 included the following:

ACT on proposed ordinary dividend of £49,000	£21,000
Mainstream corporation tax for the year ended 31 March 19X4 due 1 November 19X5 after set-off ACT amounting to £21,000	£75,000

(b)   No under or over provision for taxation arose following the agreement of the 19X4 computation.

(c)   The tax computation for the year to 31 March 19X5 may be summarized as follows:

Profit on ordinary activities before taxation	£780,000
Add: disallowable items	20,000
depreciation	543,000
	1,343,750

Less: gain on disposal of fully depreciated plant		25,000
Less: capital allowances		818,750
Corporation tax due on		500,000

(d) The proposed ordinary dividend for the year to 31 March 19X5 was held at the same level and is due to be paid on the same date as in the previous year.

(e) The book written down value of assets attracting capital allowances at 31 March 19X5 amounted to £2,310,000 which exceeded their tax written down value by £2,100,000 at that date.

(f) Forecasts for the three years to 31 March 19X8 are:

	Depreciation £	Profit on ordinary activities before taxation £	Expenditure on plant £	Proceeds of disposals of plant £
19X6	560,000	700,000	800,000	110,000
19X7	655,000	650,000	1,145,000	–
19X8	635,000	700,000	1,185,000	–

You are required to:

(a) Show the journal entries relating to taxation in the accounting records for the year ended 31 March 19X5.

(b) Show how taxation would be disclosed in the financial statements for the year ended 31 March 19X5.   (*26 marks*)

Notes:

1   ACT should be taken at 3/7 throughout.

2   Corporation tax rates are:

Financial year 19X3	50%
19X4	45%
19X5	40%
19X6	35%

3   Capital allowances on plant are:

First year allowance:	from 1 April 19X5 to 31 March 19X6	50%
	from 1 April 19X6	nil
Writing down allowance		25%

Institute of Chartered Accountants in Scotland, Part 1 Examination, Financial Accounting

2   Turner Ltd has purchased items of fixed plant costing £282,000. The company's depreciation policy on such plant is to write the cost off evenly over ten years. In due course the company received a regional development grant of 20 per cent. Mr Whistler, the company accountant, proposes to take the whole of the grant to the credit of the profit and loss account in the year in which it is received. Mr Whistler also raises, with you, the question of advance corporation

tax. The company paid a first and final dividend on 29 April 19X4 of £63,000 for the accounting year ended 30 April 19X4.

You are required to state the advice which you would give to Mr Whistler regarding:

(a) Both of the acceptable methods of accounting for the regional development grant received showing the appropriate workings.

(*6 marks*)

(b) The accounting treatment for advance corporation tax in connection with the dividend paid on 29 April 19X4.   (*8 marks*)

Institute of Chartered Accountants in England and Wales, Professional Examination 1, Financial Accounting 1

3   Rock Estates Ltd was formed many years ago as a property investment company owning blocks of terraced houses in a large city. Due to increased repair costs and restrictions on rental increases it is company policy to sell off houses when vacant possession is obtained. Dividends are paid out of realized gains, as authorized in the company's memorandum and articles of association, to supplement the reduced dividends payable out of income. The advance corporation tax on dividends paid out of property realizations has been treated by the company as part of the cost of the dividend as an appropriation of the profits.

You are required to:

(a) Explain the requirements of SSAP8 in relation to the treatment of advance corporation tax in a company's financial statements.

(*7 marks*)

(b) Comment on the treatment by Rock Estates Ltd of its irrecoverable advance corporation tax.   (*3 marks*)

(*Total 10 marks*)

Institute of Chartered Accountants in England and Wales, Professional Examination 1, Financial Accounting 1

7 Cash flow and funds flow statements

The profit and loss account and the balance sheet are the two financial statements which traditionally have provided users of accounts with information concerning an organization's business activities. The profit and loss account describes what has occurred between two accounting dates at which balance sheets are prepared, whilst a balance sheet provides a statement of financial position at a given date. Apart from technical and other problems associated with their preparation, several difficulties can be identified with profit and loss accounts and balance sheets.

Profit and loss accounts emphasize the matching of revenues and costs, not the flows of resources, cash and otherwise, into and out of an organization over a period of time. They concentrate only upon operating activities, not the effects of other very important aspects of organizational activity, such as financing and investment decisions. The profit and loss account may thus not give a useful indication of what has happened to an organization during a period. For example, it may not be clear whether an organization, although having recorded a profit, has sufficient cash to pay its bills. The balance sheet, although concentrating upon financing and investment, liabilities and assets, does so in snapshots. One may make inferences about the investment and financing activities of an organization by comparing the appropriate totals from opening and closing balance sheets for a period, but such information is not shown directly.

This chapter deals with two statements, the cash flow statement and the funds flow statement, which attempt to deal with some of the deficiencies just noted.

126

Cash flow statements

Cash is the most important resource possessed by any organization. Cash is what gives an organization command over resources and, perhaps of greatest importance, cash allows an organization to meet its commitments and thus remain in existence. Ultimately business transactions involve cash: wages and salaries are paid in cash, as are dividends, and so are tax liabilities and creditors. Failure to meet contractual obligations, for example, interest on borrowings or payments to creditors, may result in bankruptcy. Failure to make profits need not have the same result, at least in the short-term.

The profit and loss account does not show flows of cash into and out of the business. The profit and loss account may show a favourable position but the business may have insufficient cash to meet its immediate needs. Although in the long run making profits will have the affect of increasing the cash resources of a business, in any given year this may not be the case. There are several reasons for this. First, the application of the accruals concept means that expenses are matched with sales, rather than cash disbursements being matched with cash receipts. Revenue which accrues to a period may not involve the receipt of cash until later due to sales being made on credit. Similarly, expenses which are matched against those revenues may not involve cash outflows, e.g. depreciation or purchases on credit. Profit needs to be adjusted for such accruals if it is to be brought nearer to cash flow. Second, cash resources may have been affected by transactions other than of an operating nature, such as the acquisition or sale of fixed assets. Third, cash may come from sources other than the operations summarized in the profit and loss account, e.g. new issues of shares, and may be used for non-operating purposes, such as the redemption of debt.

A cash flow statement accounts for changes in a company's cash flow position during a stated period of time, irrespective of the sources of those changes. Receipts of cash originate from cash sales, debtors who pay their debts, sales of fixed assets, and issues of shares and other securities. Payments of cash include cash expenses, payments to creditors, payment of dividends, interest and taxation, purchase of fixed assets, and the redemption of company securities. The preparation of a cash flow statement involves the data contained in both a company's profit and loss account and balance sheet and we shall illustrate this by using the summarized accounts of Rivelin plc, reproduced in Example 7.1.

We can determine the change in the company's cash position over the period covered by these accounts by identifying the cash transactions, receipts and payments. Example 7.1 shows Rivelin plc to have made a net profit of £32,000 for the year ended 31 December 19X6. This profit figure is based upon sales of £106,000. However these were on credit. The amount of cash generated from sales in the year will depend upon the settlement of debtors from the previous year as well as the amount of debtors outstanding at the end of the current year. Thus if we combine the change in debtors over the year, with the year's sales we obtain:

	£000
Debtors at 31 December 19X5	16
Sales during year	106
	122
Less: Debtors at 31 December 19X6	(20)
Cash from sales	102

Example 7.1
Rivelin plc produces the following information:

Balance sheet as at:	31 December 19X5		31 December 19X6	
	£000	£000	£000	£000
Fixed assets at cost		200		212
Less depreciation to date		72		80
		128		132
Current assets				
Stocks	20		38	
Debtors	16		20	
Cash	8		4	
	44		62	
Creditors: amounts falling due within one year				
Trade creditors	24		26	
Net current assets		20		36
		148		168
Creditors: amounts falling due after more than one year				
9% debentures		20		32
		128		136
Capital and reserves				
Called up share capital		40		40
Profit and loss account		88		96
		128		136

Profit and loss account for the year ended 31 December 19X6

	£000	£000
Sales (on credit)		106
Opening stock	20	
Purchases	80	
	100	
Less closing stock	38	
Cost of goods sold	62	
Depreciation	8	
Expenses	4	

	£000
	74
Net profit	32
Dividend paid	24
Retained profit	8

Note: Taxation is ignored
£12,000 of fixed assets were purchased in 19X6

Similarly, the profit and loss account includes £80,000 of purchases, some of which will be on credit. We isolate cash purchases by adjusting for opening and closing amounts of creditors, hence:

	£(000)
Creditors at 31 December 19X5	24
Purchases during year	80
	104
Creditors at 31 December 19X6	(26)
Purchases for cash	78

Examination of the accounts indicates that several other cash transactions took place:

(a) Fixed assets were purchased for £12,000 (see notes to the accounts).
(b) Debentures were issued to the value of £12,000 (shown by the increase in the value of 9 per cent debentures between the two balance sheet dates).
(c) Dividends were paid to the value of £24,000 (profit and loss account).
(d) Expenses of £4,000 were incurred (profit and loss account).

These items, together with the cash receipts and payments associated with debtors and creditors, can be brought together in a cash flow statement.

Cash flow statement

	£(000)	£(000)
Receipts:		
From sales		102
From issue of debentures		12
		114
Payments:		
To creditors	78	
To purchase of fixed assets	12	
To expenses	4	
To dividends	24	(118)
Decrease in cash (net cash outflow)		(4)

The cash flow statement shows that cash payments over the year exceeded cash receipts by £4,000, meaning that a net cash outflow of that amount took place. This can also be seen from the comparative balance sheets, where cash fell from £8,000 at 31 December 19X5 to £4,000 at 31 December 19X6. One might argue that since a comparison of the cash figures in the balance sheets gives the same answer, a cash flow statement is superfluous. This is not correct. The cash flow statement shows where cash came from and where it went to. This detail is arguably at least as important as the net cash flow. For example, the cash flow statement shows that Rivelin spent twice as much cash on paying dividends as on fixed asset acquisition. Also, the value of its spending on fixed assets was equal to the cash raised by its debenture issue, thus the company may be financing long-term assets by long-term liabilities, financial management which most analysts would approve of.

Funds flow statements

The Oxford English Dictionary defines 'funds' as a permanent stock of something ready to be drawn on. In the case of a business, funds are not necessarily permanent but require replenishment. Figure 7.1 illustrates how funds are applied to business activities and where they are derived from.

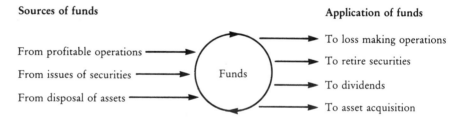

Figure 7.1   *Sources and applications of funds*

Clearly, if the value of sources exceeds that of applications, funds increase, or vice versa.

For most people the funds at the centre of Figure 7.1 are synonymous with cash and hence a common view of the funds of a business is that they are represented by its cash resources. Consequently, a statement showing the flow of funds into and out of an organization (a funds flow statement) would show movements of cash in much the same way as the cash flow statement just considered, and the net increase or decrease in funds would be the increase or decrease in cash.

An alternative to this cash view of funds is to consider funds as working capital. There are three main reasons for adopting this broader view. The first is that an emphasis on cash alone may give an incorrect indication of the funds at the disposal of an organization. Consider Rivelin's position at 31 December 19X6 with £4,000 of cash, £38,000 of stock and £20,000 of debtors. If stock and debtors were converted into cash during the following year with no other changes taking place, Rivelin would have £62,000 of cash. If the company's funds are judged as cash, Rivelin would have almost sixteen times the funds of 31 December 19X6. However, if viewed from a working capital point of view, its funds position is unchanged. Working capital is net current assets and as the following shows, the conversion of stocks and debtors to cash leaves working capital at £62,000.

	At 31 December 19X6	After conversion of all current assets to cash
Current assets:	£000	£000
Stocks	38	–
Debtors	20	–
Cash	4	62
	62	62
Creditors: amounts falling due within one year	(26)	(26)
Net current assets	36	36

All that has happened is that the composition of working capital has changed in favour of cash, but the fund from which the company can draw to finance its activities remains the same.

This leads us to the second argument in favour of a working capital approach to funds. Working capital is the focus of a business's activities, hence its name. With fixed assets it provides the operating capability of the business. An expansion in working capital may be necessary to expand business operations, but this will require an investment of funds, possibly at the expense of the use of funds elsewhere. Conversely, a reduction in investment in working capital frees funds for investment elsewhere or removes the necessity to obtain additional funds in the first place. Although cash is the most useful resource to a business, it is fundamentally only the purchasing power which is directed to obtaining and supporting operating capability which in its turn supports business operations. Working capital is at the centre of the cycle of business operations. A company acquires goods on credit, converts them into debtors on sale, then debtors are converted to cash, which is then used to pay short-term creditors, for the cycle to be repeated. This cycle is summarized in the two flows of Figure 7.1, 'From profitable operations' and 'to loss making operations'. Figure 7.1 shows the other ways in which the fund of working capital may be augmented or depleted.

A third advantage of defining funds as working capital rather than cash is that the latter is more susceptible to manipulation ('window dressing'), than the former. Despite the existence of SSAP17, '*Post Balance Sheet Events*', aimed at remedying this problem, it is still possible to adjust a company's cash balance advantageously by, for example, delaying the payment of creditors or cash purchases by a matter of days. On the other hand, 'window dressing' the overall figure for working capital is much more difficult and therefore, working capital is more reliable as an indicator of funds.

Preparation of a funds flow statement based on working capital

The seven flows of funds in Figure 7.1 summarize the items to be included in a funds statement. Although varying degrees of complexity can be utilized these seven flows represent the only ways in which a company's working capital can alter and we shall utilize them in preparing a funds flow statement for Rivelin based on the company's accounts in Exhibit 7.1.

It is usual to begin by determining funds from operations using data from the profit and loss account. Profit (or loss) from operations is adjusted for any non-funds items included in it. Thus, Rivelin's profit for the year to 31 December 19X6 was £32,000. This contains an allowance for depreciation of £8,000 which is merely a book entry which reduces profit and the recorded value of the associated asset. Thus:

	£(000)
Funds generated by operations:	
Profit	32
Adjustment for non-cash item: depreciation	8
	40

The accounts show that an additional £12,000 of debentures were issued, but that no fixed assets were disposed of. Only two applications of funds are apparent: fixed assets were acquired to the value of £12,000 and dividends of £24,000. The net value of these sources and applications of funds can be accounted for in the change or movement of working capital items over the period. A comparison of Rivelin's two balance sheets shows the following:

	31 December 19X6 £(000)	31 December 19X7 £(000)	Movement
Current assets:			
Stocks	20	38	+ 18
Debtors	16	20	+ 4
Cash	8	4	− 4
Creditors:			
Amounts falling due within one year	(24)	(26)	− 2
Working capital	20	36	+ 16

Stocks and debtors both increased (indicating increased investment of funds) whilst cash decreased (indicating the release of funds). The increase in creditors shows the availability of additional funds. The net increase of £16,000 in working capital shows additional investment of funds in this part of the business. The full funds flow statement set out in Example 7.2 shows that these funds have come from the excess of funds generated from operations and issue of securities over applications.

Example 7.2
Funds flow statement for the year ended 31 December 19X6

	£000	£000
Funds generated by operations		
Profit		32
Adjustments for non-cash items:		
Depreciation		8
		40
Other sources		
9% debentures		12
		52
Applications		
Dividends paid	24	
Purchase of fixed assets	12	36
		16
Movements in working capital		
Increase in stocks	18	
Increase in debtors	4	
Increase in creditors	(2)	
Decrease in cash	(4)	16

The last part of the statement shows changes in the components of working capital. These are not flows, but net changes in the amount of each component. They show that all the funds arising would have been in cash form had some not gone into financing increases in stocks and debtors, slightly offset by an increase in creditors.

The funds statement does not contain information that cannot be found in the profit and loss account and balance sheet. Rather, it reclassifies this information to show how the company financed its activities in 19X6. Thus, Rivelin plc financed the purchase of fixed assets from an increase in long-term loans. In particular, the large increase in stocks is highlighted.

SSAP10 – Statements of source and application of funds

Although there are no statutory requirements relating to the preparation and disclosure by companies of funds statements, SSAP10, *Statements of Source and Application of Funds* issued in 1975, requires all companies having a turnover in excess of £25,000 to include a source and application of funds statement (or funds flow statement) as part of their annual report to shareholders. According to SSAP10:

A funds statement should show the sources from which funds have flowed into the company and the way in which they have been used. It should show clearly the funds generated or absorbed by the operations of the business and the manner in which any resulting surplus of liquid assets has been applied or any deficit of such assets has been financed, distinguishing the long-term from the short-term. The statement should distinguish the use of funds for the purchase of new fixed assets from the funds used in increasing the working capital of the company.

SSAP10 does not stipulate that a particular format must be used for a funds statement but it does give a specimen layout in the appendix to the standard. This specimen statement contains a more detailed dis-aggregation than that considered above and indicates that the content of a funds statement will normally include:

(a) The sources from which funds have flowed into the company:
   (i) The profit for the period before tax
   (ii) Extraordinary items
   (iii) An adjustment for items not involving the movement of funds
   (iv) Issues of share capital
   (v) Funds raised by means of medium or long-term loans
   (vi) Proceeds from the sale of fixed and non-current assets
(b) Application of funds:
   (i) Dividends paid
   (ii) Taxation paid
   (iii) Acquisitions of fixed and non-current assets
   (iv) Repayment of medium or long-term loans
   (v) Redemptions of issued share capital
(c) The change in working capital sub-divided into its components:
   (i) Stocks
   (ii) Debtors
   (iii) Creditors
   (iv) Net liquid funds

Net liquid funds are defined as cash at bank and in hand together with cash equivalents, such as investments held in current assets, less bank overdrafts and other borrowings repayable within one year of the accounting date.

Although SSAP10 does not define the term 'funds' the illustration in the appendix to the standard implies a working capital approach. However, it may be observed that the above list excludes dividends proposed and taxation payable in favour of dividends paid and taxation paid, suggesting a cash concept of funds. In this respect, SSAP10's approach is a compromise between a cash flow statement and a pure working capital statement. Example 7.3 illustrates a source and application of funds statement based on the format suggested by SSAP10. The standard recommends that there should be a minimum of 'netting off' of items, since netting off tends to mask the significance of individually important items. For example, the proceeds from the sale of fixed assets should not be deducted from the figure for purchase of fixed assets and then shown as a net figure under 'application of funds' if purchases exceed disposals in value.

Example 7.3
Barncliffe plc: statement of source and application of funds for the year ending 31 December 19X7

	19X7 £000	19X7 £000	19X6 £000	19X6 £000
Source of funds				
Profit before tax		5,780		5,120
Adjustments for items not involving the movement of funds:				
Depreciation		1,500		1,200
Extraordinary item		(10)		–
Total generated from operations		7,270		6,320
Funds from other sources				
Increase in share capital	2,000		1,000	
Increase in loan capital	3,000		500	
Disposal of fixed assets	100	5,100	50	1,550
		12,370		7,870
Application of funds				
Dividends paid	2,200		2,000	
Taxation paid	1,800		1,500	
Purchase of fixed assets	450		100	
Loan repaid	2,000	6,450	–	3,600
		5,920		4,270
Increase/decrease in working capital				
Increase in stocks		5,300		1,500
Increase in debtors		2,650		200
(Increase)/decrease in creditors		(1,000)		2,000
Movement in net liquid funds:				
Increase/(decrease) in cash	(1,500)		1,420	
Increase/(decrease) in short-term investments	470	(1,030)	(850)	570
		5,920		4,270

Some problem areas

Some problems in drawing up the contents of a funds statement are:

Profit for the period
A loss should be treated in the same way as a profit. It appears as the first item to which depreciation is added back.

Extraordinary items

These are not dealt with specifically by SSAP10. However, generally accepted accounting practice requires that if extraordinary items involve movements of funds they should be disclosed separately in the funds statement at amounts before taxation.

Issues of shares

Issues of shares for cash and issues in exchange for assets are both shown as a source of funds. It is not necessary to disclose bonus issues which merely capitalize reserves because there is no external change in financial resources.

Acquisition or disposal of fixed assets

Incomplete information may be provided on the acquisition or disposal of fixed assets. For example, the following extracts give no information on fixed asset acquisitions or the period's depreciation charge:

	£000	
	19X8	*19X7*
Fixed assets at cost	1,637	1,550
less depreciation	(1,077)	(1,075)
Net book value	560	475

Note: During the year fixed assets which had cost £315,000 and on which depreciation of £150,000 had been charged, were disposed of for £165,000.

The missing amounts can be determined by completing accounts for fixed assets at cost and fixed asset depreciation:

£000

Fixed asset account				*Depreciation account*		
Balance b/f	1,550	Balance c/f	1,637	Disposal	153	Balance b/f 1,075
Additions	402	Disposal	315	Balance c/f 1,077	Charge for	155
(balancing	1,952		1,952	1,230	the year	1,230
figure)					(balancing	
					figure)	

The value of acquisitions which is derived (£402,000) could now be included as an application of funds with the adjustment to profit for depreciation being £155,000.

When fixed assets are disposed of and a gain or loss results, the gain or loss is added back to profit and the full proceeds are shown as a source of funds. For example, if a machine which originally cost £10,000, with a net book value of £6,000 is sold for £7,000, a profit of £1,000 is made. The funds statement will show a receipt of funds of £7,000 and £1,000 is deducted from the profit before tax:

	£
Adjustments for items not involving the movement of funds:	
Profit on sale of fixed assets	(1,000)
Funds from other sources:	
Disposal of fixed assets	7,000

Conversely, where a loss is made on the disposal of fixed assets this must be added back to the profit before tax.

Dividends paid
The original exposure draft referred to dividends paid and proposed, but this was amended to refer solely to dividends paid. The main reason for this change relates to the interval, often several months, between balance sheet date and payment of final dividend.

Taxation paid
Again, the long interval between balance sheet date and payment of tax explains why tax liabilities are excluded from working capital.

Acquisitions of fixed and non-current assets
Government grants are not mentioned in SSAP10, but if material, should preferably be disclosed either as a source of funds, or by showing the amount received separately as a deduction from the full cost of the relevant assets. To the extent that research and development expenditure is carried forward, any increase should be shown as an application of funds. Amounts subsequently written off must then, like depreciation, be adjusted in the funds statement as an item not involving the movement of funds.

Evaluation of SSAP10

In evaluating SSAP10 we may make three observations: first, SSAP10 does not deal adequately with the objectives of fund statements. The standard states that 'the objective of such a statement is to show the manner in which the operations of a company have been financed and in which its financial resources have been used, and the format selected should be designed to achieve this objective'. This tells us little about the needs of users of financial statements and how a funds statement may assist their decision making if indeed this is the use to which such a statement is put. Second, SSAP10 does not discuss the various concepts of funds nor why it favours a particular approach. Third, because the standard does not provide a positive ruling as to the standard format and content of funds statements there remains considerable diversity in corporate reporting practices relating to funds statements despite the standard.

Usefulness of funds statements

At the beginning of this chapter we considered some of the deficiencies of balance sheets and profit and loss accounts in aiding users of financial statements in their evaluation of companies. As our discussion of cash flow and funds flow statement unfolded we were able to obtain more information on company activities and the decisions of management over the relevant accounting period. We may conclude that the funds statement, whether in its cash or working capital form, can answer, inter alia, the following questions.

(a)   Did the funds generated from ordinary trading activities cover payment of tax and dividends?
(b)   Were the funds to pay taxation and dividend obligations raised by long-term borrowing or asset disposals?
(c)   How were loans repaid?
(d)   How were the proceeds of newly issued securities utilized?
(e)   How was the increase in working capital financed?

Over a number of years a series of funds statements may provide the analyst with valuable information on liquidity trends which assist his estimates of the future.

In common with other financial statements, the funds statement can reveal what has happened but cannot tell us why. For example, it may show an increase in stocks, but it cannot tell us whether this occurred because of deliberate policy, or poor stock control, or an inability to sell the product. Similarly, an increase in share capital does not tell us whether this was the best method of raising the finance, nor whether the action could have been avoided by better asset control. Issues of this nature will be considered further in Chapter 13.

Example 7.4
From the following information we shall prepare a source and application of funds statement for the year ended 31 March 19X9, complying with SSAP10.

	Trial balances as at	
	1 April 19X8	31 March 19X9
	£	£
Credits:		
6% Debentures 1990	30,000	20,000
Ordinary shares of £0.25 each	20,000	45,000
Share premium	–	15,000
Sales	–	107,006
Creditors	7,520	9,050
Reserves and retained profit	35,963	18,963
Corporation tax due 1 January 19X9	4,200	–
Bad debt provision	9	11
Depreciation provision:		
Freehold buildings	4,023	5,164

	Trial balances as at	
	1 April 19X8 £	31 March 19X9 £
Machinery and vehicles	9,671	10,732
Profit on redemption of debentures	–	1,700
Profit on sale of machinery	–	95
Proposed final dividend	1,567	–
Provision for maintenance of properties	325	268
Bank overdraft	85	–
	£113,363	£232,989
Debits:		
Stock	8,853	10,625
Cost of sales	–	95,042
Debtors	9,577	12,024
Trade loans to customers	3,750	4,950
Fixed assets at cost:		
Freehold land	13,200	16,200
Freehold buildings	56,075	58,760
Machinery and vehicles	18,422	20,652
Investments at cost	3,486	4,024
Interim dividend	–	1,383
Balance at bank	–	9,329
	£113,363	£232,989

In addition to the above, the following transactions took place during the year:

(a) There was a bonus issue of shares of one for one to the ordinary shareholders, followed by a rights issue of one share for every eight shares held at a price of £1 per share.
(b) The freehold land was revalued from £13,200 to £16,200, the increase in valuation being transferred to reserves.
(c) Machinery costing £2,700 and with a book value of £600 was sold at a profit of £95.
(d) Part of the debentures were redeemed at a profit of £1,700.

The statement of source and application of funds is shown below:

Statement of source and application of funds year ended 31 March 19X9

	£	£
Source of funds		
Profit before tax		12,007
Adjustments not involving the movements of funds:		
Depreciation on freehold buildings	1,141	
Depreciation on machinery and vehicles	3,161	4,302
Total generated from operations		16,309

	£	£
Funds from other sources		
Proceeds of rights issue of ordinary shares	20,000	
Proceeds of sale of machinery	695	20,695
		37,004
Application of funds		
Fixed assets purchased:		
freehold buildings	2,685	
machinery	4,930	
Corporation tax paid	4,200	
Dividends paid	2,950	
Cost of redemption of £10,000 6% Debentures	8,300	
Investments purchased	538	
Payment for property maintenance	100	23,703
		13,301
Increase in working capital:		
Increase in stock	1,772	
Increase in debtors	2,445	
Increase in trade loans to customers	1,200	
Increase in creditors	(1,530)	
	3,887	
Movement in net liquid funds:		
Increase in cash	9,414	£13,301

The components of the statement are generated a follows:

Profit before taxation:
Operating profit before taxation is determined as follows:

	£
Sales	107,006
Cost of sales	(95,042)
	11,964
Credit for property maintenance	43
	12,007

   The credit taken to profit as the result of property maintenance is the difference between the payment made (£100) and the reduction in the balance on that account (£57).

Depreciation on freehold buildings:
No buildings were disposed of and the adjustment for depreciation is given by the change in balances, thus:

£5,164 − £4,023 = £1,141

Depreciation on machinery and vehicles:
This item consists of the change in balances over the year (£10,732 −

£9,671) together with the accumulated depreciation on the machinery disposed of (£2,700 − £600).

Proceeds of rights issue:
The opening balance of ordinary shares was £20,000 which at £0.25 represented 80,000 shares. The bonus issue increased the number of shares in issue to 160,000 and the rights issue, being one to eight £1 per share raised £20,000.

Proceeds of sale of machinery:
The profit of £95 on a book value of £600 represents a sales price of £695.

Purchases of fixed assets:
The change in debit balances on land represent the results of the revaluation, however for buildings, and machinery and vehicles acquisitions occurred. Since no buildings were disposed of the value of acquisitions is given by the difference between opening and closing debit balances (£58,760 − £56,075). In the case of machinery and vehicles, to the difference in debit balances (£2,230) must be added the cost value of disposals (£2,700) to give the gross value of acquisitions.

Corporation tax paid:
Given by the change in the credit balance.

Dividends paid:
Given by the sum of the changes on balances for proposed final dividend and interim dividend.

Cost of redemption of debentures:
The profit of £1,700 on the redemption of debentures of nominal value £10,000 means a funds outflow of £8,300.

Investments purchased:
This is given by the change in the debit balances.

Payment for property maintenance:
Given in notes above.

Change in stock:
This is given by the increase in debit balances.

Change in debtors:
The increase in the debit balances (£12,024 − £9,577), equal to £2,447 understates the investment in debtors during the year since the provision for bad debts has increased by £2.

Change in creditors:
This is given by the increase in the credit balances.

Change in cash:
Since the bank overdraft has reduced by £85 whilst the balance at bank has increased by £9,329, the total increase in cash is £9,414.

Questions

1   The directors of Modern Engineering plc have prepared accounts for the year ended 30 September 19X4 and are considering their funding requirements for the coming year. They wish to invest heavily in new plant to automate production but they are very aware of the high cost of robots.

The balance sheet as at 30 September 19X4 is as follows:

	£000	£000
Tangible assets		
Freehold premises		561
Plant and equipment		384
Vehicles		62
		1,007
Intangible asset		
Goodwill		50
Deferred asset		
ACT on proposed dividend		43
Current assets		
Stock	280	
Debtors	350	
Short-term investment	20	
Balance at bank	17	
	667	
Current liabilities		
Creditors	230	
Corporation tax due		
June 19X5	183	
Proposed dividend (ordinary)	100	
ACT on proposed dividend	43	
	556	
Net current assets		111
		1,211
Loan from Industrial and		
Commercial Finance		150
		1,061
Ordinary shares of 25p each		500
7% Redeemable preference shares		
of £1 each		200
Capital reserves		135
Revenues reserves		226
		1,061

The directors anticipate that the following events are likely to occur during the year to 30 September 19X5:

(a) The freehold premises will be revalued and a surplus of £100,000 is anticipated.

(b) Expenditure on plant and equipment is forecast at £240,000 and on vehicles £64,000. Equipment with a book value of £20,000 is expected to be sold at that value.

(c) Stocks, debtors and creditors are expected to increase by 10 per cent.

(d) A rights issue of 2 for 5 at 35p will be made on 31 December 19X4.

(e) A £30,000 loan will be repaid to Industrial and Commercial Finance.

(f) A full preference dividend and related advance corporation tax will be paid during the year.

(g) An ordinary dividend of 5p for the year will be proposed at 30 September 19X5.

(h) The profit before tax for the year to 30 September 19X5 is forecast as £280,000; corporation tax is estimated at £100,000.

(i) Depreciation for the year, including depreciation on all additions, is estimated to be £49,000 on plant and equipment and £21,000 on vehicles.

You are required to:

(a) Prepare a report for the directors to include:
  (i) A funds flow forecast for the year to 30 September 19X5 to show the change in the bank balance.   (*10 marks*)
  (ii) A brief commentary on the position revealed by the funds flow statement.   (*5 marks*)

(b) Comment on the usefulness of this type of information for the purpose required by the directors of Modern Engineering plc. What other information could be of use to fulfil their needs?
          (*5 marks*)
          (*Total: 20 marks*)

Chartered Institute of Public Finance and Accountancy, Professional Examination 1, Financial Accounting and Auditing

2 The summarized balance sheet and profit and loss account of the Craigleith Trading Company Ltd are set out below:

Balance sheet as at 30 April 19X5

	Note	19X5 £000	19X4 £000
Tangible fixed assets	1	491	643
Current assets	2	1,693	1,306
Creditors – amounts falling due within one year		649	603
Net current assets		1,024	703

	Note	19X5 £000	19X4 £000
Total assets less current liabilities		1,515	1,346
Creditors – amounts falling due after more than one year loans and debentures		416	555
		1,099	791
Capital and reserves:			
Called up share capital	4	840	720
Profit and loss account	5	259	71
		1,099	791

Profit and loss account for the year ended 30 April 19X5

	19X5 £000	19X4 £000
Turnover	2,930	1,563
Change in stocks of finished goods and work in progress	205	106
	2,725	1,669
Raw materials and consumables	1,015	702
Other external charges	205	107
	1,220	809
	1,505	860
Staff costs	1,154	742
Depreciation	56	45
Other operating charges	183	33
	1,393	820
Operating profit	112	40
Income from deposits	3	1
	115	41
Interest payable on loans not wholly repayable within five years	30	35
Profit on ordinary activities before taxation	85	6
Tax on profit on ordinary activities	40	2
Profit on ordinary activities after taxation	45	4
Extraordinary credit after taxation	205	–
	250	4

	Note	19X5 £000	19X5 £000
Transfer to capital redemption reserve		20	–
Proposed dividend		42	28
		62	28
Retained profit/(loss) for year		188	(24)

Notes:

	19X5 £000	19X4 £000
1 Tangible fixed assets comprised:		
(a) Freehold property:		
at cost		455
at valuation	340	

(b) Plant:	Cost £000	Cumulative depreciation £000
at 30 April 19X4	282	94
additions during year at cost	103	–
disposals	(109)	(25)
provision for the year	–	56
at 30 April 19X5	276	125

Properties which originally cost £235,000 were sold during the year for £525,000 together with related plant which realized £99,000. Corporation tax of £100,000 was payable.

	19X5 £000	19X4 £000
2 Current assets comprised:		
Stocks and work-in-progress	893	688
Trade debtors	793	608
Cash at bank and in hand	7	10
	1,693	1,306

	£000	£000
3 Creditors – amounts falling due within one year comprised:		
Trade creditors	483	563
Dividends proposed	42	28
Taxation	144	12
	669	603

	19X5 £000	19X4 £000
Called up share capital comprised:		
Redeemable preference shares of £1 each	–	20
Ordinary shares of £1 each fully paid	840	700
	840	720

5   Movements in reserves during the year comprised:

	General £000	Revaluation £000	Capital redemption reserve £000
Balance at 1 May 19X4	71	–	–
Revaluation surplus	–	120	–
From profit and loss account	188	–	20
Bonus issue	–	(120)	(20)
Balance at 30 April 19X5	299	–	–

You are required to:

Prepare a statement of source and application of funds for the year ended 30 April 19X5 so far as the information provided will permit.   (*20 marks*)

Institute of Chartered Accountants of Scotland, Part 1 Examination, Financial Accounting

8 Group accounts

A small business often starts in the form of a sole trader, becomes a partnership as additional expertise and capital becomes necessary and then turns into a limited company as further growth takes place. Once company status has been achieved, further growth is often put into effect by that company buying a controlling interest in the share capital of other companies. This gives rise to a 'group' of companies, consisting of a holding (or parent) company and one or more subsidiaries which the holding company controls.

The question then arises as to how this special holding company/subsidiary relationship should be reflected in financial statements. The Companies Act 1948 tackled the problem by requiring a holding company which has one or more subsidiaries at the end of its financial year to publish financial statements relating to the group as a whole, in addition to the holding company's own financial statements.

The group accounts could, in law, take a variety of forms but UK practice, as regulated by SSAP 14, *Group Accounts*, requires them to be produced as consolidated financial statements. These are designed to show the results of the group (consolidated profit and loss account) and financial position of the group (consolidated balance sheet) as if all the companies which make up the group formed a single entity. This will often be the case for management purposes, because key decisions relating to the subsidiaries will often be taken by, or will require the approval of, the Board of the holding company.

This chapter examines the mechanics of preparing consolidated financial statements for a simple group, i.e. one which consists of a holding company and one or more subsidiaries which are controlled directly by that holding company. The structure of a simple group is illustrated in Figure 8.1.

Other complex group structures, involving sub-subsidiaries or cross share holdings between subsidiaries can be envisaged but are not dealt with here.

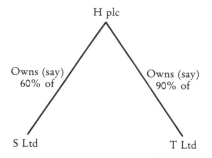

Figure 8.1

At its simplest, consolidation can be achieved by merely aggregating items in the accounts of the holding company with the same items in the accounts of the subsidiary. However, consolidation adjustments are necessary before this aggregation can be realistically achieved. These adjustments will now be considered in connection with the consolidated balance sheet, under the following headings: cancellation, minority interests, pre-acquisition reserves and inter-company trading.

The consolidated balance sheet

Cancellation

As stated above, the objective of the consolidated balance sheet is to present the financial position of the group as if it were a single entity. If this financial position is to be presented realistically, care must be taken to ensure that the assets shown are resources owned *by the group* and that liabilities shown are claims on the resources *of the group*. An unrealistic picture of the group's financial position is presented if internal items (i.e. items which are assets to one group company, but liabilities of another) appear on the balance sheet. This introduces the first principle in the preparation of consolidated accounts – the cancellation of internal items.

Example 8.1 introduces the principle of cancellation but simplifies the consolidation process by making the following assumptions:

(*a*) The holding company owns the whole of the issued capital of the subsidiary.
(*b*) That capital was purchased at par, on the incorporation of the subsidiary.
(*c*) The two companies do not trade with each other.

Each of the assumptions will be relaxed in later examples when more realistic conditions are introduced.

Example 8.1

The balance sheets of two companies, who do not trade with each other, at 31 December 19X1 are as follows:

	Gower plc		Border plc	
	£000	£000	£000	£000
Fixed assets – tangible				
Freehold land, at cost		150		50
Plant, at net book value		80		120
Investments				
100,000 £1 ordinary shares				
in Border plc, at cost		100		
		330		170
Current assets				
Stocks	60		40	
Debtors	120		30	
Cash at bank	10		20	
	190		90	
Creditors – amounts due				
within one year				
Trade creditors	(110)		(60)	
Corporation tax	(40)	40	(10)	20
Total assets less current				
liabilities		370		190
Creditors – amounts due				
after one year				
10% irredeemable debentures		–		(10)
		370		180
Capital and reserves				
Called up capital –				
ordinary shares of £1 each		200		100
Profit and loss account		170		80
		370		180

These balance sheets show that Gower plc owns the whole of the issued capital of Border plc, i.e. Border plc is a wholly-owned subsidiary of Gower plc. Note also that the balance sheet of Gower plc shows the investment in Border plc at cost, £100,000, which is equal to the nominal value of Border plc's issued capital. These two amounts (the issued capital of Border plc and the investment account held by Gower plc) represent two aspects of the same transaction – the share capital *issued by* Border plc was *issued to* Gower plc. These represent an internal item as far as the group is concerned and are cancelled in preparing the consolidated balance sheet. The consolidation of other balance sheet items is shown in the bracketed computations in the completed consolidated balance sheet reproduced below. The called up share capital which appears is that of Gower only.

Gower plc – consolidated balance sheet as at 31 December 19X1

	£000	£000
Fixed assets – tangible		
Freehold land, at cost (150 + 50)		200
Plant, at net book value (80 + 120)		200
		400
Current assets		
Stocks (60 + 40)	100	
Debtors (120 + 30)	150	
Cash at bank (10 + 20)	30	
	280	
Creditors – amounts due within one year		
Trade creditors (110 + 60)	(170)	
Corporation tax (40 + 10)	(50)	60
Total assets less current liabilities		460
Creditors amounts due after more than one year		
10% irredeemable debentures		(10)
		450
Capital and reserves		
Called up share capital		
ordinary shares of £1 each		200
Profit and loss account (170 + 80)		250
		450

Many other types of internal items may exist and require cancellation, as illustrated by Example 8.2. This example shows the summarized balance sheets at 31 March 19X1 of two companies which do not trade with each other.

Example 8.2

	Gooch plc		Wood plc	
	£000	£000	£000	£000
Fixed assets – tangible at				
net book value		210		170
Investments				
80,000 £1 ordinary shares				
in Wood plc		80		
60,000 £1.8% debentures				
19X7/X9 in Wood plc		60		
		350		170
Current assets				
Dividend receivable from				
Wood plc	20			
Others	210		180	
	230		180	

	Gooch plc		Wood plc	
	£000	£000	£000	£000
Creditors, amounts due within one year				
Dividends payable	(30)		(20)	
Others	(60)		(80)	
Total assets less current liabilities		140		80
		490		250
Creditors – amounts due after one year				
80,000 £1 8% debentures		–		(80)
		490		170
Capital and reserves				
Called up share capital ordinary shares of £1 each		250		80
Profit and loss account		240		90
		490		170

Three items appearing on the above balance sheets which are internal to the group are:

(a) The investment in Wood plc carried in the books of Gooch plc and the issued share capital of Wood plc.
(b) The dividend receivable from Wood plc by Gooch plc and the dividend payable by Wood plc.
(c) The holding of some of the 8 per cent debentures issued by Wood plc as an investment by Gooch plc.

These are merely other examples drawn from the lengthy list of possible internal items. The cancellation principle can be applied to each of these in turn in producing the consolidated balance sheet, shown below. Care must be taken in the case of the 8 per cent debentures where only 60,000 out of the 80,000 issued by Wood plc are held by its holding company.

Gooch plc – consolidated balance sheet as at 31 March 19X1

	£000	£000
Fixed assets – tangible at net book value (210 + 170)		380
Current assets, sundry (210 + 180)	390	
Creditors – amounts due within one year		
Dividend payable	(30)	
Others (60 + 80)	(140)	
		220
Total assets less current liabilities		600

	£000
Creditors – amounts due after one year (80 − 60)	(20)
	580
Capital and reserves	
Called up share capital	
ordinary shares of £1 each	250
Profit and loss account (240 + 90)	330
	580

Minority interests

We now relax the first of our assumptions applied in Examples 8.1 and 8.2 and consider a situation where the holding company controls the subsidiary but owns less than 100 per cent of its issued share capital. Example 8.3 summarizes the balance sheets, at 30 September 19X1, of two companies which do not trade with each other. The principal point to note is that Edmonds plc owns only 80 per cent of the issued capital of Bennett plc, i.e. there is a 20 per cent minority interest on the ordinary shares of the subsidiary.

Example 8.3

	Edmonds plc		Bennett plc	
	£000	£000	£000	£000
Fixed assets – tangible at book value		100		80
Investment in Bennett plc 80,000 £1 shares at cost		80		
		180		80
Current assets – sundry	120		40	
Creditors – due within one year sundry	(60)	60	(10)	30
Total assets less current liabilities		240		110
Capital and reserves				
Called up share capital ordinary shares of £1 each		200		100
Profit and loss account		40		10
		240		110

UK consolidation practice consolidates 100 per cent of the assets and liabilities of Bennett plc with those of Edmonds plc (even though only 80 per cent arc owned) and then separately recognizes the minority interest as a liability to be reflected on the consolidated balance sheet. This minority interest is computed here as 20 per cent of the subsidiary's net assets (i.e. capital plus reserves) as shown in the minority interest account below.

As we introduce more realistic consolidated balance sheet examples it becomes useful to introduce working accounts to assist in processing the necessary consolidation adjustments. In order to deal with the minority interest adjustments we shall use the following working accounts:

(a) 'Minority interest' – to calculate the amount of the subsidiary's share capital and reserves relating to non-group shareholders.
(b) 'Subsidiary's reserves' – to adjust the reserves of Bennett plc for consolidation purposes.
(c) 'Consolidated reserves' – to summarize the resulting reserves which appear on the consolidated balance sheet.

These working accounts show the following for Example 8.3:

Minority interest

	£000		£000
Balance to consolidated balance sheet	22	20% of ordinary share capital (20% × 100)	20
		20% of reserves (20% × 10)	2
	22		22

Bennett plc reserves

	£000		£000
Minority interest (20% × 10)	2	Balance	10
Consolidated reserves	8		
	10		10

Consolidated reserves

	£000		£000
Balance to consolidated balance sheet	48	Edmonds plc	40
		Bennett plc	8
	48		48

It should be noted that the adjustments are effected in the working accounts on double entry principles, thereby ensuring that the resulting consolidated balance sheet balances. The procedure is as follows:

(a) The balance on the subsidiary's reserves is placed to the credit of 'Bennett plc reserves' account.
(b) The balance on the holding company's reserves is credited to 'consolidated reserves' account.
(c) The minority interest in the issued capital of the subsidiary is credited to the minority interest account. This amounts to 20 per cent of the issued share capital of Bennett plc. It should be noted that at the cancellation stage, it is possible to cancel only £80,000 of the issued capital of the subsidiary against the investment

account in the books of the holding company. The uncancelled issued capital of the subsidiary (£20,000) belongs to the 'minority interest' and is credited to the working account.

(d)   20 per cent of the closing reserves of Bennett plc are transferred from the subsidiary's reserves to the minority interest working account.

(e)   The balance of the subsidiary's reserves is consolidated with the reserves of the holding company.

Following these adjustments and the consolidation of other items (see computations in parentheses), the consolidated balance sheet of Edmonds appears as follows:

Edmonds plc – consolidated balance sheet as at 30 September 19X1

		£000
Fixed assets – tangible at book value (100 + 80)		180
Current assets – sundry (120 + 40)	160	
Creditors – due within one year sundry (60 + 10)	(70)	90
Total assets less current liabilities		270
Capital and reserves		
Called up share capital		200
Profit and loss account (see working account)		48
		248
Minority interest (see working account)		22
		270

SSAP14, *Group accounts*, requires that the minority interest in the share capital and reserves of subsidiaries should not be classified as shareholders' funds. Hence, a sub-total of share capital and reserves is shown, with the minority interest being reflected outside this sub-total.

Example 8.4
This example is based on the same data as Example 8.3 but introduces dividends payable by the subsidiary company to its parent. The balance sheets as at 30 September 19X1 now show the following:

	Edmonds plc		Bennett plc	
	£000	£000	£000	£000
Fixed assets – tangible at book value		100		80
Investments in Bennett plc 80,000 £1 shares at cost		80		
		180		

	Edmonds plc		Bennett plc	
	£000	£000	£000	£000
Current assets:				
Dividend receivable from				
Bennett plc	8		–	
Others	112		40	
	120		40	
Creditors – amounts due within				
one year				
Dividend payable	(60)	60	(10)	30
		240		110
Capital and reserves				
Called up share capital				
ordinary shares of £1 each		200		100
Profit and loss account		40		10
		240		110

Previously we saw that inter-company dividends payable by the subsidiary and receivable by the holding company are cancelled in the process of consolidation. Where a minority interest in the subsidiary exists (20 per cent in the case of Bennett plc) the cancellation process will leave part of the dividend payable by the subsidiary outstanding as a liability in the consolidated balance sheet, i.e. the 20 per cent of the proposed dividends of Bennett plc which is due to the minority interest and not to the holding company. This uncancelled amount is classified on the consolidated balance sheet under 'creditors – amounts due within one year'. It is not added to the minority interest account because this represents in essence a long-term liability whereas the proposed dividend is in the nature of a current liability.

The same working accounts are used as those in Example 8.2 but we shall add a 'dividend elimination account' which assists the cancellation of the inter-company dividend and the treatment of any resulting balance.

Dividend elimination account

	£000		£000
Dividend receivable by		Dividend payable by	
Edmonds plc	8	Bennett plc	10
Balance: dividend due			
to minority interest	2		
	10		10

The resulting consolidated balance sheet now shows:

Edmonds plc consolidated balance sheet as at 30 September 19X1

	£000	£000
Fixed assets – tangible at book value		180
Current assets		
Sundry (112 + 40)	152	
Creditors – amounts due within one year		
Dividends payable to minority interest	2	
Sundry (60 + nil)	60	(62)	90
		270
Capital and reserves		
Called up share capital		200
Profit and loss account		48
		248
Minority interest in capital and		
reserves of subsidiary		22
		270

It may be the case that the holding company has not yet recorded its
portion of a dividend receivable from its subsidiary because it adopts a
policy of accounting for such dividends on a 'cash received' basis.
However, we would suggest that, for consolidation purposes, the
financial statements of the holding company should be adjusted to
reflect the dividend (i.e. DR dividend receivable CR profit and loss
account). The consolidation can then proceed as above, using the
dividend elimination account.

Example 8.5
In this example we introduce preference capital in which the minority
has an interest in the balance sheet of the subsidiary.
Downton plc is the holding company of Phillips plc. Their summarized balance sheets as at 30 April 19X1 show the following:

	Downton plc £000		Phillips plc £000	
Fixed assets – tangible at net				
book value		50		60
Investment in subsidiary				
30,000 ordinary shares				
at cost (£1 each)		30		
18,000 6% preference shares				
at cost (50p each)		9		
		89		60
Current assets				
sundry	60		70	
Creditors – amounts due				
within one year	(40)	20	(20)	50
Total assets less current liabilities		109		110

	Downton plc £000	Phillips plc £000
Capital and reserves		
Called up capital:		
ordinary shares of £1 each	60	40
6% preference shares of 50p each	–	10
	60	50
Profit and loss account	49	60
	109	110

No ordinary dividends have been paid or are prepared for the period by either company. The preference dividend of Phillips plc was paid on 30 April 19X1. Care must be taken in calculating the minority interest where their interest in the various types of capital differs, as in the case here. Since dividends on the preference shares have been paid up to date, the minority interest in the preference capital has no interest in the profit and loss account balance of Phillips plc.

The working accounts appear as follows:

Minority interest

	£000		£000
Balance to consolidated		Ordinary share capital	10
balance sheet	26	Preference share capital	1
		Reserves (1/4 × 60)	15
	26		26

Note
1/4 × ordinary share capital
1/10 × preference share capital

Phillips plc reserves

	£000		£000
Minority interest	15	Balance	60
Consolidated reserves	45		
	60		60

Consolidated reserves

	£000		£000
Balance to consolidated		Downton plc	49
balance sheet	94	Phillips plc	45
	94		94

Downton plc consolidated balance sheet as at 30 April 19X1

	£000	£000
Fixed assets – tangible at		
net book value (50 + 60)		110
Current assets		
sundry (60 + 70)	130	
Creditors – amount due within one year		
sundry (40 + 20)	(60)	70
Total assets less current liabilities		180
Capital and reserves		
ordinary shares of £1 each		60
profit and loss account		
(see working accounts)		94
		154
Minority interest		26
		180

Example 8.6
This example is designed to deal with all the main points relating to minority interests dealt with so far.

Embury plc is the holding company of Holland plc, but the two companies do not trade with each other. Embury plc purchased 70 per cent of the ordinary capital and 60 per cent of the preference capital of Holland plc on the incorporation of that company. The latest summarized balance sheets, as at 31 January 19X1, of the two companies are shown below:

	Embury plc		Holland plc	
	£000	£000	£000	£000
Fixed assets – tangible at net				
book value		210		160
Investment in subsidiary				
ordinary shares at cost		70		–
preference shares at cost		36		–
		316		160
Current assets				
Dividends receivable from				
subsidiary	20		–	
Other	125		75	
	145		75	
Creditors – amounts due within				
one year				
sundry	(80)		(30)	
dividends payable – ords	(40)		(20)	
– prefs	–	25	(10)	15
Total assets less current liabilities		341		175

	Embury plc £000	£000	Holland plc £000	£000
Capital and reserves				
Called up capital				
ordinary shares of £1		250		100
8% preference shares of £1		–		60
		250		160
Profit and loss account		91		15
		341		175

Note that there is a minority interest in ordinary capital (30 per cent) and preference capital (40 per cent) and that the subsidiary has proposed dividends on both types of capital. The holding company has recorded its share of each of these dividends receivable.

The working accounts appear as follows:

Minority interest

	£000		£000
Balance to consolidated balance sheets	58.5	Ordinary share capital	30
		Preference capital	24
		Reserves (30% × 15)	4.5
	58.5		58.5

Note:
Ordinary share capital 30%
Preference share capital 40%

Holland plc reserves

	£000		£000
Minority interest	4.5	Balance	15.0
Consolidated reserves	10.5		
	15.0		15.0

Consolidated reserves

	£000		£000
Balance to consolidated balance sheet	101.5	Embury plc	91
		Holland plc	10.5
	101.5		10.5

Dividend elimination account

	£000		£000
Dividends receivable by		Dividends payable by	
Holland plc		Holland plc	
ords (70%)	14	ords	20
prefs (60%)	6	prefs	10
Dividend due to			
minority interest	10		
	30		30

Embury plc consolidated balance sheet as at 31 January 19X1

		£000	£000
Fixed assets – tangible net			
book value	(210 + 160)		370
Current assets, sundry	(125 + 75)	200	
Creditors – amounts due			
within one year			
sundry	(80 + 30)	(110)	
dividends payable to			
shareholders of Embury plc		(40)	
dividends payable to minority			
interests in subsidiaries			
(workings)		(10)	40
Total assets less current liabilities			410
Capital and reserves			
Called up ordinary shares of £1			250
Profit and loss account			
(see working accounts)			101.5
			351.5
Minority interests (see working accounts)			58.5
			410.0

Example 8.7
This is a revision example designed to reinforce all the main points of
principle introduced thus far.

Taylor plc is the holding company of Thompson plc. The two companies do not trade with each other. Taylor plc purchased its entire
interest in the share capital and debentures of Thompson plc on the
incorporation of that company. The holding company's investment in
the subsidiary consists of the following:

	£000
80,000 £1 ordinary shares, at cost	80
40,000 50p 10% preference shares at cost	20
10,000 £1 12% debentures 19X8/X9, at cost	10
Total investment	110

The balance sheets of the two companies as at 31 January 19X1 appear below:

	Taylor plc £000	Taylor plc £000	Thompson plc £000	Thompson plc £000
Fixed assets – tangible				
Freehold land, at cost		250		90
Plant, at net book value		110		80
Investment				
in Thompson plc (as above)		110		–
		470		170
Current assets				
Stock	190		100	
Debtors	98		37	
Cash at X bank	102		–	
	390		137	
Creditors – amounts due within one year				
overdraft at Y bank			(10)	
trade creditors	(115)		(57)	
proposed dividends	(40)		(20)	
corporation tax	(75)	160	(15)	35
Total assets less current liabilities		630		205
Creditors – amounts due after more than one year				
8 % unsecured debentures		(120)		
12% unsecured debentures				(20)
		510		185
Capital and reserves				
Called up share capital				
ordinary shares of £1		250		100
10% preference shares of 50p		–		30
Profit and loss account		260		55
		510		185

The following additional information is available:

(a) The proposed dividends of Thompson plc consist of the following:

	£000
On ordinary shares	17
On 10% preferences shares	3
	20

(b) Taylor plc has recorded its share of the proposed ordinary dividend of its subsidiary but has made no entries in respect of the proposed preference dividend.

Although no new points of principle are introduced in this example, in contrast with earlier examples we note that the holding company has not recorded its interest in the proposed preference dividend of its subsidiary. In order to standardize the treatment of proposed dividends, the balance sheet of Taylor plc should be adjusted before consolidation starts. The normal treatment of proposed dividends via the dividend elimination account can then be adopted. We adjust the balance sheet of Taylor plc by the following journal entry:

	£000	£000
Debit debtor – dividend due for		
subsidiary (300 × 40/60)	2	
Credit profit and loss account		2

At the cancellation stage, the following treatment applies:

	£000	
(a)	12% debentures of Thompson plc	
	Liability per Thompson	(20)
	Asset per Taylor	10
	Liability for consolidated balance sheet	10
(b)	Issued capital of Thompson plc	
	Ordinary capital of Thompson plc	(100)
	Investment held by Taylor plc	80
	Minority interest	20	i.e. 1/5th
	Preference capital of Thompson plc	(30)
	Investment held by Taylor plc	20
	Minority interest	(10)	i.e. 1/3rd
(c)	Dividends payable/receivable deal with via the dividend elimination account in the consolidated workings	

Finally, the bank balance in Taylor plc and the overdraft in Thompson plc will not be offset on consolidation since they are at different banks and presumably no legal right of offset exists. The consolidation working accounts are as follows:

Minority interest: Ordinary share capital 1/5th
Preference share capital 1/3rd

	£000		£000
Balance to consolidated balance sheet	41	Ordinary share capital (1/5th × 100)	20
		Preference share capital (1/3 × 30)	10
		Reserves (1/5 × 55)	11
	41		41

Note:
Ordinary share capital 20%
Preference share capital 33%

Thompson plc – reserves

	£000		£000
Minority interests		Balance	55
(1/5 × 55)	11		
Consolidated reserves	44		
	55		55

Consolidated reserves

	£000		£000
Balance to consolidated		Taylor plc – per balance	
balance sheet	306	sheet	260
		Add preference dividend	
		from Thompson plc	2
			262
		Thompson plc	44
	306		306

Dividend elimination account

	£000		£000
Dividend receivable		Dividend payable	
by Taylor plc		by Thompson plc	20.0
per balance sheet	13.6		
add preference dividend	2.0		
Minority interest dividends	4.4		
	20.0		20.0

Taylor plc – consolidated balance sheet as at 31 January 19X1

	£000	£000
Fixed assets – tangible		
Freehold land at cost (250 + 90)		340
Plant, at net book value (110 + 80)		190
		530
Current assets		
Stocks (190 + 100)	290	
Debtors (98 − 13.6 = 84.4 + 37)	121.4	
Cash at bank	102	
	513.4	
Creditors – amounts due within one year		
Bank overdraft	(10)	
Trade creditors (115 + 57)	(172)	
Proposed dividends		
To the shareholders of Taylor plc	(40)	
To minority interest in subsidiary		

	£000	£000
(see working account)	(4.4)	
Corporation tax (75 + 15)	(90)	197
Total assets less current liabilities		727
Creditors – amounts due after more than one year		
8% unsecured debentures		(120)
12% unsecured debentures		(10)
		597
Capital and reserves		
Called up share capital ordinary shares of £1		250
Profit and loss account (see working accounts)		306
		556
Minority interests (see working accounts)		41
		597

Pre-acquisition reserves

We are now in a position to relax the second assumption introduced in connection with Example 8.1 and introduce the topic of pre-acquisition reserves. This is an important area of consolidation adjustments and therefore Example 8.8 should be studied very carefully.

Example 8.8
The following summarized balance sheets have been prepared for Ellison plc and its subsidiary Lawson plc, as at 31 December 19X5. The two companies do not trade with each other.

	Ellison plc		Lawson plc	
	£000	£000	£000	£000
Fixed assets – tangible at net book value		75		60
Investment –				
30,000 £1 ordinary shares in Lawson plc, at cost		50		–
		125		60
Current assets, sundry	85		40	
Creditors – amounts due within one year	50	35	20	20
		160		80
Capital and reserves				
Called up ordinary shares £1		100		40
Profit and loss account		60		40
		160		80

We discover that Ellison plc purchased its interest in Lawson plc in 19X3, some time after the incorporation of that company. At the time of purchase, the balance on the profit and loss account of Lawson plc stood at £10,000 and the company had no other reserves. No dividends are paid or proposed by either company for the year to 31 December 19X5.

We note here that the holding company bought an interest in a subsidiary which had already traded and whose balance sheet showed accumulated profits of £10,000 at the time of the purchase. This helps to explain why Ellison plc paid £50,000 for Lawson plc's 30,000 £1 shares. The accumulated profits will, for course, be reflected in the net assets of the subsidiary at acquisition.

From a consolidation point of view, it is clear that Ellison plc 'bought' a proportion of the reserves of Lawson plc when it purchased the shares. These reserves are treated as being non-distributable by the group and are capitalized on consolidation, i.e. they are removed from distributable reserves in the consolidated balance sheet. Additionally, it is evident that we cannot simply cancel the cost of the shares in the books of the holding company against the issued capital of the subsidiary because the two amounts are not stated at the same value.

The two problems outlined above are dealt with by the introduction of a further consolidation working account, known as the adjustment account. This account compares the cost of the investment, as shown in the books of the holding company, with the 75 per cent of the share capital and pre-acquisition reserves of the subsidiary which were purchased by the holding company, as follows:

Adjustment account

	£000		£000
Cost of shares in subsidiary	50	Ordinary share capital	30
		Pre-acquisition reserves	
		(75% × £10,000)	7.5
		Balance (see below)	12.5
	50		50.0

We can now consider the interpretation of the balance on the adjustment acount. The account indicates that Ellison plc paid £50,000 for a 75 per cent interest in the share capital and reserves of Lawson plc amounting to £37,500. This amount is, of course, also 75 per cent of the net assets of Lawson plc as at acquisition. Ellison plc therefore paid a premium on the acquisition of £12,500 in excess of the book value of the net assets acquired. This premium is called goodwill.

The other consolidation working accounts appear as follows:

Minority interest (1/4)

	£000		£000
Balance to consolidated balance sheet	20	Ordinary share capital	10
		Profit and loss account (1/4 × 40)	10
	20		20

Lawson plc reserves

	£000		£000
Minority interest	10	Balance	40
Adjustment account	7.5		
Consolidated reserves	22.5		
	40		40

Consolidated reserves

	£000		£000
Balance to consolidated balance sheet	82.5	Ellison plc	60
		Lawson plc	22.5
	82.5		82.5

We have made two adjustments to the reserves of the subsidiary:

(a) By transferring the minority interest in the total closing reserves to minority interest account (the distinction between pre- and post-acquisition reserves is *not* relevant to the minority interest).

(b) By transferring the holding company's share of pre-acquisition reserves to the adjustment account.

This allocation of the reserves of the subsidiary could be shown diagrammatically, as in Figure 8.2.

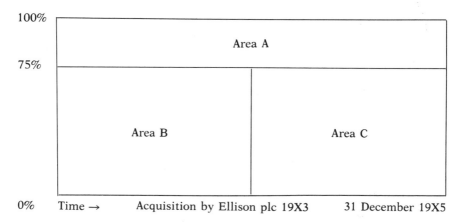

Figure 8.2 *Acquisition by Ellison plc 19X3*

Reserves of Lawson plc

Area A: i.e. 25 per cent of the *total* reserves as at 31 December 19X5 is the minority interest element.

Area B: i.e. 75 per cent of the reserves of Ellison at acquisition (19X3) is the amount to be transferred to the adjustment account.

Area C: i.e. 75 per cent of the reserves of Ellison from acquisition to 31 December 1985 is included in consolidated reserves.

Ellison plc – consolidated balance sheet as at 31 December 19X5

	£000	£000
Fixed assets – tangible at net book value (75 + 60)		135
Intangible – goodwill on acquisition of subsidiary (see working accounts)		12.5
		147.5
Current assets, sundry (85 + 40)	125	
Creditors – amounts due within one year (50 + 20)	(70)	55
Total assets less current liabilities		202.5
Capital and reserves		
Called up capital – ordinary shares of £1		100
Profit and loss account (working accounts)		82.5
		182.5
Minority interest		20
		202.5

Note that the above balance sheet does not reflect the treatment of goodwill prescribed by SSAP22, *Accounting for Goodwill*, which was mentioned in Chapter 3. The SSAP requires goodwill to be removed from the balance sheet by one of two methods. The preferred method is that goodwill should be written off immediately it is purchased against reserves. Alternatively goodwill should be amortized by a charge against profits over its useful economic life.

Any negative goodwill (i.e. a credit balance on the adjustment account) is added to reserves.

Example 8.9
This example is based on the same data as Example 8.8 except that we introduce a dividend payment from Lawson plc to Ellison plc which distributes profits accruing prior to acquisition. The data to be used is therefore:

	Ellison plc		Lawson plc	
	£000	£000	£000	£000
Fixed assets – tangible at net book value		75		60
Investment – 30,000 £1 ordinary shares in Lawson plc		47		–
		122		60
Current assets, sundry	88		36	
Creditors – amounts due within one year	(50)	38	(20)	16
Total assets less current liabilities		160		76
Capital reserves				
Called up ordinary shares of £1		100		40
Profit and loss account		60		36
		160		76

Ellison plc purchased its interest in Lawson plc in 19X3 for £50,000. At the date of acquisition the profit and loss account of Lawson plc stood at £1,000 and the company had no other reserves. The month after acquisition, Lawson plc paid a dividend of £4,000 in total, out of profits accruing prior to acquisition.

Note a difference between the cost of the shares held in Lawson (£50,000) and the figure at which the investment is stated in the balance sheet of the holding company (£47,000). This relates to the dividend paid by Lawson plc out of pre-acquisition reserves (total dividend £4000, holding company's share: 3/4, i.e. £3,000). In double entry terms, Ellison plc correctly recorded the receipt of this pre-acquisition dividend as follows:

DR   Cash   £3000

CR   Investment in subsidiary   £3000

In Example 8.8 we saw that pre-acquisition reserves are capitalized on consolidation and are not treated as distributable profit as far as the group is concerned. It is, therefore, logical that a dividend paid out of these pre-acquisition reserves is also treated as a capital sum, not distributable by the group. This explains why the credit entry is to the investment account (the pre-acquisition dividend can be seen as a refund to the holding company of part of the cost of its investment) and not to dividend income (profit and loss account). The latter would constitute an incorrect treatment because the holding company should be adjusted prior to consolidation. We can show the impact on the adjustment account, which would appear as follows:

Adjustment account

	£000			£000
Book value of share in subsidiary	47	Ordinary share capital		30
		pre-acquisition reserves $3/4 \times 10 =$	7.5	
		less pre-acquisition dividend		
		Capitalized goodwill 3.0		4.5
		Balance		12.5
	47			47

(a) The investment in the subsidiary is reflected in the adjustment account at book value, as reduced by the correct recording of the dividend.
(b) Pre-acquisition reserves are computed as previously but are then reduced by £3,000, the amount of the pre-acquisition dividend which has, in effect, already been capitalized by the holding company placing the credit entry to the investment account.
(c) The balance on the adjustment account is £12,500, as in the previous example. This must be the case because the objective of the adjustment account is to compare the cost of the investment with the net assets purchased at the date of acquisition. A pre-acquisition dividend does not affect net assets as at acquisition.

Because the other aspects of the consolidation contain no new features a full solution is not given here.

Inter-company trading

We now relax the final assumption, by allowing for the group companies to trade with each other by transferring assets, usually stocks or fixed assets, between group companies at a profit.

Example 8.10
Lamb plc is the holding company of two subsidiaries, Hilditch plc and Wellham plc. There is a significant amount of trading between the three companies. Summarized balance sheets at 30 April 19X5 include the following amounts:

	Lamb plc £000	Hilditch plc £000	Wellham plc £000
Stocks			
From Hilditch plc	30	–	5
From Wellham plc	20	10	–
Others (external)	180	60	40
Total	230	70	45

	Lamb plc £000	Hilditch plc £000	Wellham plc £000
Reserves			
Profit and loss account	100	60	40

In addition, we ascertain the following additional information:

(a) Lamb plc owns 80 per cent of the ordinary capital of Hilditch plc and 60 per cent of that of Wellham plc. Neither subsidiary has any other class of capital.

(b) There are no pre-acquisition reserves attributable to either subsidiary.

(c) Stock transfers are effected between group companies on the following terms:

   (i)   Sales from Hilditch plc – at cost plus 25 per cent
   (ii) Sales from Wellham plc – at cost plus 33.1/3 per cent

In the consolidated balance sheet stocks are stated at cost to the group (or net realizable value if lower). The value of stock for the consolidation is calculated as follows:

			£000	£000
Lamb plc:	from Hilditch 30 − (1/5 × 30)	=	24	
	from Wellham 20 − (1/4 × 20)	=	15	
	external		180	219
Hilditch plc:	from Wellham 10 − (1/4 × 10)	=	7.5	
	external		60	67.5
Wellham plc:	from Hilditch 5 − (1/5 × 5)	=	4	
	external		40	44
Total per conslidated balance sheet				330.5
Total unrealized profit is (345 − 330.5)		=		14.5

The working accounts for reserves are shown below:

Hilditch plc reserves

	£000		£000
Minority interest		Balance	60
(20% × 60)	12		
Consolidated reserves	48		
	60		60

Wellham plc

	£000		£000
Minority interest		Balance	40
(40% × 40)	16		
Consolidated reserves	24		
	40		40

Consolidated reserves

	£000		£000
Unrealized profits		Lamb plc	100
on stocks	14.5	Hilditch plc	48
Consolidated		Wellham plc	24
balance sheet	157.5		
	172		172

Note that the unrealized profit adjustment is dealt with through consolidated reserves, with the minority interests being unaffected by the adjustment.

Example 8.11
This example considers the treatment of transactions involving fixed assets between members of the group.

Gatting plc owns 80 per cent of the issued ordinary capital of Wessels plc. The shares were purchased on 1 January 19X3. On 1 January 19X4, in order to rationalize the operations of the group, Wessels plc sold a freehold factory building to Gatting plc at its then market value of £500,000. The agreed cost of the building to Wessels plc (on 1 February 19X3) was £450,000. Group accounting policy depreciates freehold buildings at 2 per cent per annum on cost, with a full year being charged in the year of acquisition. We shall now show how the building would be represented in the 31 December 19X5 balance sheets of: (*a*) Gatting plc, (*b*) the group.

As in the case of stock in the previous illustration, the freehold building must be shown on the consolidated balance sheet based at its cost to the group, i.e. £450,000. £50,000 profit on sale will therefore be eliminated on consolidation thus:

DR consolidated reserves   £50,000
CR freehold buildings   £50,000

But if the asset is valued at cost to the group, then depreciation (both accumulated and charge for the period) must be based on this same value. Extracts from balance sheets of Gatting plc and the group appear as follows:

Balance sheet (extracts) as at 31 December 19X5

	Gatting plc	Group
Fixed assets – tangible		
freehold building, at cost	500	450
less accumulated depreciation		
(2 years × 2% × 500 × 450)	(20)	(18)
Net book value	480	432

In the consolidation of the profit and loss account, the charge for depreciation of the building for the year would be 2 per cent ×

£450,000, not 2 per cent × £500,000 as in the case of Gatting plc accounts.

Summary of the consolidated balance sheet technique

Before presenting a comprehensive example on all the main points of balance sheet consolidations, it is perhaps useful to summarize a technique for dealing with the preparation of consolidated balance sheets in, for example, an examination context.

The suggested technique is as follows:

(a)   Establish the group structure and the percentage of each claim of the subsidiary's capital owned by the holding company.

(b)   Review the balance sheets of each group company for correctness and completeness. Make any necessary adjustments (e.g. record dividends receivable from subsidiaries in the balance sheet of the holding company, if not already recorded).

(c)   Cancel internal items, other than investment/share capital and inter-company dividends.

(d)   Open up the necessary consolidation working accounts and calculate the effect of any unrealized profit adjustments and record them.

(e)   Work systematically down the balance sheets of the group companies, dealing with items as follows:

	Item	Treatment
(a)	Fixed assets, other than shares in subsidiary	Aggregate and present on consolidated balance sheet
(b)	Shares in subsidiary	Record on the debit side of the adjustment account
(c)	Current assets, other than the holding company's dividend	Aggregate and present on consolidated balance sheet
(d)	Dividend due from subsidiaries	Record on the debit side of the dividend elimination account
(e)	Creditors – amounts due within one year, other than subsidiary's dividends payable	Aggregate and present on consolidated balance sheet
(f)	Subsidiary's dividends payable	Record on the credit side of the dividend elimination account
(g)	Creditors – amounts due after more than one year	Aggregate and present on consolidated balance sheet
(h)	Called up capital holding company subsidiary	Present on consolidated balance sheet Allocate between the adjustment account (credit side) and the minority interest account
(i)	Reserves subsidiary	Enter in subsidiary reserves account

Item	Treatment
holding company	Enter in consolidated reserves account
(j) Adjust the reserves of the subsidiary	In respect of each reserve:
	(i) Transfer the minority's share to minority interest account
	(ii) Transfer the pre-acquisition element to the adjustment account

(k) Balance off all workings and present the resulting balances on the consolidated balance sheet.

This technique can now be applied to the following comprehensive example.

Example 8.12
The following balances are taken from the books of two companies, Over plc and Maiden plc at 31 December 19X5.

	Over plc £000	Maiden plc £000
Debits		
Freehold land, at cost	40	–
Buildings, at book value	50	40
Plant, at book value	20	60
Stock and work in progress	50	20
Debtors	30	30
Cash at bank	5	2
Investment in subsidiary	95	–
	290	152
Credits		
Ordinary share capital (£1 shares)	150	60
10% accumulative preference shares (50p shares)	–	20
Share premium	20	10
General reserve	15	30
Profit and loss account	45	15
Trade creditors	30	9
Tax payable	20	–
Proposed dividends	10	8
	290	152

The following additional information is available:

(a) Over plc purchased 75 per cent of the issued ordinary capital of Maiden plc for £55,000 and 50 per cent of the issued 10 per cent accumulative preference shares for £10,000, both purchases being effected on 1 January 19X5. There have been no changes in the issued capital of Maiden plc since that date.

(b)   Stocks of Over plc include goods purchased from Maiden plc for £20,000. Maiden plc charged out these stocks at cost plus 25 per cent.

(c)   Over plc has not recorded its dividend.

(d)   Creditors of Over plc include £5,000 payable to Maiden plc in respect of stock purchases. Debtors of Maiden plc include £8,000 due from Over plc. The holding company sent a cheque for £3,000 to its subsidiary on 30 December 19X5, which was not received by Maiden plc until 4 January 19X6.

(e)   At 1 January 19X5, the balances on the reserves of Maiden plc were as follows:

	£000
Share premium	10
General reserve	20
Profit and loss account	10

(f)   Proposed dividend of Maiden plc includes a full year's preference dividend; the balance is proposed ordinary dividend. We shall now prepare the consolidated balance sheet of Over plc as at 31 December 19X5, in a form suitable for presentation to the members of the holding company in so far as the given information permits.

The consolidated balance sheet for Over plc, together with the relevant consolidation workings are shown below.

Over plc consolidated balance sheet as at 31 December 19X5

	£000	£000
Fixed assets – tangible		
Freehold land, at cost		40
Buildings, at net book value		90
Plant, at net book value		80
		210
Current assets		
Stock and work-in-progress		
(50 + 20 − [1/5 × 20])	66	
Debtors (30 + 30 − 8)	52	
Cash at bank (5 + 2 + 3)	10	
	128	
Creditors – amounts falling due within		
one year:		
Trade creditors (30 + 9 − 5)	(34)	
Taxation payable	(20)	
Proposed dividends		
– to group shareholders	(10)	
– to minority interest	(2.5)	

	£000	£000
Net current assets		61.50
Total assets less current liabilities		271.50
Capital and reserves		
Called up share capital		
ordinary share of £1		150
Reserves		
share premium		20
general reserve		22.5
profit and loss account (50.25 − 10)		40.25
		232.75
		38.75
Minority interest		271.50

Consolidated working accounts (£000s)

Over plc adjustment account

Cost of investment	95	Ordinary share capital	
		(75% × 60)	45
		Preference share capital	
		(50% × 20)	10
		Share premium (75% × 10)	7.5
		General reserve (75% × 20)	15
		Profit and loss (75% × 10)	7.5
		Goodwill written off to	
		group reserves on	
		consolidated balance	
		sheet	10
	95		95

Minority interest

		Ordinary share capital	
		(25% × 60)	15
		Preference share capital	
		(50% × 20)	10
		Share premium (25% × 10)	2.5
		General reserve (25% × 30)	7.5
Consolidated balance sheet	38.75	Profit and loss (25% × 15)	3.75
	38.75		38.75

Maiden plc – reserves

	Share premium	General profit and loss			Share premium	General profit and loss	
Adjustment account	7.5	15	7.50	Balance	10	30	15
Minority interest	2.5	7.5	3.75				
Consolidated reserves	nil	7.5	3.75				
	10	30	15		10	30	15

Consolidated reserves

Unrealized profit on stock (1/5 × 20)			4	Over plc	20	15	45
				Dividend due			5.50
Consolidated	20	22.5	50.25	Maiden plc	–	7.5	3.75
	20	22.5	54.25		20	22.5	54.25

Dividend elimination account

Receivable by Over plc (group reserves)			Dividend payble by	
preference	1		Maiden plc – preference	2
ordinary	4.5		– ordinary	6
Minority interest	2.5			
	8			8

The consolidated profit and loss account

The same principles which have been dealt with in the preparation of a consolidated balance sheet also apply to the consolidated profit and loss account. Therefore we are again concerned with cancellation, minority interests, capitalization of pre-acquisition profits and the elimination of unrealized profits. In this section we deal only with the application of the principles to the profit and loss account.

Example 8.13
This example illustrates a relatively simple application of the principles. The following details are taken from the draft published profit and loss accounts of Off plc and On plc, for the year to 31 December 19X5.

	Off plc £000	On plc £000
Turnover	2,000	1,500
Cost of sales	(1,400)	(1,200)
Gross profit	600	300
Distribution costs and administrative expenses	(300)	(200)
Profit on ordinary activities before taxation	300	100
Taxation on profit on ordinary activities, at 40%	(120)	(40)
Profit on ordinary activities after taxation	180	60
Dividends – proposed	(90)	–
Retained profit for the year	90	60

Statement of retained earnings

As at 1 January 19X5	150	100
Retained for 19X5	90	60
As at 31 December 19X5	240	160

Notes are available, giving additional information as follows:

(*a*) The two companies do not trade with each other.

(*b*) Off plc purchased 90 per cent of the ordinary share capital of On plc on 1 January 19X1. On plc has no preference capital in issue.

(*c*) The reserves of On plc at 1 January 19X1 amounted to £60,000.

The consolidated workings

For profit and loss account purposes, a columnar working schedule as shown below is recommended. The schedule cross-adds to the right, and the right hand column is effectively the consolidated profit and loss account.

	Off plc £000	On plc £000	Consolidated £000
Turnover	2,000	1,500	3,500
Cost of sales	(1,400)	(1,200)	(2,600)
	600	300	900
Distribution costs and administrative expenses	(300)	(200)	(500)
Profit on ordinary activities before taxation	300	100	400

	Off plc £000	On plc £000	Consolidated £000
Taxation on profit on ordinary activities	(120)	(40)	(160)
Profit on ordinary activities after taxation	180	60	240
Minority interest (10% × 60)		(6)	(6)
Profit for the financial year	180	54	234
Dividends proposed	(90)	–	(90)
Retained profit for the year	90	54	144

Statement of retained earnings

As at 1 January			
(90% × [100 – 60])	150	36	186
Retained for 19X5	90	54	144
As at 31 December	240	90	330

The following points should be noted:

(a) The minority interest in the profits for the year of the subsidiary is based on the profit after tax of On plc (£60,000) to which the minority interest percentage (10 per cent) is applied.

(b) The subsidiary was acquired several years ago and therefore all the 19X5 profits are post-acquisition. However, a proportion of the opening profits are pre-acquisition and, therefore, capitalized and removed from the consolidated profit and loss account. This is the group share (90 per cent) of the pre-acquisition reserves (£60,000).

(c) The column headed 'Consolidated' in the above working can be retitled as the consolidated profit and loss account.

Example 8.14
This example introduces further complications which may be encountered in connection with profit and loss account consolidations.

Details from the draft profit and loss accounts of Stump plc and Bail plc are given below:

	Year to 31 March 19X5	
	Stump plc £000	Bail plc £000
Turnover	6,527	2,983
Cost of sales	(5,092)	(2,007)
Gross profit	1,435	976
Distribution costs	(602)	(309)
Administrative expenses	(103)	(102)
Income from shares in group companies	51	–
Profit on ordinary activities before taxation	781	565

	Year to 31 March 19X5	
	Stump plc *£000*	*Bail plc* *£000*
Taxation on profit on ordinary activities	(300)	(250)
Profit on ordinary activities after taxation	481	315
Extraordinary income (no tax effect)	100	50
Profit for the financial year	581	365
Dividends – preference paid	–	(30)
proposed	–	(30)
ordinary proposed	(90)	(50)
Retained profit for the financial year	491	255

Additional information is available as follows:

(a) The companies do not trade with each other.

(b) Stump plc purchased 90 per cent of the ordinary capital and 10 per cent of the preference capital of Bail plc on 1 January 19X1. At that date, the reserves of Bail plc, after all dividends, amounted to £90,000.

(c) The statement of retained earnings shows:

	Stump plc *£000*	*Bail plc* *£000*
As at 1 April 19X4	609	302
Retained for the year	491	255
As at 31 March 19X5	1100	557

In preparing the consolidated profit and loss account from this information the new points of detail (although not of principle) encountered are listed and dealt with below:

(a) Inter-company dividends are cancelled. The make up of the income from shares in group companies in Stump plc is:

	£000
Preference dividends – Bail plc (10% × £60,000)	6
Ordinary dividend – Bail plc (70% × £50,000)	45
	51

(b) Extraordinary items are consolidated by adding the holding company's share (net of minority interest) of the extraordinary item of the subsidiary to its own. Thus:

	£000
Consolidated extraordinary item: = 100 + [90% × 50] =	145

(c) There is a minority interest in the preference and ordinary capital of the subsidiary. Minority interest for consolidated profit and loss account purposes must be computed with care, to properly reflect the interest of various groups of outside shareholders in the profit after tax of the subsidiary, as follows:

	£000	Minority interest £000
Profit after tax on ordinary activities	315	
Less preference dividends	60 × 90%	54
Equity shareholders profits	255 × 10%	25.5
Total minority interest for the consolidated profit and loss account		79.5

(d) The Companies Acts allow a holding company *not* to publish its *own* profit and loss accounts if it adds additional information to its published consolidated profit and loss account. This provision, of which most holding companies take advantage, requires the consolidated profit and loss account to disclose the amount of the group profit dealt with in the accounts of the holding company. This amount is the profit figure which would appear on the holding company's profit and loss account if it had been published. This profit figure will include dividends which, although eliminated on consolidation, are properly reported as profit of the holding company itself.

	Stump plc £000	Bail plc £000	Consolidated £000
Turnover	6,527	2,983	9,510
Cost of sales	(5,092)	(2,007)	(7,099)
Gross profit	1,435	976	2,411
Distribution costs	(602)	(309)	(911)
Administration expenses	(103)	(102)	(205)
Profit on ordinary activities before taxation	730	565	1,295
Taxation profit on ordinary activities	(300)	(250)	(550)
Profit on ordinary activities after taxation	430	315	745
Minority interest (note (c) above)		(79.5)	(79.5)
	430	235.5	665.5
Extraordinary income (note (b) above)	100	45	145
Group profit	530	280.5	810.5
Dividend transfer			
Prefs: 10% × 60	6	(6)	–
Ords: 90% × 50	45	(45)	–
Profit dealt with	581	229.5	810.5
Dividends proposed	(90)		(90)
Retained profit for the financial year	491	229.5	720.5

	Stump plc £000	Bail plc £000	Consolidated £000
Statement of retained earnings			
As at 1 April 19X4			
(90% × 302 − 90)	609	190.8	799.8
Retained for the year	491	229.5	720.5
As at 31 March 19X5	1,100	420.3	1,520.3

The right hand consolidated column could be rewritten as the consolidated profit and loss account, disclosing the fact that (if the holding company is not publishing its own profit and loss account) £581,000 of the group profit of £810,500 is dealt with in the accounts of the holding company.

Example 8.15
This example completes our examination of profit and loss account consolidation by introducing two new elements:

(a) Trading between the group members.
(b) An acquisition of a subsidiary part way through the current accounting period.

The first point leads to the necessity of eliminating on consolidation inter-company sales, expenses and unrealized profits. The second requires us to ensure that only the post-acquisition element of the subsidiary's current year profits are consolidated.
Details from the draft profit and loss accounts of two companies are given as follows:

	Year to 31 December 19X5	
	Victory plc £000	Ashes plc £000
Turnover	4,017	3,921
Cost of sales	(3,204)	(2,970)
Gross profit	813	951
Distribution costs and administrative expenses	(506)	(691)
Profit on ordinary activities before taxation	307	260
Taxation on profit	(150)	(120)
Profit on ordinary activities after tax	157	140
Dividends: ordinary proposed	(60)	(50)
Retained profit for the year	97	90
Statement of retained earnings		
As at 1 January 19X5	209	167
Profit for the year	97	90
As at 31 December 19X5	306	257

The following additional information is available:

(a)   Victory plc purchased 75 per cent of the equity capital of Ashes plc on 1 July 19X5. Ashes plc has no other class of capital in issue.

(b)   Since the date of acquisition, there has been significant trading between the two companies. Ashes plc has sold to Victory plc goods with a total selling price of £630,000. At 31 December 19X5, one sixth of these goods remained in stock. Ashes plc added 25 per cent to cost when selling these goods to Victory plc.

(c)   Profit and loss account items are assumed to accrue on a time basis.

(d)   Victory plc has not recorded its interest in the proposed dividend of Ashes plc.

The inter-company trading is dealt with as follows:

	£000
Consolidated turnover is reduced by	630
Consolidated cost of sales is reduced by	
an adjustment to remove unrealized profit	
in closing stock, i.e. 630 × 1/6 = 105 × 1/5	(21)
Net reduction in cost of sales	609

The above has the effect of reducing gross profit by twenty-one, the amount of the unrealized profit. The holding company acquired control of its subsidiary halfway through the current accounting period. Thus, all profits accruing up to 30 June 19X5, are pre-acquisition and only those from 1 July 19X5 are consolidated as being post-acquisition. In our consolidation working, this is effected by restricting the column of figures relating to the subsidiary to 6/12 of the year's results (1 July–31 December).

The consolidation working

	Victory plc £000	Ashes plc £000	(6/12) Adjustment £000	Consolidated £000
Turnover				
(note (a) above)	4,017	1,960.5	(630)	5,347.5
Cost of sales				
(note (b) above)	3,204	(1,485)	630	(4,080)
			(21)	
Gross profit	813	475.5	(21)	(1,267.5)
	(21)			
Distribution costs and				
administrative				
expenses	(506)	(345.5)		(851.5)
Profit as ordinary				
activities before				
taxation	286	130.0		416.0

	Victory plc £000	Ashes plc £000	Adjustment £000	Consolidated £000
Taxation on profit on ordinary activities	(150)	(60)		(210)
Profit on ordinary activities after taxation	136	70		206
Minority interest (25% × 70)		(17.5)		(17.5)
	136	52.5		188.5
Dividend transfer (6/12 × 75% × 50)	18.75	(18.75)		–
Profit dealt with	154.75	33.75		188.5
Dividends – ordinary proposed	(60)			(60)
Retained profit for the financial year	94.75	33.75		128.5
Statement of retained earnings				
As at 1 January 19X5	209	–		209
Retained for the year	94.75	33.75		128.5
As at 31 December 19X5	303.75	33.75		337.5

(a) It must be stressed that all figures in the column relating to Ashes plc are restricted to a 6/12 (i.e. post-acquisition) basis.

(b) There are a number of possible methods of reflecting the unrealized profit adjustment (£21,000). In the working above, this has been allocated into the holding company column for presentation and analysis purposes.

(c) All the retained earnings of the subsidiary at 1 January 19X5 are pre-acquisition and are therefore capitalized on consolidation.

Recapitulation of the profit and loss account technique

We have now considered all the consolidation principles in operation in preparing consolidated profit and loss accounts. The following are the major points to bear in mind:

(a) A columnar working is used, employing one column for each group company and a total (or consolidated) column on the right hand side, which is in effect the consolidated profit and loss account.

(b) The column relating to a subsidiary acquired during the current accounting period should be restricted on a time basis to post-acquisition profits only.

(c) Inter-company sales and purchases are eliminated by use of an adjustments column, which also shows the adjustment for un-realized profits as an increase in cost of sales.

(d)   If the holding company is not publishing its own individual profit and loss account, as is usually the case, the consolidated profit and loss account must show the amount of the group profit (including inter-company dividend) dealt with in the accounts of the holding company.

Example 8.16
This comprehensive example brings out other aspects of the application of the consolidation principles to profit and loss accounts.

For a holding company (Dexter plc) and its only subsidiary (Benaud plc) draft profit and loss accounts for the year to 31 December 19X5 show:

	Dexter plc £000	Benaud plc £000
Turnover	5,921	3,079
Cost of sales	(3,907)	(2,201)
Gross profit	2,014	878
Distribution costs	(603)	(284)
Administration expenses	(490)	(192)
Other operating income	80	–
Income from shares in group companies	75	–
Interest payable	(60)	
Profit on ordinary activities before taxation	1,016	402
Taxation on profit on ordinary activities	(404)	(161)
Profit on ordinary activities after taxation	612	241
Extraordinary charges	102	(50)
Profit for the financial year	510	191
Dividends – ordinary proposed	(100)	(100)
Retained profit for the year	410	91
Statement of retained earnings		
As at 1 January 19X5	609	221
Retained for 19X5	410	91
As at 31 December 19X5	1,019	312

Notes:
(a)   Dexter plc purchased 75 per cent of the issued ordinary capital of Benaud plc on 1 April 19X5. Benaud plc has only ordinary shares in issue.
(b)   All profits and losses may be treated as accruing evenly throughout the year, other than the subsidiary's extraordinary items which arise on 1 December 19X5.

(c) Since the group was formed, the following inter-company transactions have taken place:

   (i) Dexter plc sold goods to Benaud plc amounting to £250,000. All these goods were in stock at 31 December 19X5. Dexter plc's normal profit margin of 10 per cent on sales applied to this transaction.

   (ii) On 1 April 19X5, Dexter plc issued 800,000 £1 10 per cent unsecured loan stock, 20 per cent of which was acquired by Benaud plc. The subsidiary has recorded its interest income on the stock in administrative expenses.

   (iii) Since 1 April 19X5, Dexter plc has levied a management charge on its subsidiary, amounting to £1,000 per month. Both companies have accounted for this in administrative expenses.

The preparation of the consolidated profit and loss account is set out below.

	Dexter plc £000	Benaud plc £000	Adjustment £000	Consolidated £000
Turnover	5,921	2,309.25	(250)	7,980.25
Cost of sales	(3,907)	(1,650.75)	250	(5,332.75)
Gross profit	2,014	658.50	(25)	2,647.50
	(25)			
	1,989			
Distribution costs	(603)	(213)		(816)
Administrative expenses	(490)	(144)	(12)	(646)
Other operating income	80			80
Interest payable	(60)		12	(48)
Profit on ordinary activities before tax	916	301.50		1.217.5
Taxation on profit on ordinary activities	(404)	(120.75)		(524.75)
Profit on ordinary activities after tax	512	180.75		692.75
Minority interest		(45.19)		(45.19)
	512	135.56		647.56
Extraordinary charges	(102)	(37.5)		(139.5)
Profit for the financial year	410	98.06		508.06
Dividend transfer	56.25	(56.25)		–
	466.25	41.81		508.06
Dividend proposed	(100)			(100)
Retained for the financial year	366.35	41.81		408.06

	Dexter plc £000	Benaud plc £000	Adjustment £000	Consolidated £000
Statement of retained earnings				
As at 1 January 19X5	609	–		609
Retained for the year	366.25	41.81		408.06
As at 31 December				
19X5	975.25	41.81		1017.06

Notes:
(a) Unrealized profit eliminated on consolidation is calculated as: £250,000 × 10% (profit margin on sales) = £25,000.
(b) Inter-company interest is eliminated as follows: £80,000 × 10% × 9/12 = £60,000 interest payable by Dexter plc of which 20% × £60,000 = £12,000 is inter-company. This eliminates £12,000 from both the interest payable of Dexter plc and the administrative expenses of Benaud plc.
(c) There is no need to adjust for the management charge since, as this is in administrative expenses of both companies the income of one and the expense of the other automatically cancels when the columns are added together.
(d) Minority interest is calculated as follows: 25% × £180.75 = £45.19.
(e) Since the example states that the extraordinary item of the sub-sidiary arose on 1 December 19X5, this figure is not subject to the 9/12 post-acquisition adjustment as applied to the other figures relating to the subsidiary. The subsidiary's figure for this is: 75% (group share) × £50 = £37.50.
(f) The dividend transfer is: £100 × 75% (post-acquisition only) × 75% group share = £56.25.
(g) All brought forward profits of the subsidiary are pre-acquisition.

Questions

1   X plc acquired 80 per cent of the ordinary share capital of Y plc on 1 January 19X6 for £300,000. The following lists of balances of the two companies at 31 December 19X6 were:

	X plc £000	Y plc £000
Called up share capital:		
400,000 ordinary shares of £1 each.		
fully paid	400	
300,000 ordinary shares of £0.50 each,		
fully paid		150
Reserves as at 1 January 19X6	220	90
Retained profits for 19X6	20	18
Trade creditors	130	80

	X plc	Y plc
	£000	£000
Taxation	30	14
Proposed final dividend	20	10
Depreciation provisions:		
Freehold property	12	6
Plant and machinery	40	12
Current account		14
	872	394
Tangible fixed assets:		
Freehold property, at cost	120	160
Plant and machinery, at cost	183	62
Investment in Y plc	300	
Stocks	80	70
Debtors	160	90
Bank	10	12
Current account	19	
	872	394

Notes:

(a) A remittance of £2,000 from Y plc to X plc in December 19X6, was not received by X plc until January, 19X7.

(b) Goods, with an invoice value of £3,000, were despatched by X plc in December 19X6 but not received by Y plc until January 19X7. The profit element included in this amount was £400.

(c) Included in the stock of Y plc at 31 December 19X6 were goods purchased from X plc for £10,000. The profit element included in this amount was £2,000.

(d) It is group policy to exclude all profit on any inter-company transactions.

(c) No interim dividend was paid in 19X6 by either company.

(f) Ignore the ACT on the proposed final dividend

(g) Goodwill is to be written off against reserves.

You are required to prepare a consolidated balance sheet for X plc and its subsidiary Y plc as at 31 December 19X6.   (*20 marks*)

Chartered Institute of Management Accountants Stage 2, Financial Accounting, Specimen Examination Paper (New Syllabus)

2 Banquo Ltd, Angus Ltd and Ross Ltd had issued ordinary share capitals of £500,000, £250,000 and £150,000 respectively. All the companies made up their accounts to 28 February in each year. The par value of the ordinary shares of Banquo Ltd and Ross Ltd is £1 each and of Angus Ltd 25p. The following figures were extracted from the companies' accounting records for the year ended 28 February 19X6.

	Banquo Ltd £	Angus Ltd £	Ross Ltd £
Sales	2,783,400	1,256,500	1,749,100
Purchases	1,318,220	700,350	1,285,650
Administrative expenses	395,680	320,600	176,070
Distribution expenses	134,900	109,800	102,770
Stock on 28 February 19X5	219,750	61,540	113,080
Profit and loss account on 28 February 19X5	458,740	35,350	163,990
Interim dividends paid 1 September 19X5	100,000	10,000	15,000

You also obtain the following information:

(*a*)   Banquo Ltd purchased 75 per cent of the shares of Angus Ltd on 1 May 19X5 and on 1 July purchased 120,000 shares in Ross Ltd.

(*b*)   Ross Ltd sells goods for resale to Banquo Ltd with a mark up of 25 per cent on cost. In the first four months of the year the sales to Banquo Ltd totalled £39,500.

(*c*)   Ross Ltd operated a sales discount agreement with customers by way of 1.5 per cent rebate on annual sales in excess of £43,750. Provision for the rebate for the year is to be made of £8,950 which includes the rebate to Banquo Ltd of £1,620.

(*d*)   Stocks on 28 February 19X6 were: Banquo Ltd £236,000; Angus Ltd £57,290; and Ross Ltd £121,640. Included in the stock held by Banquo Ltd were goods purchased from Ross Ltd for £10,000.

(*e*)   Provision is to be made for corporation tax and final dividends as follows:

	Banquo Ltd	Angus Ltd	Ross Ltd
Corporation tax	£350,000	£45,000	£65,000
Final dividend per share	60p	6p	50p

You are required to:

Prepare a consolidated profit and loss account for Banquo Ltd and its subsidiary companies for the year ended 28 February 19X6 together with consolidation schedules.   (*26 marks*)

Note: Ignore advance corporation tax.

Institute of Chartered Accountants in England and Wales, Professional Examination 1, Financial Accounting 1

3   Full Ham plc is the listed parent company of a group engaged mainly in the food industry. At 30 June 19X4 the following share investments were held:

	Holding %	Cost £000	Market value £000	Directors valuation £000
Full Ham Manufacturing Ltd	100	3	–	53
Full Ham Pies Ltd	100	5	–	–
Full Ham Fish Ltd	100	7	–	47
Full Ham Fruit Ltd	85	16	–	17
Full Ham Management Ltd	100	–	–	–
Full Ham Farms Ltd	52	26	–	50
Full Ham Market Gardens plc	45	47	96	–
Cottage Foods Ltd	24	18	–	18
Thames Properties plc	0.5	6	7	–
15% Exchequer Stock 19X6	N/A	150	152	–
North South Foods Ltd	2	2	–	100
East Cost Growers Ltd	12	10	–	40

The following additional information is given:

(a) All holdings except the 100 per cent subsidiaries are held by Full Ham Management Ltd, a company with a £100 share capital.

(b) During the year a further 10 per cent of the capital of Full Ham Fish Ltd has been purchased at a cost of £2,000.

(c) The holding in Full Ham Farms Ltd was increased on 1 July 1983 from 42 per cent to 52 per cent a cost of £10,000.

(d) Full Ham Market Gardens plc is a listed company. There are no other holders of more than 5 per cent of the issued capital. Full Ham plc has three nominees on the seven man board of directors and has a significant influence on the day-to-day management.

(e) The remainder of the shares in Cottage Foods Ltd are held by Empire Breweries plc which effectively controls the company. Full Ham plc has no significant influence on the day to day affairs.

(f) Thames Properties plc has a full listing as has the Exchequer Stock.

(g) It has been decided to write down to a nominal £1 the value of the shares in Full Ham Pies Ltd.

(h) The profit and loss accounts for the year ended 30 June 1984 of the undermentioned companies are summarized below:

	Full Ham Farms Ltd £000	Full Ham Market Gardens plc £000	Cottage Foods Ltd £000
Profit for the financial year	54	33	76
Dividends	–	8	26
	54	25	50

	Full Ham Farms Ltd £000	Full Ham Market Gardens plc £000	Cottage Foods Ltd £000
Retained profit brought forward	86	96	124
Retained profit carried forward	140	121	174
The excess of the cost of the shares over the net assets acquired was, in each case	3	13	6
Allotted share capital and other reserves at 30 June 19X3 and 19X4	10	100	10

(*i*)   Unless otherwise indicated all holdings are of ordinary shares and there are no other classes of capital.

You are required to prepare the appropriate notes to the accounts relating to investments in a form suitable for publication in the financial statements of Full Ham plc at 30 June 19X4.   (*22 marks*)

Note: Ignore comparative figures and taxation.

Institute of Chartered Accountants in England and Wales, Professional Examination 1, Financial Accounting 1

9 Accounting for changes in price levels

In recent years there has been intense controversy over accounting for changing prices. There are two reasons for this situation. First, disagreements over the objectives of accounting produce disagreements on the methods of accounting which should be applied. Second, where there is agreement on objectives there is frequently dispute over the means of achieving these objectives.

Reservations about the usefulness of financial statements prepared under the historical cost concept during periods of inflation have been expressed because:

(a) Not all balance sheets reveal the real value of all the assets and liabilities.
(b) Depreciation is inadequate to replace the fixed assets consumed during the year.
(c) The charge for the cost of stock consumed is inadequate to replace it because stock is charged at the cost of purchase and not at the cost of replacement.
(d) The effects of holding monetary assets (e.g. cash, debtors), or owing monetary liabilities (e.g. creditors, loans), are ignored.

As a result of these inadequacies:

(a) Growth is exaggerated because no allowance is made for the fall in the value of the money used to measure the results.
(b) Their uncritical use may lead to the situation where capital, although maintained in money terms, may not be maintained in real terms and may be distributed to shareholders, employees, customers or the Inland Revenue to the detriment of the long-term viability of the business. (Inflation Accounting Steering Group, 1976.)

Reforms proposed

The ASC's proposals on inflation accounting are:

1974   Publication of Provisional SSAP7, *Accounting for Changes in the Purchasing Power of Money*, proposed the current purchasing power (CPP) method. This was withdrawn in 1978.

1976   Publication of ED18, which proposed the current cost accounting (CCA) method based upon the report of the Sandilands Committee.

1977   The lengthy and complicated proposals of ED18 were rejected and replaced by the Hyde Guidelines, an interim recommendation which proposed that listed companies prepare a supplementary statement to accompany their accounts showing a simplified version of ED18 confined to the profit and loss account only.

1980   Publication of SSAP16 *Current Cost Accounting*.

1984   ED35, *Accounting for Changing Prices*, proposed modifications to SSAP16.

1985   ED35 was withdrawn and SSAP16 classed as non-mandatory. These reforms dealt with two issues:

   (*a*)   Asset valuation for the purpose of reporting balance sheet values at a certain time.
   (*b*)   Profit measurement in which the problem of capital maintenance plays a leading role.

Asset valuation

The historical cost (HC) approach, by aggregating the values of individual assets and liabilities, although similar in character, may produce meaningless totals if items were obtained at significantly different historical values. The following reforms have been proposed:

(*a*)   Adjusted historical cost
(*b*)   Current values:
   (*i*)   Current replacement cost
   (*ii*)   Net realizable value
   (*iii*)   Present value
   (*iv*)   Value to the firm

Adjusted historical cost attempts to solve the problem of price instability by using a general price index to adjust values recorded at historical cost for changes in the general purchasing power of money. The basic rationale of these adjustments is to provide homogeneity to the measurement process so that all money equivalents are measured in the same scale. The historical cost values of items such as fixed assets or stocks are adjusted to their current purchasing power equivalents by applying the ratio:

Index of general prices at the accounting date
Index of general prices at the transactions date

Example 9.1
A factory building was purchased for 100,000 at the end of 19V6 when
the price level index was 80 and straight line depreciation of 3 per cent
per year is being taken. At the end of 19X6, when the price level index is
120, the asset would be valued for the balance sheet as follows:

	Unadjusted £000	Conversion factor	Adjusted £000
Factory building (cost)	100	120/180	150
Deduct: accumulated			
depreciation	60	120/80	90
Net book value	40		60

This calculation indicates that the carrying value of the building in
terms of 19X6 pounds is understated by £20,000. This illustrates the
approach of SSAP7 to asset valuation.

Current replacement cost values assets on the basis of the sacrifice
which would be incurred today in replacing the asset or the service
potential represented by the asset.

Example 9.2
If the factory building in Example 9.1 has, at the end of 19X6, a replacement cost of £170,000, the asset would be valued for balance sheet
purposes as follows:

	£000
Factory building	170
Deduct: accumulated depreciation	102
Net book value	68

This calculation indicates that the historical cost value of the asset is
understated in terms of its replacement by £28,000. There may be
difficulty in computing the replacement cost of assets. For many assets,
especially physical plant, there may be no ready market for which to
acquire replacement assets. In such cases specific price indices may be
used, or management estimates. It follows that substantial technological change can make this concept difficult to apply.

Net realizable value of an asset may be defined as the estimated
amount that would currently be received from the sale of the asset less
the anticipated costs that would be incurred in its disposal.

The net realizable value approach provides investors and creditors
with some measure of the risks involved in investing in or lending to a
company. Essentially this approach reflects the capacity of the enterprise to adapt to new alternatives, information which is not provided by
other valuation systems. The major disadvantage of using realizable
values is that they imply a short run approach to the analysis of

business operations. All assets are valued at exit prices even though many assets are not held for resale. Although realizable values represent values based on market prices, they do not reflect the behaviour of enterprises. In reality, firms do not sell off their assets at frequent intervals: in practice they continue in the same line, or lines, of business for a considerable time. Another problem is that of determining selling prices for highly specific assets such as items of plant where there is no ready market. Scrap values may be the only alternative for valuing such assets.

Present value is defined as the sum of the future expected net cash flows associated with the use of an asset discounted to their present value. As such it is consistent with the concept of value contained in the economic theory of income. However, in this particular context this concept of value is used to value each asset individually rather than to value the firm as a whole. Since the computations are based on future predictions the concept does not perform well in terms of objectivity and verifiability. This poses severe limitations for its practical application. Furthermore, it is only very rarely that cash flows can be identified with one individual asset. More commonly, cash flows are derived from a group of assets, with the result that wholly arbitrary allocations are necessary to assign them among individual assets.

Value to the business is designed to indicate the value of an asset to an enterprise in the light of the economic context in which it is held. One method of computing this value is to measure the loss which would be suffered if the business was deprived of the asset. This reverses the opportunity cost concept and defines opportunity value as the least costly sacrifice avoided by owning the asset. It is based on the work of Bonbright (1937) who defined opportunity value in the following terms: 'The value of a property to its owner is identical in amount with the adverse value of the entire loss, direct and indirect, that the owner might expect to suffer if he were deprived of the property.'

In no sense may historical cost be measured as the value of an asset to the business because it is not related to the amount which would have to be paid for the asset, the amount that might be gained from disposing of it, or the amount to be gained by holding it. Deprival value is not based on a single type of value but on a combination of possible values which include the three bases of valuation discussed above:

(a)   The current purchase price (replacement cost) of the asset (RC).
(b)   The net realizable value of the asset (NRV).
(c)   The present value of expected furture earnings from the asset (PV).

Six hypothetical relationships exist between these three values:

		Correct valuation basis
1	NPV > PV > RC	RC
2	NRV > RC > PV	RC
3	PV > RC > NRV	RC
4	PV > NRV > RC	RC

		Correct valuation basis
5	RC > PV > NRV	PV
6	RC > NPV > PV	NRV

In 1 and 2 above, NRV is greater than PV. Hence, the firm would be better off selling rather than using the asset. The sale of the asset necessitates its replacement, if the NRV is to be restored. We may say, therefore, that the maximum loss which the firm would suffer by being deprived of the asset is RC.

In 3 and 4 above, PV is greater than NRV, so that the firm would be better off using the asset rather than selling it. The firm must replace the asset in order to maintain PV, so that the maximum loss which the firm would suffer by being deprived of the asset is again RC.

The general statement which may be made, therefore, in respect of the first four cases 1 to 4 is that, where either NRV or PV, or both, are higher than RC, RC is the appropriate value of the asset to the business. As regards a current asset, such as stocks, RC will be the current purchase price (entry value). In the case of a fixed asset, RC will be the written down current purchase price (replacement cost), since the value of such an asset will be the cost of replacing it in its existing condition, having regard to wear and tear.

In cases 5 and 6, RC does not represent the value of the asset to the business, for if the firm were to be deprived of the asset, the loss incurred would be less than RC. Case 5 is most likely to arise in industries where assets are highly specific, where NRV tends to zero and where RC is greater than PV, so that it would not be worth replacing the asset if it were destroyed, but it is worth using it rather than attempting to dispose of it.

Case 6 applies to assets held for resale, that is, where NRV must be greater than PV. If RC should prove to be greater than NRV, such assets would not be replaced. Hence, it implies that they should be valued at NRV or RC which ever is the lower.

The Sandilands Report's acceptance of the deprival value concept attracted criticism because of the practical problem of assessing PV, as noted above. This problem arises in Case 5 in the above table where RC > PV > NRV. In 1978 the Australian provisional accounting standard rejected the deprival concept and recommended instead adoption of the 'recoverable amount' criterion. Accordingly, two questions should be asked about an asset:

(a) Is the asset to continue in use? If yes – ask question (b). If no – value at net realizable value.

(b) Can the current cost of the asset be expected to be recovered, through charges against the revenues from the continued use of the asset, and/or by its sale? If yes – value at replacement cost. If no – value at the amount of replacement cost that can be recovered (the recoverable amount).

Similarly, SSAP16 abandoned the deprival value concept and pre-scribed the recoverable amount criteria where RC does not provide the value to the business. In SSAP16 the value to the business of an asset is defined as:

(a)   RC or if a permanent diminution to below RC has been recognized.
(b)   Recoverable amount, which is the greater of NRV of an asset and, where applicable, the amount recoverable from its further use.

Profit measurement

The original thrust toward inflation accounting came from the view that profit was not being properly measured under the historical cost system. This has led to a re-examination of how profit should be mea-sured. Hicks (1946) defined the income of an individual as:

> ... the maximum value which he can consume during a week, and still expect to be as well-off at the end of the week as he was at the beginning.

Hicks' model of personal income was adapted by Alexander and subsequently revised by Solomons (see Alexander 1950), to an equiva-lent concept of corporate profit. Accordingly, Alexander defined corpo-rate profit as the maximum amount which a firm could distribute to its shareholders during a period and still remain as well off at the end of the period as at the beginning. The difficulty in applying this definition in practice is in defining what one means by 'well-offness'. Although there is general agreement that profit is a residue available for distri-bution once provision has been made for maintaining the value of capital intact difficulties begin to emerge when the discussion turns to the consideration of the meaning of 'capital maintenance'. Three inter-pretations of this concept focus on maintenance of:

(a)   The money amount
(b)   The financial capital
(c)   The operating capability

Money amount maintenance takes the view that the measurement of periodic profit should ensure that the monetary value of the share-holders' equity is maintained intact. In effect, the profit of the period amounts to the increase in monetary terms in the shareholders' equity measured between the beginning and the end of the period. It is this amount which may be distributed as dividends to ensure that the money capital is maintained intact. The money capital maintenance concept is reflected in historical cost accounting.

Financial capital maintenance seeks to maintain the purchasing power of the shareholders' equity by constantly updating the historical cost of assets for changes in the value of money. The translation of historical asset cost is effected by a retail price index, and results in the represen-tation of asset values in common units of purchasing power. This concept of capital maintenance purports to show to shareholders that their company kept pace with general inflationary pressures during the accounting period, by measuring profit in such a way as to take into account changes in the price levels. In effect, it intends to maintain the shareholders' capital in terms of monetary units of constant purchasing power. Therefore it reflects the proprietorship view of the enterprise which demands that the objective of profit measurement should focus on the wealth of equity shareholders.

Operating capability maintenance aims to maintain the physical quantities of resources at the disposal of the entity since it is these which generate the cash flows from which we obtain a measure of net profit. Therefore, profit is considered to be the residue after provision has been made for maintaining the capability of the assets to continue operations at the same level which existed at the beginning of the period.

The operating capability concept implies that in times of rising prices increased funds will be required to maintain assets. These funds might not be available if profit is determined without recognition of the rising costs of assets consumed in operations. For example, profit would not be earned on the sale for £1,000 of 100 units of stock costing £800 if their replacement cost was £1,000. In this situation, an outlay of £1,000 would be required in order to maintain the operating capability of the business in terms of 100 units of stock. In other words, the increase in the cost of the stock necessitates the investment of additional funds in the business in order to maintain it as an operating unit.

The operating capability concept does not imply that the firm is committed to replacing assets with identical items. The entity, being dynamic, may extend, contract, or change its activities in which ever way desired. The concept simply means that the operating capability should be maintained at the same level at the end of a period as it was at the beginning.

In the previous section we saw how the purchasing power adjusted money value concept views the capital of the enterprise from the standpoint of the shareholders. By contrast, the operating capability concept views the problem of capital maintenance from the perspective of the enterprise itself. This notion underlies current cost accounting, but the method of its implementation, as we shall see, is very controversial.

Holding gains

Earlier we saw that assets determined by their 'value to the business' are usually measured in terms of their replacement cost. This method of valuation divides historical cost profit into two elements:

(a) Current cost operating profit, i.e. selling price minus replacement cost of the asset sold.
(b) Holding gains, i.e. increase in the replacement price of the asset held.

Example 9.3

During the year ended 31 December 19X0 Hathersage Components Limited, a £400 equity financed company acquired an asset at a cost of £400. By 31 December 19X0 its replacement cost had risen to £600. It was sold on 31 December 19X1 for £1,000 and at the time of sale, its replacement cost was £650.

For the purpose of measuring historical cost profit, the profit arising from the sale of the asset (assuming no depreciation) would accrue in the year ended 31 December 19X1 and would be calculated as follows:

HC profit = Revenue-historical cost
         = £1,000 − £400
         = £600

For the purpose of measuring replacement cost profit three distinct gains are recognized which occur as follows:

(a) A holding gain in the year ended 31 December 19X0 measured as the difference between the replacement cost at 31 December 19X0 and the acquisition cost during the year, that is £600 − £400 = £200.

(b) A holding gain in the year ended 31 December 19X1 measured as the difference between the replacement cost at 31 December 19X0 and the replacement cost on the date of sale, that is, £650 − £600 = £50.

(c) An operating gain resulting directly from the activity of selling measured as the difference between the realized sale price and the replacement cost at the date of sale, that is £1,000 − £650 = £350.

These differing timings of profit recognition may be compared as follows:

Year ended 31 December	19X0	19X1
	£	£
Historical cost profit	–	600
Replacement cost profit		
Holding gains	200	50
Current operating gain	–	350

It is clear from this example that the differences between historical and replacement cost relate to the timing of reported gains and losses since the total gain over the two periods is £600 in each case. Furthermore, the replacement cost concept provides more detailed information than the historical cost profit for performance evaluation. Two arguments for the separation of profit into holding and operating gains have been suggested. First, the two profit categories may be used to evaluate different aspects of management activity. Secondly, they permit better inter-period and inter-firm comparisons.

Holding gains on assets which have not been sold are termed 'unrealized', after sale they are said to be 'realized'. As we saw in Chapter 2 the Companies Acts do not permit dividends to be paid from unrealized profits Additionally, when the concept of maintenance of operating capability is applied no part of the holding gain can be regarded as profit. This should be credited to a capital maintenance reserve, designated 'current cost reserve' by SSAP16. Assuming all of the £350 operating profit was distributed as dividends the condensed balance sheet of Hathersage Components Limited at 31 December 19X1 would appear as follows:

Balance sheet as at 31 December 19X1
(maintaining operating capability)

	£		£
Share capital	400	Cash (£1,000 − £350)	650
Current cost reserve	250		
	650		650

If the balance sheet of Hathersage Components Limited is prepared on a historical cost basis, and assuming the £600 profit was all distributed as dividends the position would appear as follows:

Balance sheet as at 31 December 19X1
(maintaining money amount)

	£		£
Share capital	400	Cash (£1,000 − £600)	400

This example shows clearly how under the money amount maintenance concept capital may be distributed to shareholders to the detriment of the long-term viability of the business.

Current purchasing power accounting is not designed to differentiate between operating profits and holding gains. However, it may be used to compute real gain or loss – i.e. the surplus or shortfall between the replacement cost value and what this would have been if it had behaved like prices in general (Baxter 1984). Returning to Example 9.3 assume the retail price index at 31 December 19X1 has increased by 10 per cent since Hathersage Components Limited bought the asset in question. Real gain is calculated as follows:

	£
Current replacement cost	650
Historical cost adjusted by general index	
(£400 × 110/100)	440
Real gain	210

This shows that the company has beaten the general index to make a real gain of £210. In maintenance of financial capital real holding gains form part of profit; the gain exceeds that needed to maintain the purchase which resulted in the gain. Therefore, under this concept of capital maintenance £560 (£210 + £350) would be available for distribution as dividends. If the company did take this step the balance sheet based on maintenance of financial capital at 31 December 19X1 would appear as follows:

Balance sheet as at 31 December 19X1
(maintaining financial capital)

	£		£
Share capital (£400 + 10%)	400	Cash (£1,000 − £560)	440

Monetary items

Hitherto, we have confined our attention to physical assets such as property, plant and equipment and stock. These items gain in money value in periods of inflation. Monetary items (e.g. bank balances and liabilities generally), are stated in fixed units of money which are not affected by a change in prices. However, the purchasing power of such items will change with fluctuations in the value of money. When prices are rising the purchasing powers of a bank deposit or an amount due from debtors will be falling, and it may be argued that this represents a loss to the business. Conversely, the purchasing power represented by the claims of creditors will fall during a period of inflation. It may be argued that such a reduction in the purchasing power of monetary liabilities represents a gain to the business. In order to represent this situation current purchasing power financial statements contain one type of item not represented in historical cost statements – purchasing power gains or losses on monetary items. This item is necessary to maintain the financial capital of a company.

The treatment of monetary items in proposals which seek to maintain the operating capability of a company is more complex, because supporters of the maintenance of operating capability are by no means united on a definition of capital. It is possible to identify seven different basic notions of what is meant by operating capability:

(*a*) Physical assets.
(*b*) Physical assets and monetary assets (excluding fixed or long-term monetary assets).
(*c*) Physical assets and all monetary assets.
(*d*) Physical assets and all monetary assets – current liabilities.
(*e*) Physical assets and monetary assets (excluding cash) – creditors.
(*f*) Physical assets and net monetary assets.
(*g*) Physical assets and all monetary assets – all liabilities.

All these notions have attracted supporters. SSAP16 is based on (*e*).

In the remainder of this chapter we illustrate two of the ASC's proposals on inflation accounting. SSAP7, published in 1974 and withdrawn in 1978, had the objective of maintaining financial capital. SSAP16, published in 1980, was aimed at maintaining operating capability. Detailed applications of these proposals are examined in a companion volume *Advanced Financial Accounting*.

Current purchasing power (CPP) accounting

The provisional standard SSAP7 proposed a supplementary statement designed to make adjustments for inflation using the retail price index as an index of general price change. Under CPP the balance sheets of the previous and the present accounting periods are converted into the same units, i.e. £s of current purchasing power. All items in the balance sheet and all non-monetary items including equity in the closing balance sheet are adjusted using general indices. Monetary items in the closing balance sheet require no conversion because they are already stated in units of CPP. Profit and loss account items are adjusted by reference to the average rate for the period, though depreciation is adjusted at the rate applicable to the relevant asset and opening and closing stocks according to the changes in the index between their respective dates of acquisition and the closing balance sheet date. One further calculation is required – the gains or losses that result from holding monetary assets and liabilities.

Example 9.4
Bright Limited was incorporated on 1 January 19X0 with an issued share capital of £10,000. On the same date the company received a long-term loan of £5,000, purchased fixed assets at a cost of £12,000 and stocks at a cost of £1,500. The opening balance sheet shows:

	£	£
Fixed asset		12,000
Current assets:		
Stock	1,500	
Cash	1,500	3,000
		15,000
Creditors – amounts falling due		
after more than one year:		
Loan		5,000
		10,000
Capital		10,000

The fixed asset is depreciated over six years. Stock is priced on a first-in, first-out (FIFO) basis. Stock on hand at the end of the year may be assumed to have been purchased evenly throughout the last six months of the year. Sales and purchases occur evenly throughout the year, i.e. in effect these transactions occur at the average price level of the year.
The following transactions occurred during 19X0:

Sales	£20,000
Purchases	£15,000

On 31 December 19X0, £500 interest on the loan and £1,000 dividends

were paid. £2,000 was set aside for taxation. Closing stock had cost
£3,000.

The profit and loss account and balance sheet prepared on a historical
cost basis were as follows:

*Bright Limited – profit and loss account for the year ended 31 December
19X0*

	£	£
Sales		20,000
Cost of goods sold:		
Opening stock	1,500	
Add purchases	15,000	
	16,500	
Less closing stock	3,000	13,500
		6,500
Depreciation	2,000	
Interest	500	2,500
		4,000
Taxation		2,000
Profit after taxation		2,000
Dividends paid		1,000
Retained profit		1,000

Balance sheet as at 31 December 19X0

	£	£
Fixed asset	12,000	
Less: depreciation	2,000	10,000
Current assets:		
Stock	3,000	
Debtors	5,000	
Cash	4,000	
	12,000	
Creditors – amounts falling due within one year:		
Trade creditors	4,000	
Taxation	2,000	
	6,000	
Net current assets		6,000
		16,000
Creditors – amounts falling due after more than one year:		
Loan		5,000
		11,000
Capital and reserves:		
Share capital		10,000
Profit and loss account		1,000
		11,000

The Retail Price Index during the year moved as follows:

1 January 19X0	100
31 December 19X0	112

The gains and losses resulting from changes in the purchasing power of the pound are to be computed for the year, and the financial statements are to be restated in terms of the pound at the end of 19X0.

Bright Limited – purchasing power gain or loss on monetary items for the year 19X0

	Unadjusted £	Conversion factor	Adjusted £
Cash balance 1 January	1,500	112/100	1,680
Add sales	20,000	112/106	21,132
			22,812
Less purchases	15,000	112/106	15,849
			6,963
Less other expenditure:			
Interest	500		
Taxation	2,000		
Dividends	1,000		3,500
			3,463
Closing:			
Debtors	5,000		
Cash	4,000		
	9,000		
Less creditors	6,000		3,000
			463
Add gain on loan			600
Purchasing power gain			137

Bright Limited – CPP financial statements profit and loss account for year ending 31 December 19X0

	Unadjusted £	Conversion factor	Adjusted £
Sales	20,000	112/106	21,132
Cost of goods sold:			
Opening stock	1,500	112/100	1,680
Add purchases	15,000	112/106	15,849
	16,500		17,529
Less closing stock	3,000	112/109	3,083
	13,500		14,446
Gross profit	6,500		6,686
Depreciation	2,000	112/100	2,240
Interest	500		500
	2,500		2,740
Profit before taxation	4,000		3,946

	Unadjusted £	Conversion factor	Adjusted £
Taxation	2,000		2,000
Profit after taxation	2,000		1,946
Dividends	1,000		1,000
	1,000		946
Add purchasing power gain			137
Retained profit			1,083

Balance sheet at 31 December 19X0

	Unadjusted £	Conversion factor	Adjusted £
Fixed asset	12,000	112/100	13,440
Less: depreciation	2,000	112/100	2,240
			11,200
Current assets			
Stock	3,000	112/109	3,083
Debtors	5,000		5,000
Cash	4,000		4,000
	12,000		12,083
Creditors – amounts falling due within one year:			
Trade creditors			4,000
Taxation			2,000
			6,000
Net current assets			6,083
			17,283
Creditors – amounts falling due after more than one year:			
Loan			5,000
			12,283
Capital and reserves:			
Share capital	10,000	112/100	11,200
Profit and loss account			1,083
			12,283

Appraisal of CPP

CPP protects the general purchasing power of invested capital and seeks to maintain the opportunity for alternative investment on the assumption that the existing investment could be withdrawn. A general index is used on the grounds that the suppliers of equity capital require results to be measured in terms of their own consumption.

Common pound accounting can be applied with a high degree of objectivity, as it does not depart in principle from historical cost based measurement. Price level adjustments are verifiable by reference to the index used to measure changes in the purchasing power of money, and result in alterations to historical cost measurements which are themselves objective, thereby satisfying the criteria of objectivity and verifiability.

A disadvantage of this technique is that it does not recognize the presence of changing relative prices. The possibility of reporting items at a value significantly above (or below) their current worth, may be misleading to the financial statement user. Another objection is raised by the argument that organizations and people do not see themselves as holding general purchasing power when they hold money; rather, they see themselves as holding specific purchasing power in respect of those relatively few items which they wish to purchase. Hence, the purchasing power of money should be related to those items on which money is intended to be spent. A unit of measurement which relies for its validity on the purchasing power of money assessed by reference to a set of goods and services will not be equally useful to all individuals and entities.

Moreover, the concept of profit on which these adjustments are based is not one which maintains the service potential of capital. A general price index, particularly a consumer's price index, is a weighted average of the price change occurring in a wide variety of goods and services available in the economy. Therefore, adjusting financial data for the effects of inflation is not the same as reporting current values. Additionally, controversy surrounds the treatment of gains and losses arising on monetary items. CPP accounting includes such gains and losses in the periodic profit. Hence, a company's pre-tax profit will be dramatically different, according to the nature of its financial structure, before and after these adjustments have been made. Property companies, whose largest balance sheet item is often their liabilities to banks, finance houses and other credit institutions, find their adjusted profit and loss account showing exceptionally good results. But the 'gains' resulting from these adjustments do not increase sums available for distribution as dividends to shareholders, since they are purely accounting adjustments. They could only be distributed by drawing on existing cash resources or by borrowing. Hence if the net 'gains' on monetary items are regarded as available for distribution, the users of adjusted financial reports could be seriously misled.

Although CPP accounting has limitations the underlying concepts have been incorporated to some extent by accounting standard setters. As we show in the following section the 'gearing adjustment' seeks to recognize the benefit which borrowing provides to shareholders in a period of rising prices. In the United States the Financial Accounting Standards Board (FASB) requires that CPP information be reported by large companies. The FASB does not support the view that CPP information alone is sufficient to satisfy the needs of financial statement users. However, it recognizes that selected items of financial information adjusted for general inflation may have some value.

Current cost accounting (CCA)

SSAP16 represented a substantial attempt to introduce replacement costs into financial reporting by UK companies. Its major requirements were:

(*a*)   Current cost information to be published either as a supplement to historical cost, or as the main medium of report with supplementary historical cost accounts. A current cost balance sheet and profit and loss account were to be provided.

(*b*)   The current value of assets to be determined as value to the business (or deprival value) at the balance sheet date.

(*c*)   That the capital to be maintained is determined by the operating capability of the business.

Profit and loss account requirements

Current cost profit was to be derived from historical cost profit after applying four current cost adjustments. A pro forma profit and loss account is as follows:

	£	£
Historical cost profit before interest		x
Current cost operating adjustments:		
Cost of sales	x	
Depreciation	x	
Monetary working capital	x	(x)
Current cost operating profit		x
Gearing adjustment	x	
Interest	(x)	x
Current cost profit attributable to		
shareholders		x

The purpose of the current cost operating adjustments is to adjust for the fact that in the calculation of historical cost profit only the historical cost value of resources is charged for. In a period of rising prices this will understate resource cost and overstate profit. The gearing adjustment attempts to reflect how a business's financial structure may mitigate the effects of inflation on shareholders.

The cost of sales adjustment (COSA) refers to the difference between the value to the business (normally replacement cost) of stock consumed during a period and the historical cost of that stock. Thus,

COSA = (Current cost of stock − Historical cost of stock)

The current cost of stock is calculated by revaluing individual items to their replacement cost value or by applying indices to historic costs. The indices are specific to stock items, unlike the general price level indices of CPP accounting. This is illustrated by Example 9.5.

Example 9.5
An index which is appropriate to a company's stock behaves as follows:

100	115	120
Index ⊢	⊣	⊣
1 January	Average for year	31 December

The company's historic cost of sales is adjusted to current cost by applying these indices:

(£)

	Historic cost		Current cost
Purchases	4,600		4,600
Stock movement			
Opening	700	$\times \frac{115}{100} =$	806
Closing	1,220	$\times \frac{115}{120} =$	1,036
	380		330
Cost of sales	4,220		4,370

Giving a COSA of £4,370 − £4,220 = £150.

The depreciation adjustment (DA) applies similar reasoning to fixed assets and aims to charge in each accounting period a proportion of the current value to the business of a fixed asset consumed in a period. Hence:

DA = (Current cost depreciation − Historical cost depreciation)

Like stock, fixed assets are revalued using indices specific to the particular fixed assets (or where appropriate by valuation). Assume that a machine with a five year life which cost £10,000 three years ago has a current replacement cost of £14,000. In this case, historic cost depreciation on a straight line basis would be £2,000, with current cost depreciation being £14,000 ÷ 5 = £2,800. This would give a DA of: £2,800 − £2,000 = £800.

The monetary working capital adjustment (MWCA) extends the notion of a business's operating capability beyond non-monetary assets (fixed assets and stock) to include monetary assets and liabilities. Three justifications were offered for this adjustment. First, debtors and creditors represent an integral part of operating capability, hence the collective description of working capital. Second, during inflation additional investments need to be made in debtors to maintain a business's operations, some of which may come from creditors. Third, different types of businesses have operating capability composed differently. Consider, for example, a supermarket, a bank, and an engineering company. All will have fixed assets (and hence depreciation adjustments), but the relationships between their stocks, debtors and

208   *Financial Accounting*

creditors will be different. A supermarket will have large stocks, substantial creditors, but no debtors due to its cash sales business. A bank has no stock, trade debtors or creditors, but has substantial monetary assets and liabilities (advances and customers' deposits). Finally, a manufacturing company has substantial stock, debtors and creditors. Failure to reflect these differences means failure to reflect accurately the effects of inflation on businesses. The MWCA is an attempt to reflect some of these effects.

The calculation of the MWCA requires application of a specific index to trade debtors and creditors to obtain a current cost value for monetary working capital (MWC) as in example 9.6.

Example 9.6

	Trade debtors	Trade creditors	MWC	Indexation	Current cost
Opening	1,800	(1,200)	600 ×	$\frac{110}{100}$ =	660
Closing	2,240	(1,400)	840 ×	$\frac{110}{120}$ =	770
Net increase over the accounting period			240		110

This assumes that an index specific to trade debtors and creditors has risen steadily from an opening value of 100 to a closing value of 120.
The MWCA is given by:

Historical cost difference in MWC − Current cost difference in MWC

or   £240 − £110 = £130

The implication of the calculation is that £110 is due to price changes and £130 is due to volume effects.

As the pro forma statement on page 206 indicates, the three current cost operating adjustments are applied to historic cost profit to give current cost operating profit. The final stage in adjustment to current cost profit attributable to shareholders represents an interesting innovation, the gearing adjustment. The gearing adjustment (GA) reflects the influence which financial structure (gearing) may have upon the way inflation affects a business. As Figure 9.1 shows, the net operating assets of a business are financed by a mixture of shareholders funds and net borrowing.

The value of the debt component of total capital (a monetary liability) will be fixed in money terms but will decline in real terms during times of inflation. In this way, shareholders gain at the expense of lenders because of inflation. SSAP16 attempts to show this shareholders' gain through the gearing adjustment. The GA is calculated in two stages. Stage one is the calculation of the gearing proportion. This is the ratio

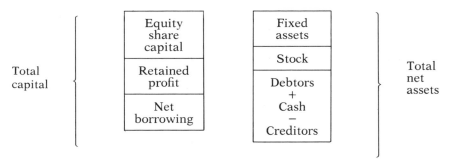

Figure 9.1

of net borrowings (B), to the total of shareholders funds, that is equity share capital and retained profits (E), and net borrowings, thus:

$$\text{Gearing proportion} = \frac{B}{E + B}$$

Stage two applies the gearing proportion to the sum of the current cost operating adjustments to obtain the GA. The GA is credited to the current cost profit and loss account as a gain to shareholders. Since lenders are compensated by being paid interest, the interest charge is off-set against the GA to obtain the net gain to shareholders. The following extract from a balance sheet illustrates the calculation of a GA:

	Opening	*Average for accounting period*	Closing
		(£)	
Share capital	2,000	2,000	2,000
Retained profit	600	1,200	1,800
10% debentures	4,600	4,800	5,000
	7,200		8,800

The gearing proportion is $\dfrac{4,800}{3,200 + 4,800} = 0.6$

Taking the sum of the operating adjustments calculated above, £150 + £800 + £130 = £1,080 and applying the gearing proportion gives:

GA = 0.6 × £1,080 = £648

Assuming a historical cost profit before interest of £2,000 and noting that debenture interest will be £460, the current cost profit and loss account appears as:

	£	£
Historical cost profit before interest		2,000
Current cost operating adjustments:		
Cost of sales	150	
Depreciation	800	
Monetary working capital	130	(1,080)
		920

	£	£
Current cost operating profit		
Gearing adjustment	648	
Interest	(460)	188
Current cost profit attributable to		
shareholders		1,108

Balance sheet requirements

The current cost balance sheet required by SSAP16 contains fixed assets and stock valued on the basis of deprival value (or value to the business). Value to the business may be net replacement cost, economic value (amount recoverable from an asset's continued use) or net realizable value. Which of these applies depends upon the application of two simple tests concerning an asset's use to the business, thus for each asset one must determine:

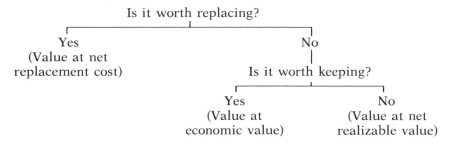

The usual basis of valuation will be net replacement cost and this is determined for fixed assets and stock by the application of specific indices as in the DA and COSA. The resulting gains due to such revaluations represent holding gains and were required to be taken to reserve and a special reserve was created for this and other purposes, the current cost reserve. The various current cost adjustments from the profit and loss account are also to be taken to current cost reserve.

The remaining assets and liabilities (cash, debtors, share capital and borrowings) are all monetary items and therefore are not subject to revaluation and appear in the current cost balance sheet at their historical cost values.

	19X0	19X1
	£	£
Net operating assets	240,314	279,188
Plus:		
Dividend	4,800	6,250
Taxation	8,000	6,660
Overdraft	20,000	16,660
	273,114	308,758
Average	£290,936	

This gives a gearing proportion of:

$$\frac{£45,660}{£290,936} = 0.157$$

and a gearing adjustment as before.

The gearing adjustment is central to the dispute over whether an entity or proprietary view is appropriate for companies. As we have noted an entity view regards the company as an entity in itself and both shareholders and creditors are regarded as being outside the company. Both provide finance for the company and require to be compensated, but no distinction has to be made between their separate interests. On a proprietary view, the company belongs to the shareholders. Those who support the entity view argue that gains on borrowing should not be included in income because the gain is not represented by cash inflows. Therefore, distribution of the gain may impair the basic assets of the company. Some who support the proprietary view critize SSAP16's gearing adjustment on the grounds that it does not reflect the full impact of inflation on monetary items. Instead, the benefits from net borrowings are associated with the other current cost adjustments and are not determined in their own right. According to this viewpoint, the COSA and depreciation adjustment arising in a particular period are unrelated to the benefit arising to shareholders from the existence of creditors.

SSAP16 defines the resulting entity and proprietorship profit concepts as follows:

(*a*) Current cost operating profit 'is the surplus arising from the ordinary activities of the business in the period after allowing for the impact of price changes on the funds needed to continue the existing business and maintain its operating capability, whether financed by share capital or borrowing. It is calculated before interest on net borrowing and taxation'.

(*b*) Current cost profit attributable to shareholders 'is the surplus for the period after allowing for the impact of price changes on the funds needed to maintain their proportion of the operating capability'.

Both the UK and Australian proposals warn against the dangers of distributing gains from gearing as dividends. The Australian proposals state:

As gearing gains on loan capital do not increase entity net profit, distributions made to shareholders from the gearing gains reserve account constitute a reduction in the operating capability of the entity unless replaced by additional equity funds or loan capital.

SSAP16 says that:

The current cost profit attributable to shareholders should not be assumed to measure the amount that can prudently be distributed. Although, the impact of price changes on the shareholders' interest in the net operating

assets has been allowed for, other factors still need to be considered ...
such as capital expenditure plans, changes in the volume of working
capital, the offset on funding requirements of changes in production
methods and efficiency, liquidity and new financing arrangements.

The progress of SSAP16

At the time SSAP16 was issued the ASC announced that it would
monitor its progress over a three year period and a monitoring working
party was established for this purpose. Over the trial period a number
of research projects into CCA were also commissioned.

By 1983 it was widely recognized that SSAP15 had declined in popu-
larity and that many people who had originally supported the standard
were questioning its usefulness. Two major reasons for this situation
were:

(a) From 1980 to 1983 the inflation rate declined constantly, feeding
     the hope that inflation and its attendant problems would go away.
(b) The government refused to consider taxing business on a basis
     consistent with CCA principles. Furthermore, the government's
     decision in 1980 to calculate stock relief by reference to the general
     all stocks' index rather than the specific indices of CCA showed that
     the government considered CCA irrelevant for tax purposes.

The monitoring working party took evidence from interested parties
and whilst they were able to identify considerable dissatisfaction with
historical cost accounting they detected little support for the CCA alternative. Critics of SSAP15 were especially hostile to the publication of
annual reports containing two totally different sets of figures whilst the
MWC and gearing adjustments received little support. Some argued
that the standard was unsuitable for companies in specialized fields
such as shipping, mining and oil. However, the working party recommended that a new standard should be issued which would require
financial statements to show the effects of changing prices when these
effects are material.

Research into the usefulness of current cost information has concluded that certain types of information are widely used by sophisticated investors. Mixed evidence was found about whether unexpected
current cost information leads to changes in share prices, but CCA profit
figures appear to be able to improve the explanation of share prices
given by historical cost profits. Many preparers, it has been found,
comply with SSAP16 from a 'sense of obligation', although preparation
costs seem low. Although this research has been the subject of considerable controversy it has been interpreted in certain quarters as
justification that CCA information should contrive to be disclosed
with limited exemptions where the concept of maintaining operating
capability is not applicable (Carsberg and Page, 1984).

In 1984, the publication of ED35, *Accounting for Changing Prices*,
contained the ASC's proposals for a standard to replace SSAP16. ED35

did not involve a departure from the concept of 'operating capability', but it did allow simpler methods for calculating the current cost adjustments. In particular, three options for calculating the gearing adjustment were allowed. ED35 proposed that current cost information be given in the main accounts, either in a note or as part of full current cost accounts, rather than in supplementary cost accounts.

ED35 provoked generally adverse comment and the lack of consensus led to its withdrawal in 1985. Shortly afterwards, SSAP16 was declared non-mandatory. However, the ASC has reaffirmed its view that, where historical cost accounts are materially affected by changing levels, information about the effects of changing prices is necessary for an appreciation of a company's results and financial position. The ASC has announced that it intends to develop a new accounting standard on accounting to take the place of SSAP16 in due course. It is intended that the proposed new standard will allow more choice of method than SSAP16 and that the SSAP methodology will be one of those that will comply with the new standard.

Questions

1 'Although some businesses may see defects in CCA, they are not immune to the effects of inflation. Indeed, fluctuating rates of price change in recent years have made mental adjustment of historical cost figures a science beyond managements' or investors' abilities. A formal system for reflecting the effects of price changes in the accounts of all business is vital if accounts (and accountants) are to retain their credibility. Can any proposal or set of proposals be both theoretically sound and workable in practice?' (Newman).

You are required to comment on the above quotation in the light of past proposals and the current debate on the future of a system of accounting for inflation.   (*20 marks*)

Chartered Institute of Public Finance and Accountancy, Professional Examination 1, Financial Accounting and Auditing

2 Following the high rates of inflation in the 1970s some accounting theorists lost faith in historical cost accounting, resulting in the issue, in March 1980, of the Accounting Standard on Current Cost Accounting (SSAP16).
You are required to:

(a) Outline the main shortcomings of accounts prepared under the historical cost convention.   (*10 marks*)
(b) Discuss the ways in which the adjustments recommended by SSAP16 endeavour to solve these problems and their effectiveness in doing so.   (*10 marks*)
(*Total: 20 marks*)

Chartered Institute of Public Finance and Accountancy, Professional Examination 1, Financial Accounting and Auditing

3   The current assets and current liabilities of a high class retail company at the beginning and end of the year to 31 December 19X8 are summarized below:

	Opening £000	£000	Closing £000	£000
Current assets				
Stock	54		75	
Debtors	40		50	
Cash	21		15	
		115		140
Less current liabilities	50		60	
Trade creditors	30		50	
Bank overdraft				
		80		110
Net current assets		35		30

The bank overdraft is considered a permanent source of finance. Stock at the end of each year represents purchases made equally during the preceding three months. Debtors represent sales in the preceding two months. The monthly index of stock prices and the general price index was:

		Stock price index	General price index
19X7	October	115	162
	November	117	164
	December	118	167
19X8	January	120	170
	February	124	174
	March	126	178
	April	129	175
	May	132	176
	June	132	177
	July	134	179
	August	134	180
	September	135	181
	October	138	182
	November	140	184
	December	141	186
	Average for year	132	177

You are required to:

(a) Explain the purpose of the monetary working capital adjustment.   (*3 marks*)

(b) Calculate   the   monetary   working   capital   adjustment   in

accordance with SSAP16 by reference to the data given above
(work to the nearest £100). *(4 marks)*
(c) Explain briefly why some authorities do not consider that a
monetary working capital adjustment is necessary. *(3 marks)*
(Total: 10 marks)

Institute of Chartered Accountants in England and Wales, Professional
Examination II, Financial Accounting 2

4 The five year financial record of a company as presented in the
published accounts prepared on the historical cost basis is shown
below:

	Year ended 31 December (£m)				
	19X0	*19X1*	*19X2*	*19X2*	*19X4*
Capital employed					
Capital and reserves	631	499	421	377	323
Loans	149	29	34	33	35
	780	528	455	410	358
Fixed assets	764	460	326	297	268
Net current assets:					
stock	10	15	25	24	26
net monetary assets	6	53	104	89	64
	780	528	455	410	358
Profit after taxation	152	78	44	54	37

The indices which represent the price changes appropriate to the
particular assets held by the company and the general price index
over the year were:

	Year ended 31 December				
	19X0	*19X1*	*19X2*	*19X3*	*19X4*
Beginning of year					
General prices	188	168	146	117	100
Fixed assets	165	144	121	110	100
Stocks, other current assets and current liabilities	180	160	140	120	100
Average during year					
General prices	197	182	157	135	108
Fixed assets	172	154	133	116	105
Stocks, other current assets and current liabilities	190	170	150	130	110
End of year					
General prices	204	188	168	146	117
Fixed assets	180	165	144	121	110
Stocks, other current assets and current liabilities	200	180	160	140	120

You are required to:

(a) Present a revised five year financial record which reflects the application of inflation or current cost accounting principles in so far as the data provided permits, explaining any calculations you make.   (*14 marks*)

(b) Comment on three significant differences between this new record and the original data.   (*6 marks*)

Institute of Chartered Accountants in England and Wales, Professional Examination II, Financial Accounting 2

5   SSAP16 deals with current cost accounting. Wigwam Ltd trades as agricultural merchants and contractors. Its stocks at two successive year ends were as follows:

	31 October	
	19X1	*19X0*
	£000	*£000*
Goods for resale	884	675
Seasonal stocks	87	121
Wheat futures	55	54
Contract work-in-progress	–	47
	1,026	897

   The following further information is given:

(a) The goods for resale consist of the normal stocks of the business which are offered for sale via the warehouse and retail outlets. They have been valued on a unit cost basis. They include certain old stocks which have been valued at their net realizable value at 31 October 19X1 of £138,000 (1980 £123,000). It has been estimated that the remaining stock, valued at cost, was purchased equally over the preceding four months in 19X1 and three months in 19X0.

(b) It has always been Wigwam's policy to buy produce when there has been a particularly good year and to store it by the appropriate means so that it can be released to the processor later during the winter. The seasonal stocks at 31 October 19X0 consisted of raspberries purchased during August 19X0 and at 31 October 19X1 consisted of apples purchased during October.

(c) The company deals on the commodity futures market. At each year end, the stocks consist of wheat purchases which have been made on the commodity futures market and for which delivery has not been taken. These stocks have been valued consistently at the price paid for the futures contracts. Subsequent to each year end, and prior to delivery date, the contracts have been sold at a profit on the futures market.

(d) From time to time the company also undertakes construction contracts for farmers using mainly sub-contract labour. At 31

October 19X0 there was a single contract for the construction of grain silos and driers. The contract ledger for this job showed the following entries:

				Dr	Cr
19X0	October	31	Balances brought forward	47,340	–
	November	30	Costs	15,167	–
	December	31	Costs/cash	14,183	10,000
19X1	January	31	Costs	10,300	–
	February	28	Costs (final)	2,250	–
	March	31	Cash	–	90,000
	October	31	Balance to profit and loss account	10,760	–
				100,000	100,000

The opening balance on the contract arose equally over the preceding 5 months.

(e) The relevant mid-month indices supplied by the Central Statistical Office are:

	Stocks held by corn, seed and agricultural merchants		Construction stocks	
	19X0	19X1	19X0	19X1
January	105.2	142.0	109.4	137.2
February	106.7	143.9	111.6	139.8
March	107.0	145.5	113.0	141.0
April	110.6	146.1	115.3	142.4
May	115.7	146.6	119.2	144.8
June	117.7	148.3	121.6	145.9
July	120.8	147.7	124.6	148.5
August	124.3	144.0	126.8	149.0
September	127.6	141.8	128.2	149.0
October	132.6	138.7	121.1	150.4
November	136.1	137.5	133.4	151.1
December	138.5	136.9	134.6	151.3

You are required:

(a) For those items for which it is appropriate, to calculate the cost of sales adjustment using the averaging method for the year ending 31 October 19X1. *(14 marks)*

(b) To state where it would not be appropriate to use a cost of sales adjustment in Wigwam Ltd and to give the alternative approach you would adopt. *(6 marks)*

(c) To explain briefly the term 'purchasing skills' and state how this affects the application of SSAP16. *(5 marks)*

Make calculations to the nearest £ hundreds. *(Total: 25 marks)*

Institute of Chartered Accountants in England and Wales, Professional Examination II, Financial Accounting II

References

1   Alexander, S. S., 'Income Measurement in a Dynamic Economy. Five Monographs on Business Income.' American Institute of Certified Public Accountants, 1950. Revised by D. Solomons in Baxter W. T. and Davidson S. (eds), *Studies in Accounting Theory*, Sweet and Maxwell, 1962.
2   Hicks, J. R., *Value and Capital* (second edition), Oxford University Press, 1946.
3   Richardson Committee, *Report of the Committee of Inquiry into Inflation Accounting*, New Zealand, 1976.
4   Sandilands Committee, *Report of the Inflation Accounting Committee*, HMSO, Cmnd 6225, 1975.
5   Taylor, P. J. and Underdown, B., *Advanced Financial Accounting*, Heinemann and Chartered Institute of Management Accountants, 1988.

10 Public sector accounting

In a mixed economy such as the UK, the public sector is extremely important both economically and politically. Indeed, the description 'mixed economy' is a testament to this importance. The public sector encompasses both of the types of not-for-profit organization which we identified in Chapter 1, business and governmental. Within each of these two categories there are many examples of organizations, each with their own unique features. Our concern in this chapter is with the most important aspects of financial accounting in such organizations, rather than with the whole range of financial and accounting characteristics. The extensive range of public sector organizations precludes a detailed treatment of them all. We shall confine our attention to central government, local government, and the nationalized industries, but we shall include a brief section devoted to observations on other types of organization.

Central government accounting

The central government's main periodic financial reports are presented to Parliament. These are the supply estimates, the appropriation accounts, the financial statement and budget report, the Chief Secretary's Memorandum and the Public Expenditure White Paper. Several of these reports are discussed at greater length in this chapter. In addition, other accounts are maintained by central government.

Appropriation accounts

Appropriation accounts are drawn up annually for government departments. These accounts follow the form of the supply estimates and present information under equivalent vote headings and sub-headings.

The purpose of these accounts is to report on the disbursement of funds voted by Parliament. In particular, the accounts show:

(a) How much has been spent compared with the sums provided by Parliament.
(b) The composition of shortfalls and excesses where they arise.
(c) Receipts appropriated to particular votes.
(d) Sums surrendered to the Exchequer.
(e) Additional information giving supporting explanations and indicating special payments and so on.

The appropriation accounts are subject to audit by the Comptroller and Auditor General (CAG) and are also examined by the Public Accounts Committee (see below).

Trading accounts

Certain government departments carry on trading or industrial activities on a commercial basis in conjunction with their activities funded from the supply vote. For example the Stationery Office prints documents for government use, but also sells a wide range of items commercially through its shops. Similarly, the Royal Ordnance Factories supply the UK armed forces and other approved customers. These and similar departments are required to prepare trading accounts for such activities and these accounts are audited by the CAG. Certain of these departments have, since the Government Trading Funds Act 1973, been switched to a trading fund, reliant upon the supply vote. Under this arrangement trading departments are supplied with capital funding and are required to pay the Exchequer dividends from annual profit, as opposed to surrendering their annual surpluses.

Central Exchequer accounts

The central Exchequer accounts comprise the basis of central government financing. The accounts of the Consolidated Fund are prepared annually. The Consolidated Fund is the account of the Exchequer held at the Bank of England into which gross tax revenues, less repayments, together with other Exchequer receipts not directed to other places are paid. Sums issued from the Fund include those to meet supply votes. The Fund derives its name from the fact that several separate funds were consolidated to form it in 1787.

The Budget is traditionally the annual financial statement which the Chancellor of the Exchequer makes in the House of Commons in either late March or early April at the end of each financial year. The Budget statement includes an account of the revenue expenditure of the previous financial year, together with forecasts for the coming year. Tables 10.1 and 10.2 summarize the budget accounts for 1986–7. Table 10.3 shows the detail of receipts of the Consolidated Fund which

Table 10.1   *Summary of central government transactions 1985–6*

	£m
Consolidated Fund	
Revenue	105.8
Expenditure	(110.2)
Deficit met from National Loans Fund	(4.4)

Table 10.2   *Consolidated fund expenditure 1985–6*

		£m
Supply issues		98,100
Standing services		
Payment to the National Loans Fund in respect of		
service of the national debt	7,700	
Northern-Ireland, share of taxes, etc.	1,700	
Payments to the European Communities	2,600	
Other services	100	
Total standing services		12,100
Total consolidated fund expenditure		110,200

appeared as £105.8 millions in Table 10.1. This Fund covers gross tax revenue and all other public monies payable to the Exchequer. Table 10.2 shows total Consolidated Fund expenditure divided into the categories of supply issues and consolidated fund standing services. The former are monies paid from the Consolidated Fund to department's cash accounts with the Paymaster General for spending on supply. Supply (see below) is voted each year by Parliament. Standing services are a series of standing charges against Consolidated Fund revenue.

The National Insurance Funds accounts show the financial position of the contributing social insurance shares. A series of National Insurance Acts established the system of insurance benefits provided by the UK government to meet specified contingencies such as unemployment, sickness, old age and widowhood. Benefits are paid for, partly by insured persons' contributions, partly by employers' contributions on behalf of their employees, and partly by Exchequer contributions financed from general taxation.

The National Loans Fund was established in 1968. This fund serves to separate current and capital items in the central government accounts. The National Loans Fund records the majority of the government's domestic lending activity as well as transactions relating to the National Debt.

The National Loans Fund is the fund from which central government

Table 10.3   *Consolidated Fund revenue*

	1985–6		1986–7 forecast	
		(£m)		
Inland Revenue				
Income tax	35,200		38,500	
Corporation tax	10,100		11,700	
Petroleum revenue tax	8,200		2,400	
Capital gains tax	790		1,050	
Development land tax	55		35	
Capital transfer tax (inheritance tax)	760		910	
Stamp duties	1,100	56,200	1,430	56,025
Customs and Excise				
Vat	18,300		20,700	
Fuel duties	6,500		7,300	
Tobacco duties	4,300		4,700	
Duties on alcholic drinks	4,200		4,400	
Betting and gaming	700		800	
Car tax	760		980	
Other excise duties	20		20	
Duties accountable to EEC	1,500	36,300	1,460	40,360
Other revenues				
Vehicle excise duties	2,500		2,500	
National Insurance surcharge	30		–	
Gas levy	520		500	
Broadcasting receiving licences	790		1,000	
Interest and dividends	870		840	
Other	9,200	13,910	7,400	12,240
Total Consolidated Fund revenue		106,500		108,625

makes loans to local authorities, nationalized industries, and other public sector bodies. The Fund is administered by the Treasury and is held at the Bank of England. Central government hence borrows on the money and capital markets on its own behalf and on behalf of other public sector bodies. The central government's power to borrow is contained in the National Loans Act 1968. This act sets no upper limit on the total which may be borrowed nor upon the form or terms of borrowing. These matters are determined by consultation between the Treasury and the Bank of England.

The National Loans Fund is an example of a consolidated fund. It is a centralized fund which brings together the capital funds borrowed by central government on its own behalf and on behalf of the rest of the public sector. Similar arrangements are found within local authorities (see below) and other public bodies which operate consolidated loan funds.

National Loans Fund receipts and payments 1985–6

	£m
Receipts	
Interest on loans, profits of the Issue Department of the Bank of England	6,600
Service of the National Debt, balance met from Consolidated Fund	7,700
Total receipts	14,300

	£M
Payments	
Service of the National Debt	
Interest	14,130
Management and expenses	170
Total service of the National Debt	14,300
Loans to:	
Nationalized industries	90
Other public corporations	260
Local authorities	4,800
Private sector and within central government	90
Total National Loans Fund lending	5,240
Consolidated Fund deficit	4,500
Total payments	24,040

As the payments side of the above shows, central government, as well as meeting its own Consolidated Fund deficit, provides capital funds to the rest of the public sector through loans from the National Loans Fund. The extent to which the central government borrows for these purposes is seen by the receipts entry 'net borrowing by National Loans Fund'. This figure does not represent either the central government's overall borrowing requirement nor the Public Sector Borrowing Requirement. The former is obtained by adjusting the net borrowing of the National Loans Fund for, primarily, the surplus on the National Insurance Fund, and for deficits or surpluses on departmental balances. Thus:

Net borrowing by the National Loans Funds	. . .
Less surplus of National Insurance Fund	. . .
Plus (*less*) deficit of departmental balances (surplus)	. . .
= Central government borrowing requirement	

The Public Sector Borrowing Requirement is the amount borrowed by the public sector as a whole from other sectors of the UK economy and overseas. Thus:

Central government borrowing requirement	. . .
Plus Nationalized industries net borrowing from other sources	. . .

Plus   local authorities net borrowing
         from other sources   . . .
Public Sector Borrowing Requirement

Parliamentary control of expenditure

The expenditures of central government departments are controlled by Parliament through the 'supply' system. The system is illustrated in Figure 10.1. Under this procedure each government department is required to prepare estimates of its expenditure for the financial year commencing in the coming April. Once these estimates have been

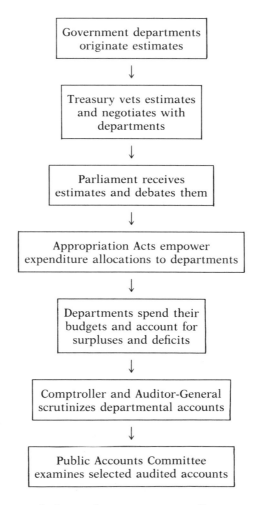

Figure 10.1 *The control of central government expenditure*

Table 10.4 *Central government supply services 1986–7*

		Number of votes	£m
I	Ministry of Defence	6	18,486
II	Foreign and Commonwealth Office	7	1,856
III			
IV	Ministry of Agriculture, Fisheries and Food	6	932
V	Department of Trade and Industry	9	1,973
VI	Department of Energy	6	1,439
VII	Department of Employment	6	3,117
VIII	Department of Transport	8	2,675
IX	Department of the Environment, Housing	2	1,916
X	Department of the Environment, Other Environmental Services	9	10,125
XI	Home Office and Lord Chancellor's Department	6	4,439
XII	Department of Education and Science	12	3,393
XIII	Office of Arts and Libraries	12	283
XIV	Department of Health and Social Security, Health and Personal Social Services	4	13,108
XV	Department of Heath and Social Security, Social Security	6	21,575
XVI	Scotland	25	5,465
XVII	Wales	13	2,383
XVIII	Northern Ireland	2	1,449
XIX	Department of the Chancellor of the Exchequer	16	1,984
XX	House of Commons Administration	1	21

agreed with the Treasury, the department responsible for government financial matters, they are submitted to Parliament for approval. The estimates comprise a description of the expenditures for which funds are sought, as well as the services which they represent. The estimates themselves are shown in aggregate and by various sub-divisions, including division by functional programme. Comparisons are made between the sums for which provision is sought for the coming year, and the previous year's provision or likely actual expenditure. In addition, expenditure is classified into current and capital components. It has become the practice to present these estimates (or 'votes' as they are also termed) in the annual Budget on Budget Day but the estimates themselves are debated by Parliament on 'supply days' set aside in the Parliamentary calendar. Table 10.4 shows the supply estimates for 1986–7 as set out in the Budget Statement and Financial Report presented to Parliament in March 1986.

This procedure for the voting of supply is a lengthy one and ends before the summer recess of Parliament with the passing of the Consolidated Fund (Appropriation) Act which gives authority for the provision of funds to meet estimates. In order to ensure that the time-table of Parliamentary control of expenditure does not prevent government departments' proper spending activities interim authority is provided for expenditure to begin on the first day of the financial year by 'votes on account'. These are put before Parliament in the December preceding the beginning of a new financial year and normally represent around half of the annual estimates. The passing of a Consolidated Fund Appropriation Act provides statutory authority for the interim expenditure.

The supply procedure is an exercise in budgeting and as such may require correction or adjustment. The system contains three mechanisms for the adjustment of estimates:

(a)   Provision for the submission of Revised Estimates before the summer Consolidated Fund (Appropriation) Act.
(b)   Provision for the submission of Supplementary Estimates during the year. Such estimates would be for additional funds. In contrast, Revised Estimates are submitted when estimates are to be reduced or responsibilities switched between government departments.
(c)   Use of the Contingency Fund, a fund established to meet un-expected expenditures. Funds may be transferred from it to meet urgent needs under other votes if Treasury approval is given. The Fund is limited to 2 per cent of the preceding year's total authorized supply. Drawings on the Fund must be repaid once specific authorization has been given for the additional expenditure by Parliament.

Virement
One of the purposes of establishing budgetary control procedures is to prevent unauthorized expenditures. This may involve the prevention of fraud or ensuring that policies are carried out without waste within agreed spending limits. Rigidity in budgets would therefore appear necessary if this is to be achieved. On the other hand some flexibility within budgets is necessary to allow those responsible for managing programmes subject to budgets to react to circumstances which have changed since budgets were set or to unanticipated events. Since many assumptions must be made in setting a budget there may be considerable need for such flexibility. One means of introducing flexibility is to permit the transfer of underspent balances from one part of a budget to programmes requiring spending above that provided for in the budget. Meeting overspending from underspending elsewhere is known as 'virement'.

In addition to allowing flexibility, virement reduces the need to make supplementary budgets. However, there are disadvantages. Clearly, it weakens budgetary control and in addition may encourage managers to 'pad' their budgets by introducing items into their spending pro-grammes which are likely to be underspent. To combat this and related problems public authorities impose controls on the circumstances under which virement is permitted. In the case of central government departments Treasury sanction is required for virement. Similarly, in local government the re-allocation of funds is subject to approval by the finance committee or senior finance officers. An obvious criterion to apply to the sanction of virement is to permit it if resources are made available by cost reductions or additional efficiency within the department concerned. Conversely, if savings are due to uncontrollable factors, then the funds normally revert to the central authority (e.g. the Treasury).

Public expenditure survey
The system of estimates and voting supply discussed above emphasizes a short-term view of public expenditure. Until the 1960s, with the exception of certain departments, such as Defence, where operating characteristics of programmes necessitated a long-term view, this short-term view prevailed. As a response to concerns over the adequacy of public expenditure planning and control precedures, the government established the Plowden Committee. The committee's report, *The Planning and Control of Public Expenditure*, was issued in 1961, and recommended that regular surveys of public expenditure covering several years ahead should be made in the light of prospective resources, and decisions involving significant future expenditure should be taken in the light of such surveys. Furthermore, the Plowden Committee recommended that the Chancellor of the Exchequer might make his proposals for future levels of public expenditure from his judgement of the prospects for the economy. A forward-looking survey of public expenditure would provide an appropriate framework for such proposals. A main purpose of the annual survey was to allow the allocation of funds to the public sector (and allocation of funds within the public sector) to be made in the light of broad macroeconomic considerations.

The recommendations of the Plowden Committee were accepted by the government and a Public Expenditure Survey Committee (PESC), consisting of senior officials from spending departments, was established and given the responsibility of implementing an annual survey of public expenditure. As Figure 10.2 shows, the main purpose of the public expenditure survey was to aid in decisions about the planned level and composition of future public expenditure. Once prepared, the survey provided Ministers and the Chancellor of the Exchequer with an information input into their deliberations. Out of these deliberations emerged a plan for future public spending to provide information on which Ministers might make decisions.

After preparation, the survey was circulated to Ministers and the Chancellor of the Exchequer put forward his own proposals, in the light of his expectations and assumptions about general economic activity. Together, this additional information and the DES provided the basis for Ministerial decision on planned public spending. From these deliberations and decisions emerged the annual Public Expenditure White Paper. This document contains a large amount of information on

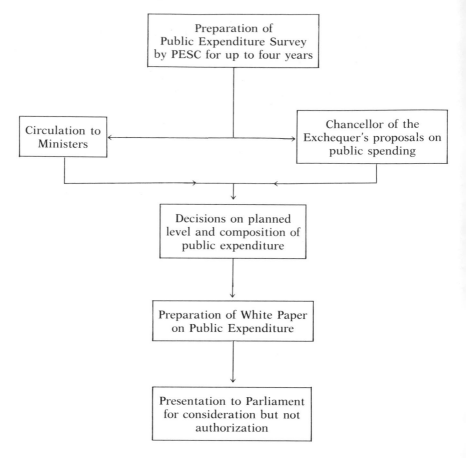

Figure 10.2

government's expenditure plans and how they relate to wider economic policy considerations. The White Paper analyses future spending plans by programme, and by current and capital components, and includes estimates for local authorities and nationalized industries as well as central government.

The inter-relationship of public expenditure plans and broader macroeconomic considerations must be stressed. In making proposals for public expenditure the Chancellor must make assumptions about economic prospects and make judgements about the relationship between public spending and major economic aggregates. During the life of the public expenditure survey various assumptions have been made, reflecting both economic expectations and government policies towards the economy.

The Public Expenditure Survey was initially based upon the determination of the expected future costs of continuing existing policies.

Later, the emphasis changed to the forward projection of existing levels of approved expenditure. This may appear to be a semantic difference, but it masks an important difference of principle. As Henley *et al.* (1983), points out, the former approach seeks to answer the question, 'how much will this cost?', while the latter considers 'how much can be bought for this level of expenditure?' The survey was drawn up in terms of constant prices (of the base year for each survey), implying that the basis of planning was the volume, not the value, of public expenditure. Such an approach may be quite satisfactory in times of relatively stable prices but when inflation is rapid, as was the case in the UK in the 1970s, a volume-based system is an unsatisfactory means of controlling expenditure, since planning the volume of activity effectively means providing for all cost and price increases as they arise. Although the supply system formally provides for the provision of cash funding limits for programmes, the granting of supplementary estimates to fund inflationary overspending in order to meet volume targets in practical terms removes this control. Budgeting in real or volume terms provides no effective motivation for managers to attempt to control inflationary cost increases. These problems are exacerbated if there is marked variation in particular inflation rates, say for different types of costs or wages, within an overall high inflation rate, or if there are substantial variations in inflation from year to year. As well as not providing incentives for cost control, a volume-based planning system gave little guidance as to the likely amounts which would be spent in the future, thereby seriously reducing its usefulness as a means of controlling public expenditure. Further problems with the volume-basis were that it could not be applied to certain spending programmes of central government, in particular social security expenditures, which were necessarily expressed in cash terms, and the local government component of public spending was based upon local governments' cash budgets.

Cash limits and cash planning

The planning and controlling of public expenditure on a volume basis became increasingly difficult in the 1970s as the general rate of inflation accelerated in the UK. These problems were made more difficult by the different specific rates of inflation which were present within the general inflation. Such problems, coupled as they were with an increasing emphasis in central government macroeconomic policy with the curbing of inflation, led to a very significant change in public sector finance, the switch to a system of cash limits and cash planning.

The cash limit system was introduced in 1976–7 and gradually extended through central government. The main characteristics of the cash limit system were:

(*a*) The setting of cash limits for as many programmes as possible.
(*b*) The cash limits to be treated as firm and only exceeded in exceptional circumstances and with Treasury approval.

(c) The basing of cash limits in volume figures agreed for the White
     Paper on Public Expenditure and government assumptions about
     inflation rates.
(d) The disaggregation of inflation rates into rates appropriate to
     various segments of the total public spending programme.
(e) As the system developed cash limits were aligned with votes in the
     Parliamentary supply estimates.

Cash limits are very similar in nature to the arrangements for cash
budgeting in the public sector in other countries. From their inception
the cash limits system had been attached to the volume based planning
system of the Public Expenditure Survey. However, in 1982–3 the
government introduced important changes in the constant price, real
terms basis of the PES by introducing cash planning. Public expenditure planning was to require the updating of prices used in surveying
public expenditure and the introduction of the government's assumptions about inflation rates during the planning period. The emphasis
was shifted from planning the volume of public spending to planning
the amount of cash to be made available to meet future public
spending.

In explaining the new system the Treasury identified the advantages
of cash planning as follows:

(a) Ministers would be forced to consider the cash actually to be spent,
     and as a consequence, the cash which would have to be financed
     from taxation or borrowing.
(b) Expenditure plans would cease to be viewed as entitlements which
     were carried forward from year to year regardless of costs.
(c) Emphasis is switched from maintaining a given volume of provi-
     sion regardless of cost, to maintaining planned cash expenditure.
(d) Managers in the public sector would be forced to consider the level
     of service which could be provided by a given amount of cash.
(e) Managers may have greater flexibility to trade off price and
     volume effects within cash budgets.

Against these advantages must be set the potential disadvantage that
establishing plans in cash terms under significant rates of inflation may
cause resources to be squeezed to an unacceptable extent. However, it
must be acknowledged that even within cash planning assumptions
must be made about the volume of goods and services to be purchased
during the year. A further disadvantage was that it is very difficult for
central government to introduce cash planning across the whole public
sector. In particular, individual local authorities are able to set their
own levels of expenditure based, if they wished, upon constant or
increasing volumes of service under inflationary conditions. Cash
planning and cash limits were introduced indirectly to this part of the
public sector by central government through the inclusion of the Rate
Support Grant (RSG) in the cash limits systems. The RSG, which is
discussed more fully below, is the central government's grant-in-aid

contribution to local government expenditure and supplements locally raised revenues. From 1976 to 1977 central government fixed the level of RSG in cash terms and has subsequently introduced more direct means, via RSG, of controlling local government spending. Similarly, nationalized industry spending was not subject to central control in cash terms initially, but as the cash limits system developed, it was extended to nationalized industries through the setting of External Financing Limits for them. External Financing Limits restrict the amount which a nationalized industry can raise in a financial year from external sources. The limit is the difference between an industry's capital requirements and its own internally generated funds.

Auditing central government
The audit of central government is a long established function. The audit requirements for central government are contained in several acts, notably the Exchequer and Audit Department Acts of 1866 and 1921 and the National Audit Act of 1983. A central feature of the legislation is that the appropriation accounts of government departments are examined by the Comptroller and Auditor General (CAG) on behalf of Parliament. Prior to the 1983 Act the CAG was head of the Exchequer and Audit Department (EAG). Following that Act, the EAG was replaced by the National Audit Office. The CAG is an officer of the House of Commons and is responsible to it and works in conjunction with the House's Public Accounts Committee, a Select Committee interested in the examination of departmental and other accounts laid before Parliament and in financial management generally.

The statutory role of the CAG is to satisfy himself that money expended has been applied to the purpose for which it was intended when provided by Parliament and that the expenditure conforms to the authority for it. The statutory audit has come to be viewed as having two components: the financial, relating to the accuracy of appropriation accounts, and the regulatory, relating to the authority for expenditure. The scope of the audit was extended in 1983 to encompass the economy, efficiency and effectiveness of expenditure although these considerations do not form a mandatory part of the audit examination.

Accounting for local government

Local government in the UK is very important, not only in the public sector, but in the economy as a whole. They are large employers of labour, provide a very wide range of services, and amongst other things, are very important landlords. There are different systems of local government in England and Wales, Northern Ireland, and Scotland, and the systems, particularly those in England and Wales, have been subject to significant organizational change in recent years. The most major recent reorganizations took place in 1974 in England and Wales, excluding London, and 1975 in Scotland. Following the 1974–5

Table 10.5   *Structure of local government in mainland UK following 1974–5 reorganization*

| | **England and Wales** | | | **London** | **Scotland** | |
	Metropolitan districts or joint board	*Non-metropolitan* *County*	*District*	*Borough or joint board*	*Region*	*District*
Consumer protection	*	*		*	*	*
Education	*	*		(a)	*	
Environmental health	*		*	*		*
Fire service	*	*		*	*	
Housing	*		*	*		*
Industrial development	*	*	*	*	*	*
Libraries	*	*		*		*
Planning Structure	*	*		*	*	
Planning Control	*		*	*		*
Police	*	*		(b)	*	
Rating	*		*	*	*	
Recreation	*	*	*	*		*
Refuse	*	*		*		*
Roads	*			*	*	
Social services	*	*		*	*	
Transport	*	*	*	*	*	

Notes:
(a)   Education provided by the Inner London Education Authority
(b)   The police service is the responsibility of the Home Office

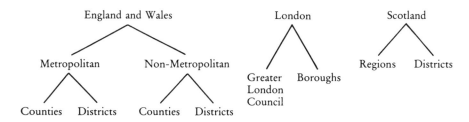

Figure 10.3   *Structure of local government in mainland UK following 1974–5 reorganization*

reorganization the structure of local government in mainland UK was as shown in Table 10.5 and Figure 10.3.

The Metropolitan Counties and the GLC were abolished in April 1986. The functions formally undertaken by the abolished authorities have been taken over by the relevant District or Borough Councils, or by joint boards covering several authorities. The range of functions are set out in Figure 10.3. Responsibility for functions, and authority to carry them out, derives from Parliament as do the arrangement for financing local government. Legislation passed by Parliament concerning local authority responsibilities largely imposes duties, i.e. mandatory powers to provide services. Much less frequent are discretionary powers allowing local governments the freedom to provide services. This dichotomy is too simple a categorization since few types of expenditure are either totally mandatory or totally discretionary. A variety of pressures and influences, and advice and encouragement all contribute to determining the level and composition of local government expenditure.

However, since local governments have legislative requirements set for them, the classification of their expenditure reflects this by being classified into various funds. Four general types of fund may be recognized:

(*a*)   Rate funds
(*b*)   Housing funds
(*c*)   Trading funds
(*d*)   Special funds

The rate fund is the most important of the funds, representing over three-quarters of local government revenue expenditure and around a half of capital expenditure. The major categories of rate fund expenditures are education, environmental services, local transport, law and order, social services and housing. Despite its name, rate fund expenditure is far from entirely rate financed. Rates are the local tax levied on the notional rental value of properties. The base of the tax is a property's rateable value and the tax rate is the rate poundage, set by a local government for the year. The basic rate poundage is reduced for domestic properties by domestic rate relief. Rate fund expenditure is also financed by grants from central government, both block and specific, and fees and charges for services. Hence, the rate fund may be represented by the following equation:

$$E = R + RSG + SG + F + B$$

where E = rate fund expenditures
           R = rate revenue
       RSG = Rate Support Grants from central government
         SG = Specific Grants from central government
           F = Income from fees and charges
           B = Changes in balances

Grants from central government (RSG and SG) have traditionally provided over half of total rate fund income. This means that, as a minority source of finance, locally set rates (R) can change quite dramatically if expenditure is increased, with RSG and SG constant, or if expenditure is maintained in the face of reductions in RSG and SG.

The housing activities of local government are recorded in the

Housing Revenue Account. The main part of revenue expenditure on this account comprises loan charges to service borrowing raised to finance the creation of local government housing. An important source of income on this account is subsidies from central goverment.

Fund accounting

Identifying local government finances under the headings of various funds emphasizes the fundamental nature of accounting for local government, although fund accounting is widely practiced in the public sector generally. A fund for this purpose is a set of accounts which brings together cash and other financial resources and related liabilities, and segregates them for the purpose of pursuing particular activities or objectives, subject to restrictions. Fund accounting is appropriate where resources are earmarked for particular uses and cannot be regarded as a general pool to be used in any way management think fit. There may be varying degrees of earmarking. Central government makes specific grants to local government for the relief of domestic rates, the subsidization of local authority housing, or the police. In these cases there is a high degree of earmarking and funds so granted cannot be redirected to other uses. On the other hand, RSG is a general block grant.

Local governments account for their activities on the basis of various funds. Above, we mentioned four, but typically these will be more since the ones referred may be sub-divided. Rate funds may be divided into rate accounts, which record items concerned with rate collection, including RSG, and General Rate Fund which records all expenditure legally chargeable to rates. There are various special funds, for example loans funds, capital funds, trust funds and so on. The purpose of fund accounting is to match income and expenditure items to ensure that the one is appropriated to the other. Hence, separate operating statements and balance sheets are provided for each fund to reflect their separateness. However, they are not kept entirely separate since transfers may be made between funds, say, from General Rate Fund to Housing Revenue Account if the decision is taken (and is permitted by law) that ratepayers are to help meet the local authority's housing expenditures. Figure 10.4 illustrates the general composition of two funds and their relationship.

Fund accounting may be criticized on several grounds. It may lead to undue emphasis on parts of the organization at the expense of a consideration of the whole. It may lead to uninformative financial reports, items are offset against each other and net figures only disclosed. The system may also be costly to operate.

Capital finance and expenditure

Important changes occurred in the system of local government planning and control of capital expenditure as a result of the Local Government

General Rate Fund revenue account		Housing revenue account		
Income		*Income*		
Rates	x	Rent		x
Government grants	x	Subsidies		x
	x	Miscellaneous		x
Expenditure				x
Education	x	*Expenditure*		
Housing	x	Maintenance	x	
Social services	x	Administration	x	
etc.	(x)	Other	x	
Transferred to revenue	x (x)	Debt charges	x	(x)
balance		Surplus of expenditure over income		(x)
		Rate fund contribution		x
		Balance carried forward		x (x)

Figure 10.4 *General composition of two funds and their relationship*

Planning and Land Act 1980. Prior to this legislation, although restrictions were placed upon local government borrowing, they were generally given considerable freedom to engage in capital expenditure financed in other ways, such as from the proceeds of asset disposals, from revenue sources, or by leasing. This freedom clearly reduced central government's control over local government capital spending.

The new system introduced 'prescribed expenditure' as the basis for control, in place of borrowing limits. This was in effect a cash limit on total local government capital expenditure on a national basis. Under this system each local authority had capital resources allocated to it and thus could in turn be allocated by the authority as it wished under five service headings, housing, education, transport, social services, and other. A capital allocation could be supplemented in four major prescribed ways:

(a) Receipts from asset sales.
(b) Carrying forward unspent balances from previous years (up to 10 per cent of the current year's allocation).
(c) Transfers from another local authority's allocation.
(d) The use of current cost profit from trading undertakings.

The new system involved closer and more detailed monitoring of capital expenditure by local authorities and more frequent reporting to the Department of the Environment.

Capital accounting

In company accounting there is no clear distinction between capital and operating accounts, except in certain circumstances where the identification of capital (and its maintenance) is important. In many types of public sector organization it is critical that such a distinction is drawn for similar reasons to those put forward for fund accounting. Elements of such a distinction could be seen in central government's accounts (witness the National Loans Fund), but the distinction is far from hard and fast since the Consolidated Fund provides funding for capital and current projects and the supply votes contain provisions for both capital and current expenditure. Other types of public sector organizations account for capital differently. Nationalized industries' capital accounting is similar to that of companies even though their capital structures and sources of capital are different. Local government has a system of capital accounting which is peculiar to itself. This unique character is due partly to law and partly to the development of practice over time. The law requires that local government debit to relevant operating statements sums equal to an instalment of principle and interest for capital items which have been financed by borrowing. This in effect requires loans to be amortized over specified periods. Since local government must balance their budgets, such charges to operating statements will ultimately be covered by rate charges.

In most local authorities strict earning of loans to capital expenditures is not practised. Instead, loans are managed in a manner similar to that of the National Loans Fund of central government described above. Local authority borrowings are maintained in a centralized fund (usually termed a Consolidated Loans Fund (CLF)), which receives all borrowed monies. This is used to finance operating departments' capital financing needs. Operating departments in effect 'borrow' from the CLF and then make annual payments to the CLF on their borrowings. These payments comprise interest and repayment of principal. Interest charges borne by the local authority, as well as the management costs of the CLF, are apportioned by the CLF to operating departments. As payments are made by operating departments to the CLF, they can be recycled by it into further lending to departments. The ability to do this is one advantage of a CLF approach. Another, is that it allows borrowing to be determined as a whole, and need not be constrained by the characteristics of individual capital projects. This allows the authority to borrow on the most appropriate terms, bearing in mind interest rate and other considerations, thereby establishing the best terms of loan repayment, whilst charging its operating departments loan redemption terms relevant to the project.

The operation of a loan redemption account requires a separate set of ledger accounts and final accounts to be prepared. The relevant ledger accounts are a cash account, distinguishing capital and revenue items, an account itemizing loans to operating departments, an account for deferred charges (charged with discounts and expenses for loans raised), an investment account, an interest account, a loans fund expenses account (for the day-to-day running expenses of the CLF), and a profit and loss account for selling investments and redeeming loans.

The CLF final accounts normally comprise a balance sheet, a capital transactions statement, a revenue transactions account, and a statement showing borrowing powers and details of borrowings outstanding.

Accounting for planning and control

Like any organization a local government requires accounts for internal purposes of planning and control and to meet external financial reporting needs. An important feature of local government accounting is that, unlike other parts of the public sectors, significant variety is present. Different means have been found at the local level of meeting the requirements to plan and control activities and to meet externally imposed requirements. Despite the presence of variety there are also common features, the most important of which is the annual budget. This provides the focus of local government accounting, as Figure 10.5, derived from Henley *et al.* 1983, page 71), indicates.

The local government annual budget is thus derived from a longer term policy plan covering several years and incorporating the council's priorities, and based on data on the costs and other characteristics of policy alternatives. This policy planning will necessarily be conducted within the framework set by central government's plans for spending by

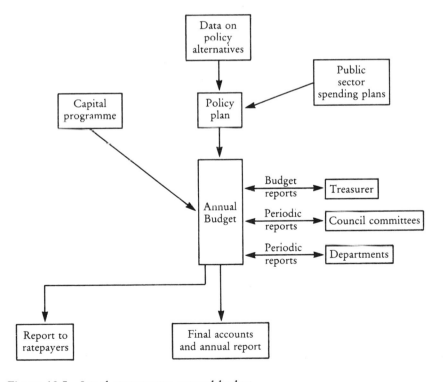

Figure 10.5 *Local government annual budget*

the public sector as a whole and recorded in the Public Expenditure White Paper. Although accounting for revenue and capital programmes is likely to be separated in the annual budgeting process, the programmes themselves must necessarily be integrated. Setting the budget will require the involvement of council committees and council officers responsible for both finance and spending departments. The interactive process of budget preparation is indicated by the links between budget and Treasurer, council committees and departments in Figure 10.5. Those links also represent the information flows which occur once the budget has been set. Officers responsible for spending departments receive the details of their departmental budgets and report actual expenditure periodically so that performance with respect to the budget can be monitored. The responsibility of the Treasurer is with combining departmental reports and with overall monitoring. At the departmental level chief officers will have overall responsibility for budgetary control but typically they will have beneath them a management structure down which authority and responsibility is delegated. Corresponding to this will be a structure of accountability for managers. The final part of Figure 10.5 concerns external financial reporting by local government.

External reporting

External reporting by local government is not confined to the formal statutory financial reports which they are required to prepare since a range of reporting media exist and are used by different local governments.

The major piece of legislation governing local authority accounts is the Local Government Finance Act of 1972. This statute sets quite general requirements upon local government, in particular:

(a)   Rating authorities are to maintain a general rate fund, county councils a county fund, and the Greater London Council a general fund. Accounts are to be kept of payments to, and receipts from such funds.

(b)   Arrangements should be made for the proper administration of a local authority's financial affairs.

(c)   Accounts are to be drawn up by local authorities to 31 March and are to be audited in accordance with the Accounts and Audit Regulations 1974 and other applicable legislation. An auditor must be satisfied that proper accounting practices have been observed.

(d)   The Secretary of State is empowered to make regulations about the amounts of local authorities.

Item (c) refers to the requirement to prepare annual accounts. These financial accounts represent the fundamental vehicle for external reporting by local government. The position of local governments is similar to that of companies in that substantial discretion is allowed in pursuing the 'proper accounting practices' of (c) above. Significant attempts have been within the sphere of local government to introduce a greater degree of harmonization into local government accounts. Notably the Institute of Municipal Treasurers and Accountants and the Chartered Institute of Public Finance and Accountancy (CIPFA) have sought to advance standardization. A significant external influence of growing importance has been the ASC with its accounting standards programme. The applicability of accounting standards for the public sector are considered later in this chapter.

Following controversy over proposals to include in the Local Government Planning and Land Act 1980 statutory requirements on detailed annual reports and other documents, a series of codes of recommended practice have been issued on the publication of information by local authorities on the discharge of their functions. These codes of practice have concerned information to be issued with rate demands, manpower information, quarterly reports on various topics including planning applications and, most important, annual reports and financial statements. Such reports are the central element in corporate reporting under the Companies Acts and are designed to serve a similar purpose for local government as documents providing a statement of stewardship for the benefit of both members of the council and of the public. In particular, three objectives were associated with annual reports:

(a) The provision of information to ratepayers on council activities.
(b) To aid judgements and comparisons of performance of authorities by interested parties.
(c) To help councillors judge the performance of their own authority.

Despite specifying over thirty performance indicators which were to be included in annual reports the code of practice allowed considerable freedom to local authorities by expressing the indicators in simplistic terms and by leaving it to the discretion of the local authority whether additional documents might be necessary to supplement the annual report.

In addition to problems of variety and lack of comparability local government accounts have been criticized on other grounds. In particular that:

(a) They are often too detailed and presented in a form which is not informative to users of them.
(b) They often fail to report sufficiently fully on capital programmes in general, and their implications for revenue considerations.
(c) The historic cost of capital assets is often not reported despite CIPFA recommendations to show in the accounts capital assets at acquisition cost until disposal or the end of their notional life. Many authorities show the cost of assets net of loan repayments, effectively amortizing as the loan is repaid. Where assets are not financed by loans but by a direct contribution from revenue for example, many authorities do not show the assets at all.

(*d*) The matching principle is frequently not applied in dealing with certain capital assets. If capital assets are funded from revenue or the receipts of asset disposals no periodic charge may be made against revenue for asset depreciation. The asset is thus fully depreciated in its year of acquisition. Such an accounting treatment has important effects. It makes the estimation of the costs of service provision difficult if no attempt is made to match capital costs to benefits derived. Moreover, revenue surpluses of authorities using different accounting methods (or different methods of financing capital acquisitions) may not be comparable performance measures.

(*e*) In similar vein to (*d*), there is no standard definition of trading surplus or deficit for trading activities.

(*f*) Current replacement costs are not included in the accounts of trading activities. This is part of the broader issue of accounting for inflation and is considered in more detail below.

Auditing local government

The external audit of local government was very significantly changed by the Local Government Finance Act of 1982. Prior to 1982 local authorities could choose whether their accounts were audited by a district auditor or an 'approved auditor'. The former were civil servants in the Department of the Environment and under the control of the Minister. However, theirs was a statutory office and this, together with tradition, made them independent of the Minister in the exercise of their duty and answerable to the courts. 'Approved auditors' were members of professional firms and were 'approved' for the purpose of local government audit by the Secretary of State for the Environment.

As a result of the 1982 act the Audit Commission for Local Authorities in England and Wales was set up. Its members are appointed by the Secretary of State and it is headed by a chief officer, the Controller of Audit. The major task of the commission is to appoint the external auditors of local authorities. The auditor appointed must be either an officer of the Commission or an outside accountant or firm of accountants. The statutory requirement for the audit is also contained in the 1982 act. It requires that the auditor:

(*a*) Satisfy himself that the accounts have been prepared:
   (*i*) In accordance with regulations established by the Secretary of State and any other statutory provisions.
   (*ii*) In accordance with proper practices.

(*b*) Satisfy himself that the body whose accounts are being audited has made proper arrangements for securing economy, efficiency, and effectiveness in the use of resources.

(*c*) Comply with the code of audit practice in force at the time.

(*d*) Consider whether he should, in the public interest, make a report on any matter coming to his notice.

The auditor has the power to apply to the courts for a judgement on whether an item is lawful and the court has power to recover any amounts declared unlawful. Moreover, the auditor has the responsibility to certify that certain sums are due from individuals. This may occur where sums have not been brought into account or where losses have been incurred or deficiences caused by wilful misconduct.

The nature of the local government audit is significantly different from that of a company, as the legal powers and responsibilities just noted indicate. There are other differences. For example, the public has the right to inspect accounts and supporting documents and to question the auditor. Also, the audit is potentially more wide-ranging than for a company as the reference to economy, efficiency and effectiveness indicates. This introduces an issue which has assumed increasing importance in public sector accounting in recent years, namely the notion of value for money auditing.

Value for money

Although value for money (VFM) is considered in the context of local government interest it has not been confined to this part of the public sector. The term VFM is not subject to a generally acceptable definition. The conventional interpretation has been that VFM involves the identification and removal of extravagance and waste. It has also been associated with the detection of fraud or the pursuit of cost reduction or increased efficiency. Suggestions as to how some or all of these aims of VFM could be achieved have also varied. Modification to the external audit, to the internal audit, use of management consultants, increased disclosure of information and the privatization of services have all had their adherents. The most obvious mechanism for the achievement of VFM might seem to be the external audit. In both central and local government there is statutory obligation to incorporate VFM into the external audit. In other parts of the public sector different arrangements exist. In nationalized industry the sponsoring department (see below) may require a VFM component in the external audit. Similarly, the external auditors of health authorities in certain regions may be asked to undertake VFM work. As might be expected, the extent to which internal auditors carry out VFM reviews varies widely.

Although the idea of VFM is appealing its pursuit is fraught with problems. We have already referred to the confusion over what VFM investigations are for. The narrower the objectives of VFM investigations (e.g. the detection of fraud), the more likely, are the problems posed, to be familiar to the auditor. The wider the objectives (e.g. assessing effectiveness) the more likely it is that unfamiliar and less tractable problems will be posed. These may be serious where activities are hard to measure, where qualitative judgements replace quantification. In such circumstances the VFM investigator risks the accusation of challenging the objectives of the policy maker by his own value judgements.

Accounting for nationalized industries

The nationalized industries represent not only an important part of the public sector but a significant part of the economy of the UK. The list of nationalized industries has changed significantly since the most active period of nationalization activity in the late 1940s.

Since that time some organizations and industries have been added to the list (e.g. British Leyland) whilst others have been deleted (e.g. British Telecom). Others have changed ownership more than once (British Steel). Clearly, nationalized industries are very sensitive to government policy.

A practical reflection of this is the fundamental importance of legislation for the industries. Each industry is subject to a nationalization act and these have been supplemented in most cases by subsequent legislation. A specific government department (the 'sponsoring' department) is responsible for each industry. This means that the government department concerned is responsible for government policy towards the industry and for dealing with the Treasury and other departments on behalf of the industry concerned. Additionally, the Minister for the department is responsible to Parliament for implementing legislation concerning the industry and for government policy towards it. Thus, the Department of Energy (and its Secretary of State) is responsible for British Coal, British Gas, and the Electricity Council, whilst the Department of Transport sponsors British Rail.

Most of the funds provided by the government are as loans from the National Loans Fund. Interest is payable on these loans at a rate established when the loans are taken out. Additionally, the industries borrow more on the domestic or overseas capital markets subject to government approval and Treasury guarantee. In addition to loan capital from the government some industries have capital finance provided in the form of Public Dividend Capital. This is effectively equity capital on which dividends are payable out of trading profits. The advantages and disadvantages of debt and equity finance are broadly the same to nationalized industries as to companies.

As we noted above, the nationalized industries have been brought into the government's cash planning system by the setting of External Financing Limits. These are set annually and reflect an industry's capital requirements and capacity to meet them internally. These financing limits are set by agreement between sponsoring department and industry since there is no statutory power to enforce them. However, Ministerial sanction is required for major capital projects and borrowing agreement can be obtained by government.

The legislation which set up each industry contains a statement of financial objectives together with non-financial duties. For example, British Rail is obliged to: provide railway services in Great Britain; to provide other services and facilities as appear expedient, with due regard to efficiency, economy and safety. In addition, the combined revenue of the industry must be sufficient to meet the combined charges to revenue one year with another. Since most industries have had a financial performance target set for them as a percentage rate of return on assets accounting assumes a considerable importance for the nationalized industries. Specific accounting issues are considered below. The target chosen seeks to reflect the circumstances of each industry, and is generally calculated in current cost terms with earnings measured before interest and tax. Where the circumstances of an industry effectively mean that it is likely to be a loss-maker the target will be expressed as a target profit or loss.

External reporting

Given their nature, it is not surprising that nationalized industries' accounting practices are much closer to those of companies than is the case for the rest of the public sector. Since the industries are required by their governing legislation to provide accounts in a form approved or specified by the sponsoring Minister with the approval of the Treasury there is variety. Some statutes require a true and fair view to be disclosed, others dictate that the best commercial practice be adhered to. Both of these requirements in different ways imply that, potentially at least, much of the subject matter of those chapters of this book which refer to companies' published accounts applies to nationalized industries. In practice, however, this is not the case. The objectives of the accounts of nationalized industries and companies differ, if only because they are directed to different users. Likewise, the activities of the nationalized industries are diverse and these differences will be reflected in the same ways that different operating circumstances are reflected in the accounts of companies. Furthermore, although accounting standards represent best commercial practice, they do not cover substantial areas of accounting and are not universally appropriate to nationalized industries.

However, there remain sufficient similarities for it to be easiest to identify the differences between company accounts and those of nationalized industries. The chief difference is in the way in which information in profit and loss accounts is compiled. Given the form of the rate of return target, current cost accounts assume a considerable importance. An enduring difference has been in the treatment of the gearing adjustment (as required by SSAP16, *Current Cost Accounting*), to reflect the extent of loan finance in the long-term capital structure and the beneficial effects of inflation on borrowings. The justification for a gearing adjustment is that borrowers gain during inflation as the real value of their loan diminishes. Hence, the adjustment is usually a credit to profit. Nationalized industries, it might be argued, are little different from companies in that they are financed by a combination of equity and debt. On the other hand, the long-term financing arrangements of the nationalized sector are demonstrably different from those in the private sector since their use of the loan market is not determined solely by financial management considerations. Consequently, the Finance

Panel of the Nationalized Industries' Chairmen's Group (a self-regula-tory coordinating body for the nationalized industries) recommended that commercial practice be followed by showing the effects of inflation on gearing in the profit and loss account, but the special position of the industries be recognized by showing the effect in a note to the accounts and not on their face.

Other differences between companies and nationalized industries are that the latter generally disclose more detailed information (as a reflection of their broader accountability responsibilities), but in a less standardized form. There is significant variety in terminology, format and accounting treatment. The extent to which SSAPs can be made applicable will to some extent determine whether a solution can be found to this problem independently of efforts towards standardization by government and the Finance Panel themselves.

Accounting for other public bodies

In this section of the chapter we shall refer briefly to accounting con-siderations relevant to other public bodies. The bodies which might be included are diverse indeed. Their common characteristic is that, whilst administered under the ultimate control of central government, they exhibit considerable autonomy. The British Broadcasting Corporation is a good example of such an organization with its semi-autonomous funding through licence fees and operating independence. Two other such public bodies are considered below: the National Health Service and universities.

National Health Service

The National Health Service (NHS) is the largest employer in Western Europe. It is administered by the Department of Health and Social Security (DHSS) and almost all its funding is provided by central government.

The NHS is organized into Regional Health Authorities (RHAs) which have responsibility for allocating financial resources to the District Health Authorities (DHAs) in their regions. Budgetary control is the most important way in which treasurers in the NHS effect financial control. Budgets and all other accounting systems in health authorities, with the exception of capital expenditure accounting, are on an accruals basis. The NHS is unique amongst bodies financed by central govern-ment in the extent to which it can exercise virement between capital and revenue, and the extent to which it can carry forward unspent funds.

Individual health authorities have no statutory responsibility to publish annual reports. However, both DHAs and RHAs are required to report to RHAs and the DHSS respectively. These reports include performance data (e.g. patients treated and manpower employed) and financial data, not conventional accounting reports. Rather, the latter are itemized records of expenditures and costs. This is not to say that at local levels voluntary reports are provided to the public and media.

Universities

Universities are technically private institutions, being governed by Royal Charters. Despite the importance of independent sources of income to some institutions, the university sector is heavily dependent upon central government, through the medium of the University Grants Committee (UGC) for funding, both current and capital. However, the liberality of their charters, tradition and the buffer of the UGC gives them considerable operating independence. This independence has been amply reflected in their accounting systems and financial reporting practices. They are required to make periodic financial returns to the UGC in a standard form and this has exerted some influence towards the standardized collection and recording of information for their own internal and external reporting purposes. Other standardizing influences have been their charitable status, the need to adopt fund accounting imposed by the existence of numerous bequests and trusts and by the rules of the UGC, and movements to harmonize instigated by the Committee of Vice Chancellors and Principals.

None the less, substantial variety remains in external financial reports. Although all universities produce the equivalents of balance sheets and income and expenditure accounts there are marked differences in terminology, accounting treatment and format. There is a distinct movement towards the adoption of the formats and terminology of company accounts, encouraged perhaps by their external auditors who are exclusively firms of private sector auditors.

Accounting standards and the public sector

There are two senses in which we can talk of accounting standards and the public sector. One concerns whether there are accounting standards within the public sector. The other concerns whether the statements of accounting practice, both SSAPs and SORPs, developed by the ASC (and discussed earlier in the book), do or should apply in the public sector. We have necessarily had to stress the diversity of accounting and financial reporting in the public sector. This suggests little standardization at present and little prospect for the future, but this is valid if considered for the public sector as a whole. Within sub-sectors, for example, nationalized industries and local government, strong movements for standardization are apparent. However, whilst this is evidence of some grounds for optimism for standardization in the first sense noted above, the second sense of standardization is perhaps more important. The Explanatory Foreword to SSAPs describes them as applying to all financial accounts intended to show a true and fair view of financial position and profit and loss. Clearly, on a narrow interpretation SSAPs are not applicable outside the private sector. However, the statements of the ASC are authoritative, relatively numerous and present an opportunity of standardization between public and private sectors. Since the boundary between the sectors is continually shifting, this suggests benefits.

There is evidence that in some parts of the public sector, the influence of SSAPs is increasing although this cannot be said of central government when the accounting environment and problems are perhaps too different. It can be said, however, of local authorities. CIPFA and the ASC have issued guidance notes on the application of SSAPs to local authorities and several standards have been judged relevant or partly relevant. Of the list of standards reproduced in Table 3.1 on page 56 SSAPs 1, 2, 4, 5, 6, 9, 10, 13, 14, 17 and 18, 19 have been judged relevant or are under consideration.

As noted above, the requirement on nationalized industries to reflect best commercial practice in their accounts suggests the applicability of accounting standards, despite the areas of accounting difference which we identified. In contrast, the substantially different reporting practices of the health authorities gives little hope for the adoption of SSAPs in the NHS. Indeed, the central government's reaction to such suggestions in the past has been distinctly negative.

At a more general level the ASC has formally considered its role in setting accounting standards in the public sector and has decided:

(*a*) To initiate consultation with preparers and users of public sector accounts to formulate a framework for standard setting.
(*b*) To ensure that a statement is issued by authoritative persons in the public sector on the subject.
(*c*) To issue a statement of its own on the matter.
(*d*) To formulate a programme of work in the light of that already undertaken by its Public Sector Sub-Committee.

Questions

1   You are required to:

(*a*) Explain the main features of a Consolidated Loans Fund and how it operates in a local authority.   (*15 marks*)
(*b*) Identify the advantages of operating such a Fund.   (*5 marks*)
                                                        (*Total: 20 marks*)

Chartered Institute of Management Accountants Stage 2, Financial Accounting, Specimen Examination Paper (New Syllabus)

2   You are requred to:

Compare and contrast the role of an auditor of a nationalized industry with the role of an auditor of a public limited company.
                                                             (*20 marks*)

Institute of Chartered Accountants of Scotland, Part 1 Examination, Auditing 1

3   The government is adopting a policy of operating some public sector trading organizations under the provisions of the Companies Act. Explain the major accounting implications when such a change is made. *(16 marks)*

Institute of Public Finance and Accountancy, Professional Examination 2, Public Sector Accounting

4   The Checkit Corporation is a public sector organization which is required to ensure that, taking one year with another, income is sufficient to meet expenditure. The following balances have been taken from the corporation's accounts:

31 March 19X4		31 March 19X5
£000		£000
3,940	Debtors	5,980
3,235	Creditors	4,760
2,825	Work-in-progress	3,220
1,380	Income on account	–
4,920	Investments	4,550
3,210	Capital reserve	3,210
40	Depreciation	180
50 CR	Cash at bank	20
490	Fixed assets at cost	840
4,260	Revenue account	6,460

It is subsequently found that certain adjustments need to be made to the accounts for 19X4–X5:

(a)   Income of £375,000 has been credited to the revenue account. It represents payments on account for work-in-progress.
(b)   Investment income of £50,000 was credited to the investment account.
(c)   Work-in-progress at March 19X5 has been overvalued by £110,000.
(d)   Redundant equipment was sold in the year for £5,000. This was credited to revenue in error. The equipment cost £40,000 and depreciation of £35,000 has been provided.

Taking into account these adjustments you are required to produce the balance sheet at 31 March 19X5 and the source and application of funds statement for 19X4–X5. *(18 marks)*

Chartered Institute of Public Finance and Accountancy Professional Examination 2, Public Sector Accounting

5   Your local authority operates a direct labour undertaking and during 19X4–5 the following historic cost trading position has been produced:

	Expenditure £	*Income* £
New work (under £50,000)	346,700	349,400
General maintenance	1,892,000	1,879,600
Highways	1,076,800	1,082,400

The DLO operates from a single depot which is held on lease from another Committee at a rent of £12,000 p.a. which is included in the expenditure figures above, together with debt charges of £2,000 on adaptations. Premises costs are apportioned 10 per cent new work, 60 per cent maintenance and 30 per cent highways. The premises are valued at £90,000 and have an expected life of sixty years. Land is not depreciated.

The expenditure totals also include £85,600 in respect of contributions to vehicle and plant renewal funds. Usage of vehicles and plant by each work category is 5 per cent new work, 50 per cent maintenance and 45 per cent highways. The value of vehicles and plant is estimated at £353,100 and depreciation costs for the year would be £64,200 in current cost terms.

Stores issues during the year totalled £535,000 and were priced on a last-in first-out basis. Average stockholdings based upon usage were £4,300 new work, £30,000 maintenance and £50,100 highways.

You are required to:

(a) Produce a statement showing the current cost adjustments to the historic cost accounts. (*8 marks*)

(b) Determine the required return on capital employed in each work category. (*4 marks*)

(c) Comment briefly on the results. (*4 marks*)

(*Total: 16 marks*)

Chartered Institute of Public Finance and Accountancy, Professional Examination 2, Public Sector Accounting

Reference

1   Henley, D., Holtham, C., Likierman, J. A., and Perrin J. R., *Public Sector Accounting and Financial Control*, Van Nostrand Reinhold, 1983.

11 Branch accounting

This chapter is concerned with the type of accounting systems that exist when a head office/branch relationship exists. The chapter deals with domestic branches only and in this context a convenient analysis of the types of accounting system that can be adopted is as shown in Figure 11.1.

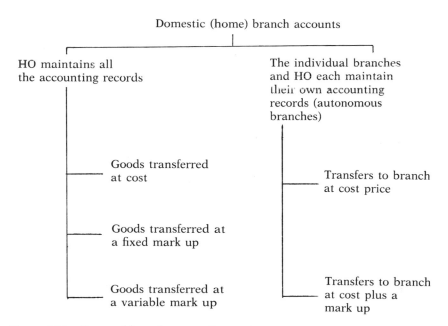

Figure 11.1 *Types of branch accounting system*

Mark up calculations

In branch accounts mark up calculations (usually based on percentages) often have to be made. These can be divided into three main categories:

(a)   Calculations where *goods* are transferred between the head office and branches at a price above cost.
(b)   Calculations where *stocks* include a profit element.
(c)   Commission payments.

In calculations where goods are transferred between the head office and branches at a price above cost the difference between the cost price and the transfer price can be expressed as a percentage of the cost price or the transfer price.

Example 11.1
Head office transfers goods originally costing £800 to a branch in Newcastle at a value of £1,000. Thus the relationship between the cost price and the transfer price can be displayed as follows:

Cost price   £800
Mark up   £200
Transfer price   £1,000

If the mark up is expressed as a percentage of cost the mark up is
$\frac{£200}{£800} \times 100 = 25\%$.

If expressed as a percentage of selling price the mark up is
$\frac{£200}{£1,000} \times 100 = 20\%$.

Clearly therefore it is of the utmost importance that all examination questions be carefully examined to identify whether the mark up percentage is based on cost price or selling price.

The following examples illustrate the principles involved.

Example 11.2
If goods are invoiced at cost plus 20 per cent and the selling price is £12,000, what is the cost price?

Cost price   100   £10,000
Mark up   20   £2,000
Selling price   120   £12,000

Since the mark up is 20 per cent of cost, then in the example above cost is given the value 100. Thus selling price has a value of 120. Thus if selling price is £12,000 the mark up value can be calculated by $\frac{20}{120} \times £12,000 = £2,000$. Therefore cost price must be £12,000 − £2,000 = £10,000.

Example 11.3
Goods originally costing £12,000 are sold to give a mark up (a gross margin) of 25 per cent on the sales value.

Sales value	100	£16,000
Mark up	25	£4,000
Cost	75	£12,000

Since the mark up is 25 per cent of sales value, then call sales value 100. Thus if sales value is 100 and mark up 25, then cost must be 75. Appropriate values can then be substituted.

In calculations where *stocks* include a profit element in principle the situation is indentical to that discussed above in that the profit (mark up) can be expressed as a percentage of cost price or selling price. Thus the same approach to solving the problem is required.

Example 11.4
Goods are transferred at cost plus 20 per cent from head office to branches. At year end the Blackpool branch had goods in stock valued at £24,000 at transfer price.

What is the cost price of the goods and the profit element included in the stock value of £24,000?

Cost price stock	100	£20,000
Profit (mark up)	20	£4,000
Transfer value of stock	120	£24,000

As can be seen the calculations are identical to Example 11.2 above.

With commission payments a branch manager may be given a *commission* based on profits. The commission may be based on profits *before* the commission is charged as an expense, or on the profit *after* charging the commission.

Example 11.5
A branch earns a profit of £20,000 *before* charging manager's commission. The manager is entitled to a commission of 10 per cent of the branch's profit *before* charging the commission. How much is the commission?

In this case the commission is simply £20,000 × 10% = £2,000.

Example 11.6
A branch earns a profit of £44,000 *before* charging manager's commission. The manager is entitled to a commission of 10 per cent of the branch profit *after* charging commission. How much is the commission?

Since the 10 per cent is based on the amount of profit *after* charging commission then let that amount equal 100. Thus the profit before charging commission must equal 110 (i.e. 100 + 10). Therefore the amounts can be calculated as follows:

Profits before charging commission   110   £44,000 (given)

− Commission   10   £4000 $\left(\dfrac{10}{110} \times £44,000\right)$

= Profits after charging commission   100   £40,000$\left(\dfrac{100}{110} \times £44,000\right)$

Branch accounts when head office maintains the accounting records and goods are transferred to the branch at cost

The major objectives of a system of branch accounts are as follows:

(*a*)   To monitor and control branch stocks.
(*b*)   To monitor and control branch cash.
(*c*)   To monitor and control branch expenses and profit.

To achieve these objectives in a branch accounting system where the head office records all the transactions and goods are transferred at cost price the following accounts are required:

Account title	*Purpose of account*
Goods to branch	To record value of goods sent to branch by head office and also goods returned by branch.
Branch stock	To record details of stock movements at the branch.
Branch expenses	To record the expenses required by the branch during the accounting period.
Branch debtors	To record credit sales and payments received from debtors.
Branch cash	To record cash receipts and payments by the branch.
Branch sales	To record sales made by the branch.
Branch profit and loss	To identify branch profit or loss for the period.

The accounting entries can be summarized as follows:

Nature of transaction	*Accounting entries*	
Goods sent to branch from head office	Debit:	Branch stock account
	Credit:	Goods to branch account
Goods returned to head office by branch	Debit:	Goods to branch account
	Credit:	Branch stock account
Branch expenses	Debit:	Branch expenses account (which may be sub-classified by nature of expense)

Nature of transaction	Accounting entries
	Credit: Bank account or creditors account dependent upon whether cash or credit transaction
Branch sales	Debit: Bank or branch debtors account
	Credit: Branch sales account
Branch sales at cost	Debit: Branch cost of sales account or profit and loss account
	Credit: Branch stock account

At the end of the accounting period the accounts are closed as follows:

Account	Accounting entries
Goods to branch account	Debit: Goods to branch account
	Credit: Head office trading account

This entry ensures that the goods sent to branch are not double charged as an expense

Branch expenses account	Debit: Branch profit and loss account
	Credit: Branch expenses account
Branch sales account	Debit: Branch sales account
	Credit: Branch profit and loss account
Branch cost of sales account	Debit: Branch profit and loss account
	Credit: Branch cost of sales account
Branch stock account	At year end a physical stocktake would normally take place and the closing stock will be carried down in the normal way. This will reveal any stock differences which will be transferred to branch profit and loss account

Example 11.7
On 1 March Distributors Limited opened a branch in Leeds and the following transactions took place during the month:

Transaction no	Description	
1	Goods sent to the branch at cost	£28,000
2	Sales made by the branch	
	– cash (cost £13,200)	£18,000
3	– credit (cost £8,800)	£12,000
4	Branch expenses paid by head office	£4,000
5	Closing stock	£6,000
6	Cash received from debtors	£9,000

From this information we shall write up the necessary accounts and prepare a branch profit and loss account for March.

Goods to branch account

	£			£
Purchases	28,000	Branch stock	(1)	28,000

Branch stock account

		£			£
Goods to branch	(1)	28,000	Profit and loss		
			(cost of goods sold)		22,000
			Closing stock	(5)	6,000
		28,000			28,000
Opening stock	(5)	6,000			

Branch expenses account

		£			£
Bank	(4)	4,000	Profit and loss	(4)	4,000

Branch sales account

	£			£
Profit and loss	30,000	Bank (cash sales (2))		18,000
		Debtors (credit sales (3))		12,000
	30,000			30,000

Branch debtors account

		£			£
Branch sales	(3)	12,000	Bank	(6)	9,000
			Balance		3,000
		12,000			12,000
Balance		3,000			

Branch profit and loss account

	£		£
Cost of goods sold	22,000	Sales	30,000
Expenses	4,000		
Profit	4,000		
	30,000		30,000

Note: The numbers in brackets refer to the individual transactions.

The above is the simplest form of branch accounting. In rather more sophisticated systems goods are transferred from head office to branches inclusive of a fixed or varying mark up. These systems are described below.

Branch accounts where head office maintains the accounting records and goods are transferred to the branch at selling prices which include a fixed mark-up

Under this system of branch accounting goods are transferred to branches at a value which represents cost plus a fixed profit margin, the transfer value itself being the estimated selling price of the goods by the branch.

The objectives of the system are the same as those specified in the previous section though the method of achieving those objectives is slightly different. Since the head office maintains the accounting records the accounting system is, in principle, similar to that detailed above but because the transfer (or invoice) price to the branch includes a profit element there are of necessity detailed differences.

Under this system of branch accounting the following accounts are necessary.

Account title	*Purpose of account*
Goods to branch	This account is identical to that described above. Note that although goods are invoiced to the branch at selling price they are recorded in this account at *cost*.
Branch stock	This account is identical to that described above except that the account is maintained at the invoiced (selling) prices.
Branch adjustment	This account 'links' the goods to branch account and the branch stock account since the mark up (gross margin) is entered in this account. In principle, the balance on this account at the end of the period represents the gross profit of the branch.
Branch expenses	As described in the previous section.
Branch debtors	As described in the previous section.
Branch cash	As described in the previous section.
Branch profit and loss account	As described in the previous section.

The accounting entries are as follows:

Nature of transaction	*Accounting entries*
Goods sent to branch from head office	Debit: Branch stock account – with invoice (selling) value Credit: Goods to branch account – with cost of goods Adjustment account – with mark up of the goods sent to branch
Goods returned to head office from branch (i.e. reverse of transaction above)	Debit: Goods to branch account – with cost of goods Adjustment account – with mark up of goods returned to head office Credit: Branch stock account – with invoice (selling) price

Nature of transaction	*Accounting entries*	
Branch expenses	Debit:	Branch expenses account (which may be sub-classified by nature of expense)
	Credit:	Bank or creditors dependent upon whether cash or credit transaction
Branch sales (at normal selling price)	Debit:	Branch debtors account or cash with sales value
	Credit:	Branch stock account with sales value of goods sold

Branch sales (at a price below normal selling price)

Debit: Branch debtors account ⎫ With actual
Credit: Branch stock account ⎬ sales value of goods sold

Debit: Adjustment account ⎫ With the
Credit: Branch stock account ⎬ reduction in the normal selling price

Since the reduction in the selling price will cause a corresponding reduction in the gross profit so as to maintain the balance in the stock account at normal selling prices the account must be credited with the reduction; whilst the adjustment account must be debited to recognize the partial loss of the normal gross profit.

Stock losses at branch	In this case since the goods have not been sold by the branch the gross profit has not been earned. Therefore the *gross profit* must be removed from the adjustment account and the *cost* of the lost goods charged to profit and loss account. Thus:
	Debit: Profit and loss account with cost price. Adjustment account with mark up
	Credit: Branch stock account with selling price
Cash losses at branch	Where cash has been stolen the gross profit on the goods sold which gave rise to the cash has been earned, therefore the adjustment account does not require amendment. The entire loss will be written off to the profit and loss account. Thus:
	Debit: Profit and loss account ⎫ With amount of cash stolen
	Credit: Branch stock account ⎬
Small losses or gains	The *full* amount is simply transferred from the branch stock account to the adjustment account

Example 11.8
Ajax Limited operates from a head office and central warehouse in Manchester with selling branches in the main centres of population. Goods are transferred from head office to branches at a fixed selling price representing cost plus 25 per cent. Details of transactions between the head office and the Stafford branch for March are as follows:

Transaction number	Description
1	Goods to branch at cost £80,000.
2	Goods returned from branch to head office at selling price £500.
3	Branch expenses paid by head office £1,200.
4	Stock stolen from branch and not recovered £1,250 (at selling price).
5	Branch sales £81,600.
6	Cash stolen from branch £1,500.
7	Closing stock of goods at branch at selling price £15,000.

We shall use this information to record the above transactions and prepare the branch profit and loss account for March.

Goods to branch account

		£			£
Branch stock	(2)	400	Branch stock	(1)	80,000
Head office trading account		79,600			
		80,000			80,000

Branch stock account

		£			£
Goods to branch	(1)	100,000	Goods to branch	(2)	500
			Stock loss		
			– profit and loss (cost)	(4)	1,000
			– adjustment account (mark up)	(4)	250
			Cash loss		
			– profit and loss	(6)	1,500
			Branch debtors (sales)	(7)	81,600
			Branch adjustment – stock loss	(8)	150
			Closing stock c/d	(7)	15,000
		100,000			100,000
Closing stock b/d	(7)	15,000			

Branch adjustment account

		£			£
Branch stock	(2)	100	Branch stock	(1)	20,000
Branch stock	(4)	250			

		£			£
Branch stock (stock loss)	(8)	150			
Branch profit and loss (gross profit)	(9)	16,500			
Closing stock c/d (profit element)	(7)	3,000			
		20,000			20,000
			Closing stock b/d	(7)	3,000

Branch expenses account

		£			£
Bank	(3)	1,200	Branch profit and loss	(10)	1,200

Branch debtors account

		£
Branch stock	(7)	81,600

Branch profit and loss account

		£			£
Branch stock	(4)	1,000	Branch adjustment (gross profit)	(9)	16,500
Branch stock	(6)	1,500			
Branch expenses	(10)	1,200			
Net profit		12,800			
		16,500			16,500

Notes:

(a) The stock loss of £150 credited in the branch stock account is the balancing figure and is treated as a 'small stock loss'.

(b) Note carefully how the profit element in the closing stock (£3,000) is carried down on the adjustment account. This amount is offset against the balance on the stock account to arrive at the value of the stock at cost.

(c) The net profit can be reconciled with the sales as follows:

Sales		£81,600
Normal gross profit thereon $\frac{£81,600 \times 25}{125}$		£16,320
Less: stock loss	1,000	
cash loss £1,500 $\times \frac{100}{125}$	1,200	
small stock loss £150 $\times \frac{100}{125}$	120	
branch expenses	1,200	
		£3,520
Net profit		£12,800

Branch accounts where head office maintains the accounting records and goods are transferred to the branch at selling prices which include varying mark up rates

This type of branch accounting can be used where:

(a) Branches sell a variety of goods with differing rates of mark up (gross margin).
(b) The proportions of the products carrying the differing rates of gross margin are the same at head office and each of the branches. Clearly it is *very rare* that this condition applies and thus the application of this system is extremely restricted in practice.

Under this system the following accounts are required:

Account title	Purpose of account
Branch stock	As in the previous section.
Branch debtors	As in the previous section.
Branch expenses	As in the previous section.
Branch sales	To record the sales for the period.

The accounting entries can be summarized as follows:

Nature of transaction	Accounting entries	
Goods sent to branch from head office	Debit:	Branch stock account
	Credit:	Branch sales account
Goods returned to head office by branch	Debit:	Branch sales account
	Credit:	Branch stock account
Branch expenses	Debit:	Branch expenses account (which may be sub-classified by nature of expenses)
	Credit:	Bank account or creditors account dependent upon whether cash or credit transaction
Branch sales	Debit:	Bank account or debtors account dependent upon whether cash or credit transaction
	Credit:	Branch sales account
Cash stolen	Debit:	Branch profit and loss account
	Credit:	Branch stock account
Stock losses	Debit:	Branch sales	} With sales value of loss
	Credit:	Branch stock	
	Debit:	Profit and loss account	} With cost of stock loss
	Credit:	Purchases in trading account	

At the end of the accounting period a physical stock-take will be carried out at the branch. The resultant stock figure, *at selling prices*, will be carried down on the branch stock account and the branch sales account. These balances will, therefore, cancel out. The closing stock of the branch *at cost* will be created via the trading account in the normal way.

The *total* purchases figure in the head office books (which will of course include the goods sent to branches) is transferred to a combined trading account (less of course any stock losses).

Example 11.9

Retailers Limited have a warehouse and sales outlet at York and a selling branch in Harrogate. Goods are transferred to Harrogate from York at selling price. Transactions for June are as follows:

Transaction no	Description	
1	Goods sent to Harrogate branch	£90,000
2	Goods returned from Harrogate to York	£4,000
3	Branch expenses paid	£7,000
4	Cash stolen from branch	£2,000
5	Branch sales on credit terms	£73,000
6	Closing stock at branch at month end – at selling price (the cost price of the stock was £4,000)	£8,000

From this information we shall prepare the accounts relating to the Harrogate branch for June, and prepare a combined branch and head office trading and profit and loss account for the month, assuming that (*a*) the cost of the branch stock loss is £2,250, (*b*) total head office purchases for the month are £190,000, (*c*) the total head office sales for the period are £150,000, (*d*) head office closing stock at cost is £20,000, (*e*) head office expenses for the month are £16,000.

Branch stock

		£			£
Branch sales	(1)	90,000	Branch sales	(2)	4,000
			Profit and loss		
			(cash stolen)	(4)	2,000
			Branch debtors	(5)	73,000
			Branch sales stock loss		
			(balancing figure)		3,000
			Closing stock c/d	(6)	8,000
		90,000			90,000
Closing stock b/d	(6)	8,000			

Branch sales

		£			£
Branch stock	(2)	4,000	Branch stock	(1)	90,000
Branch stock		3,000			

		£			£
Trading account					
(sales for period)		75,000			
Closing stock c/d	(6)	8,000			
		90,000			90,000
			Closing stock b/d	(6)	8,000

Branch debtors

		£
Branch stock	(5)	73,000

Branch expenses

		£		£
Cash	(3)	7,000	Profit and loss	7,000

Trading and profit and loss account for June

	Head office	Branch	Total
	£	£	£
Sales	150,000	75,000	225,000
Purchases			190,000
Less: cost of stock loss			(2,250)
closing stock			(24,000)
			163,750
Gross profit	40,833	20,417	61,250
Cash stolen	–	2,000	2,000
Expenses	16,000	7,000	23,000
Cost of stock loss	–	2,250	2,250
Net profit	24,833	9,167	34,000

Note: Since under this method of branch accounting the assumption is
that the mix of sales and therefore the gross profit to sales percentage is
the same for the head office and the branch, the total gross profit is
apportioned on the basis of sales.

Head office $\frac{£150,000}{£225,000} \times £61,250 = £40,833$

Branch $\frac{£75,000}{£225,000} \times £61,250 = £20,417$

Autonomous branches – transfers of goods to branches at cost price

Under this system of branch accounting the branches are treated as
separate, independent businesses. Thus *each* branch will keep a
complete set of accounts to record *its own* business transactions, and
will also prepare its own profit and loss account and balance sheet.

Transactions between the head office and branches will be recorded through *current accounts*. For example, if A Limited opens a branch in Liverpool and in order to establish the branch sends goods to the value of £50,000 and cash to the value of £90,000, the accounting entries are as follows:

In head office books
Goods sent to branch account
　　Liverpool branch current account　　　　　　　　　　　　　£50,000

Head office bank account
　　Liverpool branch current account　　　　　　　　　　　　　£90,000

Liverpool branch current account
　　Goods sent to branch account　　　　　　　　　　　　　　　£50,000
　　Head office bank account　　　　　　　　　　　　　　　　　£90,000

In branch books
Goods from head office account
　　Head office current account　　　　　　　　　　　　　　　　£50,000
Liverpool branch bank account
　　Head office current account　　　　　　　　　　　　　　　　£90,000
Head office current account
　　Goods from head office account|　　　　　　　　　　　　　　£50,000
　　Liverpool branch bank account|　　　　　　　　　　　　　　£90,000

The following points should be noted carefully:

(*a*)　The balance on the branch current account in the head office books (£140,000) is an asset to the head office and represents the net investment by the head office in the branch.
(*b*)　The balance on the head office current account in the branch books (£140,000) is a liability to the branch and represents its capital (i.e. the head office is financing the branch to the extent of £140,000).
(*c*)　The balances on the two current accounts should equal each other. Where they do not, the discrepancy will be due to cash or goods in transit.

Cash and goods in transit

Where either cash or goods are in transit between the head office and branch then entries will only have been made in the transferor's books. Thus if both sets of accounts are balanced for final accounts purposes the two current accounts will not agree.

Example 11.10
During March head office despatched eight batches of goods to its Cannock branch, each batch was invoiced at £1,000. During the same period the branch remitted to head office three cheques each for £2,000. At month end the branch had received only seven batches of goods, and the head office had received only two cheques.

Head office books

Goods to branch account

| | Cannock branch current account (8 batches) | £8,000 |

Head office bank account

| Cannock branch current account (2 cheques) | £4,000 |

Cannock branch current account

| Goods to branch account | £8,000 | Head office bank account | £4,000 |

Cannock branch books

Goods from head office account

| Head office current account (7 batches) | £7,000 |

Branch bank account

| | Head office current account (3 cheques) | £6,000 |

Head office current account

| Branch bank account | £6,000 | Goods from head office account | £7,000 |

Thus at the end of March the balances on the current accounts are different, £4,000 compared with £1,000, because of the items in transit. To remedy the situation entries will be made in a cash in transit account and a goods in transit account as follows:

Head office books

Cannock branch current account

Goods to branch account	£8,000	Head office bank account	£4,000
		Goods in transit account (1 batch)	£1,000
		Cash in transit (1 cheque)	£2,000

Goods in transit account

| Cannock branch current account (1 batch) | £1,000 |

Cash in transit account

| Cannock branch current account | £2,000 |

The current accounts now have equal and opposite balances, and the balances on the cash in transit and goods in transit accounts in the head office books will appear in the head office balance sheet at the end of March.

Stock losses

These are normally dealt with by debiting the profit and loss account and crediting the trading account of the trading entity where the stock loss took place. This method has two possible advantages;

(a)   It highlights the loss in the profit and loss account for management control purposes.
(b)   It maintains the normal gross profit percentage in the trading account.

Branch expenses paid by head office

When the head office pays expenses on behalf of the branch they must be charged *out* of the head office accounts and *into* the branch accounts through the respective current accounts, as follows:

Head office books
    Debit: branch current account
    Credit: bank account or the appropriate expense account if the entry has already been made therein

Branch books
    Debit: appropriate expense account
    Credit: head office current account

Treatment of branch profit

The branch net profit for the period must be transferred into the head office profit and loss account. Again this is done through the current accounts, the accounting entries being:

Head office books
    Debit: branch current account
    Credit: profit and loss account

Branch books
    Debit: profit and loss account
    Credit: head office current account

Example 11.11
On 1 April a new company, Sellers Limited, was formed with a head office in Matlock and a branch in Tipton. The company's initial share capital was 10,000 £1 ordinary shares fully subscribed in cash, and transactions for the month of April were as follows:

Head office	£
Goods purchased on credit	114,000
Sales: cash	30,000
credit	40,000
Goods sent to branch	38,000
Branch expenses paid	2,000

	£
Cash received from debtors	15,000
Cash paid to suppliers	50,000
Head office expenses paid	4,000
Fitting purchased for: head office	1,800
branch	1,200
Cash received from branch	10,000

Branch	£
Goods received from head office	33,000
Expenses paid	3,000
Sales: cash	20,000
credit	10,000
Cash sent to head office	12,000
Cash received from debtors	4,000

On 30 April stocks were: head office	18,000
branch	12,000

Depreciation on fittings is to be provided at 20 per cent per annum on cost. Fixed assets are all recorded in head office books.

From this information we can:

(a) Write up the necessary ledger accounts in the books of the head office and the branch.
(b) Extract a trial balance at the end of April.
(c) Prepare separate trading, profit and loss accounts for the head office and branch for the month of April, and separate balance sheets as at 30 April.

Head office books

Share capital account

		£
	Bank	10,000

Bank account

	£		£
Share capital	10,000	Branch current account	2,000
Sales	30,000	Creditors	50,000
Debtors	15,000	Expenses	4,000
Branch current account	10,000	Fittings	3,000
		Balance	6,000
	65,000		65,000
Balance	6,000		

Purchases account

	£		£
Creditors	114,000	Trading	114,000

Creditors account

	£		£
Bank	50,000	Purchases	114,000
Balance	64,000		
	114,000		114,000
		Balance	64,000

Sales account

	£		£
Trading	70,000	Bank	30,000
		Debtors	40,000
	70,000		70,000

Debtors account

	£		£
Sales	40,000	Bank	15,000
		Balance	25,000
	40,000		40,000
Balance	25,000		

Goods sent to branch account

	£		£
Trading	38,000	Branch current account	38,000

Branch current account

	£		£
Goods sent to branch	38,000	Bank:	
Bank:		Cash from branch	10,000
branch expenses	2,000	Balance	30,000
	40,000		40,000
Balance	30,000		

Expenses account

	£		£
Bank	4,000	Profit and loss	4,000

Fittings account

	£		
Bank	3,000		

Branch books

Goods from head office account

	£		£
HO current account	33,000	Trading	33,000

Head office current account

	£		£
Bank	12,000	Goods from HO	33,000
Balance	23,000	Expenses (paid by HO)	2,000
	35,000		35,000
		Balance	23,000

Bank account

	£		£
Sales	20,000	Expenses	3,000
Debtors	4,000	HO current account	12,000
		Balance	9,000
	24,000		24,000
Balance	9,000		

Expenses account

	£		£
Bank	3,000	Profit and loss	5,000
HO current account	2,000		
	5,000		5,000

Sales account

	£		£
Trading	30,000	Bank	20,000
		Debtors	10,000
	30,000		30,000

Debtors account

	£		£
Sales	10,000	Bank	4,000
		Balance	6,000
	10,000		10,000
Balance	6,000		

Trial balance: head office

	£	£
Share capital		10,000
Bank	6,000	
Purchases	114,000	
Creditors		64,000
Sales		70,000
Debtors	25,000	
Goods to branch		38,000
Branch current account	30,000	
Expenses	4,000	
Fittings	3,000	
	182,000	182,000

Trial balance: branch

	£	£
Goods from head office	33,000	
Head office current account		23,000
Bank	9,000	
Expenses	5,000	
Sales		30,000
Debtors	6,000	
	53,000	53,000

From the trial balances it can be seen that the current accounts do not agree. This is caused by the cash in transit from the branch to head office of £2,000 and the goods in transit from the head office to the branch of £5,000. To bring the current accounts into balance the following entries are required in the *head office books*:

	£	£
DR Goods in transit	5,000	
DR Cash in transit	2,000	
Branch current account		7,000

Thus after this adjustment the current accounts will have equal and opposite balances of £23,000. The final accounts can now be prepared.

Trading and profit and loss accounts for the month of April

	HO £	Branch £		HO £	Branch £
Purchases	114,000		Sales: cash	30,000	20,000
Goods from HO		33,000	credit	40,000	10,000
Gross profit	12,000	9,000	Goods sent to branch:		
			received	33,000	
			in transit	5,000	
			Closing stock	18,000	12,000
	126,000	42,000		126,000	42,000
Expenses	4,000	5,000	Gross profit	12,000	9,000

	HO £	Branch £		HO £	Branch £
Depreciation	30	20			
Net profit	7,970	3,980			
	12,000	9,000		12,000	9,000
Transfer to HO		3,980	Net profit	7,970	3,980
Balance c/f	11,950		Transfer from		
			branch	3,980	
	11,950	3,980		11,950	3,980

Balance sheets as at 30 April

	HO £	Branch £		HO £	Branch £
Fittings: cost	3,000		Share capital	10,000	
Less depreciation	50				
	2,950		Profit and		
			loss account	11,950	
			HO current		
			account		27,000
Stock:					
in hand	18,000	12,000			
in transit	5,000		Creditors	64,000	
Debtors	25,000	6,000			
Bank:					
in hand	6,000	9,000			
in transit	2,000				
Branch current					
account	27,000				
	85,950	27,000		85,950	27,000

The current account balances of £27,000 are arrived at as follows:

	HO £		Branch £	
Balance as trial balance	23,000	CR	30,000	DR
Less cash and goods in transit			7,000	
	23,000	CR	23,000	DR
Add branch expenses paid				
by HO (depreciation)	20		20	
	23,020	CR	23,020	DR
Add transfer of branch profit				
to HO books	3,980		3,980	
Balance as balance sheet	27,000	CR	27,000	DR

Autonomous branches – transfers of goods to branches at cost plus a mark up

In this system of branch accounting the general principles applied are, with one exception, the same as for autonomous branches where goods are transferred from HO at cost. The sole exception concerns the problem of unrealized profits.

The problem of unrealized profits

It is not uncommon for the head office to invoice goods to the branch at cost plus, i.e. inclusive of a profit element. The branch then adds a further profit element before finally selling the goods.

It is important to realize that the existence of the head office mark up is of no consequence to the branch. It will simply treat the goods received from head office as the equivalent of purchases. Indeed the branch may not be aware of the amount or even existence of the mark up.

However, if at the end of an accounting period the branch stock includes goods received from head office, and those goods have been transferred at cost plus, then from the *company's* viewpoint the stock includes an unrealized profit element.

Example 11.12
Head office transfers to its Droitwich branch goods to the value of £1,500. These goods had an original cost of £1,000. At the end of the accounting period the goods were still held in stock by the branch.

The profit and loss accounts of the HO and branch will appear as follows:

Profit and loss accounts

	HO £	Branch £		HO £	Branch £
Purchases	1,000		Goods to branch	1,500	
Goods from HO		1,500	Closing stock		1,500
Profit	500				
	1,500	1,500		1,500	1,500

The following points should be noted:

(a)   The HO profit of £500 has not yet, from a company viewpoint been realized since the goods to which the £500 relates are still held in stock by the branch.

(b)   Therefore:

(i)   The £500 profit must be eliminated from the *HO* profit and loss account.

(ii)   In the *company's* balance sheet the stock must be reduced to cost (£1,000).

This is done as follows:

(i)   The HO profit and loss account will be debited, and an unrealized profit account credited with the amount of the unrealized profit. The letter account will be shown in the HO balance sheet. Thus the adjustments are made in the HO books.

(ii) In the *company* balance sheet the unrealized stock profit of £500 will be deducted from the branch stock value of £1,500 to leave stock at cost of £1,000.

(c) In subsequent years the head office profit and loss account and the unrealized profit account will contain entries relating to increases or decreases in the amount of unrealized profit in stocks.

Taking Example 11.12 above, if we now assume that the unrealized stock profit at the end of the subsequent accounting period is £750, then the balance on the unrealized profit account must be increased to £750 by debiting the head of profit and loss account and crediting the unrealized profit account with £250 (i.e. the amount of the increase).

Preparation of final accounts

At the end of an accounting period the head office and branch will each balance their own set of books, extract a trial balance and prepare final accounts. In principle the procedure is identical to that shown in Example 11.11, but because the HO transfers to branch include a profit element the total company profit cannot be calculated simply by adding together the HO and branch profit. Instead a combined profit and loss account in *memorandum form* must be prepared.

When preparing the memorandum profit and loss account for the company the following should be noted:

(a) Goods from HO in the branch trading account will be offset against goods to branch in the HO trading account.
(b) Goods in transit will be shown in the combined trading account at cost, as will opening and closing stocks.
(c) The sum of the branch and head office net profits will equal the total company net profit.

When the *company* balance sheet is prepared the current account balances in the HO and branch balance sheets respectively will cancel out, whilst closing stocks will be valued at cost.

Example 11.13
Dealers Limited have a head office and retail outlet in Oswestry and a retail branch at Chester. Goods are transferred to Chester at cost plus 10 per cent, and to this price the branch adds a further 15 per cent to arrive at the ultimate selling price. The trial balances of the HO and branch on 31 December 19X1 are as follows:

Trial balance 31 December 19X1

	HO Dr £	HO Cr £	Branch Dr £	Branch Cr £
Sales		210,000		126,500
Goods to branch		66,600		
Wages and salaries	21,000		16,000	

	HO		Branch	
	Dr	Cr	Dr	Cr
	£	£	£	£
Rent and rates	6,000		4,000	
Insurance	2,000		1,800	
Heat and light	3,100		2,400	
Fixtures and fittings – cost	40,000		25,000	
Motor vehicles – cost	12,000		8,000	
Goods from HO			60,000	
Stocks	30,000		6,400	
Purchases	190,000		22,000	
Unrealized profit provision		400		
Current accounts	26,200			16,900
Bank	7,800		5,600	
Share capital		20,000		
Debtors	4,600		3,800	
Creditors		16,100		2,600
Depreciation provision:				
Fixtures and fittings		18,000		5,800
Motor vehicles		5,600		3,200
Profit and loss account		6,000		
	342,700	342,700	155,000	155,000

Notes:
(a) On 31 December 19X1 the closing stock at HO was £28,000, and at branch £7,600. Included in the branch closing stock were local purchases originally costing £2,100.
(b) Wages and salaries accrued amounted to:
    HO £2,000, Branch £1,500.
(c) Depreciation is provided at the rates of:
    Fixtures and fittings 10 per cent per annum on cost
    Motor vehicles 25 per cent per annum on cost
(d) On 31 December 19X1 a remittance of £2,700 from the branch had not been received by HO.

Trading and profit and loss account for the year ended 31 December 19X1

	HO	Branch	Total
	£	£	£
Sales	210,000	126,500	336,500
Goods to branch (including GIT)	66,600	–	–
	276,600	126,500	336,500
Opening stock	30,000	6,400	36,000
Purchases	190,000	22,000	212,000
Goods from HO	–	60,000	–
	220,000	88,400	248,000

	HO £	Branch £	Total £
Closing stock	28,000	7,600	41,100
Cost of goods sold	192,000	80,800	206,900
Gross profit	84,600	45,700	129,600
Wages and salaries	23,000	17,500	40,500
Rent and rates	6,000	4,000	10,000
Insurance	2,000	1,800	3,800
Heat and light	3,100	2,400	5,500
Depreciation:			
fixtures and fittings	4,000	2,500	6,500
motor vehicles	3,000	2,000	5,000
Increase in profit provision	700	–	–
	41,800	30,200	71,300
Net profit	42,800	15,500	58,300

Balance sheets as at 31 December 19X1

	HO £	Branch £	Total £
Fixed assets at NBV			
Motor vehicles	3,400	2,800	6,200
Fixtures and fittings	18,000	16,700	34,700
	21,400	19,500	40,900
Current assets			
Stock	28,000	7,600	{35,100
Goods in transit (GIT)	6,600	–	{6,000
Debtors	4,600	3,800	8,400
Bank	7,800	5,600	13,400
Cash transit	2,700	–	2,700
Current account	16,900	–	–
	66,600	17,000	65,600
Less current liabilities			
Creditors and accruals	18,100	4,100	22,200
Unrealized profit provision	1,100	–	–
	19,200	4,100	22,200
Net current assets	47,400	12,900	43,400
Capital employed	68,800	32,400	84,300
Represented by:			
Share capital	20,000	–	20,000
Profit and loss account	48,800	15,500	64,300
Current account	–	16,900	–
	68,800	32,400	84,300

Notes:
(a) The current account balances in the trial balance are out of balance by £9,300 (£26,200 − £16,900). This is due to goods in transit of £6,600 and cash in transit £2,700.
(b) The profit provision increase is calculated as follows:

	£
Profit provision in closing stock at branch $\left(£7,600 - £2,100 \times \dfrac{10}{110}\right)$	500
Opening provision	400
	100
Plus unrealized profit on goods in transit $\left(\dfrac{10}{110} \times £6,600\right)$	600*
Therefore increase in profit provision	700

* Since HO takes credit for the goods in transit in its own profit and loss account.

(c) The opening and closing stocks and goods in transit are valued at cost in the total (company) column.

Questions

1 Bond, a retailer of household appliances, keeps records of his Trafford Park, Warwick Road and Stretford branches at a head office in Salford. Goods are invoiced at selling price which contains no fixed profit margin and the sales mix at head office and branches are broadly similar. Stocks are included in previous year's balance sheet (30 September 19X6) at £36,000, and during the year total stocks have grown by £8,000 at cost. Purchases amounted to £100,320 and sales are £40,000 for head office, £30,000 for Trafford Park and £30,000 for Warwick Road. The manager at the Stretford branch was dismissed at the end of September 19X7 and he is thought to have taken cash with him but, as the books at head office have not been written up, the exact amount is still unknown. After further enquiries you ascertain that the opening stock at Stretford is £7,000 at selling price, that £400 worth of goods were lost (head office cost £320), and that £42,000 was invoiced to Stretford where credit sales of £44,000 and cash sales of £15,000 were made. Physical stock was taken and found to be £8,600 at selling prices before marking down shop-soiled goods by £100.

You are required to:

(a) Prepare the branch stock account and branch sales account.
(b) Prepare combined trading and profit and loss account for the year ended 30 September 19X7.

2 Lofthouse has traded for some years from a head office (at Burnden) and one branch (Bromwich Street). The branch receives goods from head office (by whom it is invoiced at selling price less 15 per cent). The branch also buys goods directly from outside suppliers. Both head office and branch sell the goods purchased by head office at a fixed selling price. The sales by head office to its customers generate

a uniform gross profit of 35 per cent on the fixed selling price and all branch sales of goods received from head office were made at the fixed selling price. The following figures appeared in the books at 31 May 19X6 before adjustment was made for any of the matters noted below:

	Bromwich Street		Burnden	
	£	£	£	£
Fixed assets at cost:				
Branch	375		750	
Head Office			2,000	
Accumulated depreciation				1,175
Balances at bank	175		1,227.5	
Purchases	3,375		39,250	
Capital account				5,000
Sales		24,750		36,000
Selling and general expenses	1,712.5		2,900	
Goods received by/ sent to branch	14,250			15,000
Debtors/creditors	9,175	4,487.5	13,120	13,197.5
Stock 1 June 19X5 at invoiced cost	1,800			
Stock 1 June 19X5 at cost	850		1,600	
Branch/head office: Current account		7,600	9,925	
Provision for unrealized profit at 1 June 19X5				400
	£36,712.5	£36,712.5	£70,772.5	£70,772.5

Adjustments to the above are required in respect of the notes:

(*a*) The branch stock on 31 May 19X6 of items purchased from outside sources was £1,225.

(*b*) It is the practice to record all branch fixed assets in the head office account. Depreciation is to be provided at 20 per cent on cost at the year-end.

(*c*) Goods invoiced by head office to the branch during May 19X6 at £750 were not entered by the branch until June 19X6.

(*d*) Head office did not receive or record until after the balance sheet date a receipt of £1,575 made by the branch during May 19X6.

(*e*) Branch sales of goods obtained from head office total £13,125.

(*f*) Stocktaking at the branch showed, in respect of goods received from head office:

    (*i*) A shortage of goods, selling value £300.

    (*ii*) Damaged goods, selling value £550 which it was decided should be written down to £187.5 for stock purposes. Head office agreed to allow the branch credit of £75 against these goods.

(g) Apart from the foregoing, all stocks at 31 May 19X6 were to be valued at cost for the purpose only of the separate branch trading account; cost of goods originating from head office is to be taken as invoice price from head office.

You are required to prepare for the head office, branch and the entire business:

(a) Trading and profit and loss accounts for the year ended 31 May 19X6.

(b) Balance sheets at 31 May 19X6.

3   Painter commenced a merchanting business on 1 April 19X0 with a head office and one branch. Goods sent to the branch by head office were charged to the branch at selling price less 25 per cent. The branch also bought goods from other suppliers. Sales by head office to its customers produced a uniform gross profit of 30 per cent on a fixed selling price and all branch sales of goods received from head office were made at the fixed selling price. The following trial balances as on 31 March 19X1 were extracted from the books before any of the adjustments contained in the notes:

	Head office £	Head office £	Stanley Park £	Stanley Park £
Painter: capital		46,400		
drawings	14,400			
Purchases	181,000		28,500	
Goods sent to branch		67,860		
Goods from head office			76,500	
Sales		120,000		106,000
Expenses	21,600		16,800	
Debtors/creditors	19,400	17,900	10,800	3,400
Current account				
Head office				18,600
Branch	19,860			
Balance at bank	5,800		1,400	
	£262,160	262,160	134,000	134,000

Notes:

(a) Foods returned to head office by the branch in March 19X1, originally invoiced by head office for £1,360 were not received by, or entered in the accounts of head office, until April 19X1.

(b) The stocktaking at the Stanley Park branch on 31 March 19X1 of goods received from head office disclosed:

(i)   Shortage of goods worth £400 (selling prices).

(ii) Damaged goods of a selling value of £1,800 which had to be written down for stock purposes to £600. Head office agreed to allow Stanley Park a credit of £730 against these goods.

(c) Apart from (a) and (b) all stocks on 31 March 19X1 were to be valued at cost. For the purposes only of the separate branch trading account, cost of goods originating from the head office is to be at the price charged by head office.

(d) Stanley Park's stock on 31 March 19X1 of goods purchased from other suppliers was £4,000 (at cost).

(e) Head office purchases include an item of £1,500 charged in error to head office by outside suppliers for goods obtained by Stanley Park.

(f) The branch sales for the year of £106,000 include £80,000 in respect of goods received from head office.

You are required to prepare for the head office, branch and entire business:

(a) Trading and profit and loss acounts for the year ended 31 March 19X1.

(b) Balance sheets at 31 March 19X1.

12 Other specialized transactions

This chapter considers several accounting problems that need special techniques to record the transactions involved. These are:

(*a*)   Hire purchase/credit sale/leasing
(*b*)   Bills of exchange
(*c*)   Royalties
(*d*)   Containers
(*e*)   Joint ventures

Hire purchase

There are three basic types of instalment credit transactions:

(*a*)   Hire purchase (HP) – under this system the buyer agrees to pay for the goods by an agreed number of instalments over a specified period of time. The legal title to the goods remains with the seller until the purchaser has made all the payments and has exercised his option to purchase, usually by payment of a nominal sum to the seller. Should the purchaser default on payment the seller has the right, subject to certain statutory limitations, to repossess the goods.

(*b*)   Credit sale – the purchase price is satisfied by instalments but the legal title to the goods passes to the purchaser on delivery. Thus the seller cannot repossess the goods, the remedy is to sue for the outstanding debt.

(*c*)   Leasing – under this type of agreement the user has the right to the use of the goods, but the legal title remains with the suppliers. On completion of the contract the goods are returned to the supplier (although purchase options may be included in the lease agreement).

Hire purchase – general principles

When goods are sold on HP terms the HP selling price will normally be more than the cash selling price. The difference in the prices is intended to compensate the seller for waiting for the full amount of the cash, for the risk of default, and for the extra administration costs. The price difference is usually described as HP interest.

Example 12.1
A typewriter with a cash price of £400 is sold at an HP price of £480, payable by twenty-four equal monthly instalments calculated as follows:

	£
Cash price	400
HP interest	80
HP price	480
Therefore each instalment equals	20

Hire purchase accounting – the buyer's books

Since the legal title to the goods purchased on HP remains with the seller until the final payment has been made, it could be argued that the goods should not be included as fixed assets (as most HP purchases are of that asset type) in the purchaser's balance sheet until that final payment is made. However, under the provision of SSAP21 the accounting concept of 'substance over form' is usually applied and such assets are normally included in the purchaser's balance sheet. The asset is recorded in the balance sheet at the *cash price*, the HP interest (which represents a financing charge) being charged as an expense in the profit and loss account.

Thus, if on 1 January 19X1 a company purchased an asset with a cash price of £100 and paid for it by six instalments of £20 then:

(a) The asset would be shown in the balance sheet at its cash price of £100.
(b) The profit and loss account would be charged with the full amount of the HP interest of £20 (i.e. 6 × £20 − £100), assuming that the company's year end was 31 December.

In the above illustration the transaction was started and completed in the same accounting period and the whole of the interest charge (£20) is a legitimate expense of that period. However, where a transaction encompasses two or more accounting periods the total interest charge must be apportioned between those accounting years.

In order to do this accurately the *'true' rate* of interest (or actuarial rate) must be known. This is the interest rate which when applied to the amount outstanding will, after the last payment has been made, reduce the amount outstanding to nil.

Example 12.2   (Showing accounting entries when the 'true' rate of interest is known)
A Limited purchased a motor vehicle from B Limited on 1 January 19X1. The HP price was £15,000 to be paid for by three equal instalments of £5,000 commencing 31 December 19X1. The cash price was £10,531 and the true rate of interest 20 per cent. The vehicle is to be written off over three years using the straight line method of depreciation.

Machinery account

1 January 19X1 B Ltd	10,531

B Ltd account

	£		£
31 December 19X1 Bank	5,000	1 January 19X1	
		Machinery	10,531
31 December 19X1		31 December 19X1	
Balance c/d	7,637	Interest (20%)	2,106
	12,637		12,637
31 December 19X2 Bank	5,000	1 January 19X2	
		Balance b/d	7,637
31 December 19X2		31 December 19X2	
Balance c/d	4,164	Interest (20%)	1,527
	9,164		9,164
31 December 19X3 Bank	5,000	1 December 19X3	
		Balance b/d	4,164
		31 December 19X3	
		Interest	836
	5,000		5,000

HP interest account

	£		£
31 December 19X1 B Ltd		31 December 19X1	
	2,106	Profit and loss account	2,106
31 December 19X2 B Ltd		31 December 19X2	
	1,527	Profit and loss account	1,527
31 December 19X3 B Ltd		31 December 19X3	
	836	Profit and loss account	836

Provision for depreciation account

	31 December 19X1	
	Profit and loss account	3,510
	31 December 19X2	
	Profit and loss account	3,510
	31 December 19X3	
	Profit and loss account	3,511

Note that the rate of interest is applied to the balance outstanding on B Limited account at the beginning of each year. The interest amounts have been rounded off each year, as have the depreciation charges.

The interest charge can also be written off to the profit and loss account in equal amounts over the term of the agreement, or the sum of digits method may be used. Using the example above the interest charge would be:

Year	Equal £	Sum of digits £		True rate (above) £
1	1,489	3/6	2,234	2,106
2	1,490	2/6	1,490	1,527
3	1,490	1/6	745	836
	4,469		4,469	4,469

Note that the sum of digits method and the true (actuarial) rate rate of interest 'front load' the interest charges and therefore reflect the fact that the amount of finance being provided by the seller reduces as the instalments are paid. Thus the amount of interest in each payment becomes smaller and the capital repayment larger. Note also that these methods are acceptable under SSAP21, but that the straight line method is not recommended.

Thus in the final accounts at year end the following will be shown:

Profit and loss account:
(a) The interest charge relating to the year.
(b) The depreciation charge relating to the asset.

Balance sheet:
(a) The asset will be shown at cost less depreciation in the usual way. The balance sheet should distinguish between assets owned and those held under hire purchase agreements.
(b) The liability to the seller (excluding any future interest charges) will be shown as a current (or deferred) liability as appropriate.

Hire purchase accounting – the seller's books

When goods are sold on HP terms the seller earns two 'profits' (a) the normal trading profit, and (b) the finance charge levied. If for example a trader purchases TV sets at a cost of £100, and his normal cash price is £150 then his trading profit is £50. But if the HP sales price is £175 his financing charge (profit) is a further £25. The treatment of these two profits must be considered separately.

(a) *Normal trading profit* – this can be:
    (i) Treated as a profit entirely in the period during which the goods are first sold.
    (ii) The profit can be apportioned over the total period of the agreement in the proportion that the cash received during a particular accounting period bears to the total cash receivable (i.e. the hire purchase price).

    SSAP21 recommends that the whole of profit be credited to the profit and loss account in the year of sale.

(b)   *Interest/finance charge* – the same apportionment problems apply here as in the buyer's books. Thus the true (actuarial) interest rate, the sum of digits method or the straight line method can be used as a basis to apportion the interest charge to the credit of the profit and loss account, though SSAP21 recommends the use of the first two methods only.

Example 12.3   (details as for Example 12.2)
A Limited purchased a motor vehicle from B Limited on 1 January 19X1. The HP price was £15,000 to be paid for by three equal instalments of £5,000 commencing 31 December 19X1. The cash price was £10,531 and the true rate of interest 20 per cent. The cost of the vehicle was £8,000. Assuming that B Limited:

(a)   Takes credit for the whole of the trading profit in the year of sale.
(b)   Uses the true (actuarial) rate of interest to apportion the finance charge,

the accounts of B Limited will appear as follows:

HP sales

	£		£
		19X1 HP debtors	
19X1 Profit and loss	10,531	(cash price)	10,531

HP debtors (A Ltd)

	£		£
19X1 HP Sales	10,531	19X1 Bank	5,000
P&L – interest	2,106	Balance	7,637
	12,637		12,637
19X2 Balance	7,637	19X2 Bank	5,000
P&L – interest	1,527	Balance	4,164
	9,164		9,164
19X3 Balance	4,164	19X3 Bank	5,000
P&L – interest	836		
	5,000		5,000

Profit and loss (extract) 19X1

	£		£
Cost of sales	8,000	Sales	10,531
Gross profit	2,531		
	10,531		10,531
		Gross profit	2,531
		HP interest	2,106

In relation to the above example note that:

(a)   The 'normal' gross profit of £2,531 is taken credit for in the year of sale.
(b)   The interest is apportioned to the profit and loss account on the actuarial method.

(c) The balance on the HP debtors account will appear as follows in the balance sheet:
  (i) Current asset – payments due within the next twelve months (less finance charges)
  (ii) Fixed asset – payment due in the following periods (less the finance charges).

Credit sale

The accounting treatment for credit sale agreements is the same as for hire purchase agreements, and will not, therefore, be further discussed.

Leasing

SSAP21 distinguishes between finance leases and operating leases. The definitions are:

(a) Finance lease: a lease that transfers substantially all the risks and rewards to ownership of an asset to the lessee. Conditions to be satisfied for finance leases are:
  (i) The lease term is for the major part (normally 75 per cent or more) of the useful economic life of the asset.
  (ii) The present value of the minimum lease payments amount to substantially all (normally 90 per cent or more) of the fair value of the leased asset to the lessor at the start of the lease.
(b) Operating lease: a lease other than a finance lease (this chapter is not concerned with operating leases).

Finance leases

A finance lease is very similar to an HP agreement, the major difference being that at the end of the lease period the asset being leased is returned to the lessor, although the lease may contain an option to purchase.
  In the books of the lessee the accounting treatment is as follows:

(a) Balance sheet:
  (i) The finance lease is recorded as an asset and also as a liability to pay future rentals.
  (ii) The asset is depreciated over the shorter of the lease term or its useful life.
(b) Profit and loss account: – the finance charge (or interest charge) included in the rentals paid is apportioned to the profit and loss account using the true (actuarial) basis or the sum of digits method (as in hire purchase).

Example 12.4   (Details as for Example 12.2)
A Limited leases a motor vehicle from B Limited. The lease period
commences at 1 January 19X1. The annual lease payments are £5,000
for three years commencing on 31 December 19X1. The cash price of the
vehicle is £10,531. The true rate of interest charged is 20 per cent.

Leased asset
£
1 January 19X1   B Ltd.   10,531

B Ltd (leasing creditor)

	£		£
31 December 19X1 Bank	5,000	1 January 19X1	
		Leased asset	10,531
31 December 19X1 Balance		31 December 19X1 Balance	
	7,637	P&L (interest)	2,106
	12,637		12,637
31 December 19X2 Bank	5,000	1 January 19X2 Balance	7,637
31 December 19X2		31 December 19X2	
Balance	4,164	P&L (interest)	1,527
	9,164		9,164
31 December 19X3 Bank	5,000	1 January 19X3 Balance	4,164
		31 December 19X3	
		P&L (interest)	836
	5,000		5,000

Provision for depreciation

	£
31 December 19X1	
Profit and loss	3,510
31 December 19X2	
Profit and loss	3,510
31 December 19X3	
Profit and loss	3,511

Profit and loss

	£
31 December 19X1	
Interest	2,106
Depreciation	3,510
31 December 19X2	
Interest	1,517
Depreciation	3,510
31 December 19X3	
Interest	836
Depreciation	3,511

Note that the accounting entries above are similar to those relating to hire purchase shown above.

In the balance sheet the asset would be shown at cost less depreciation under the heading of leased assets, whilst the the balance account of B Limited would be shown as a liability under the heading of 'Obligations under finance leases' (effectively a creditor).

In the *books of the lessor* the accounting entries are similar to those of a hire purchase seller. Thus Example 12.4 above serves also as the illustration of the accounting entries required in the books of the lessor in relation to finance leases. In the final accounts the following would appear:

Profit and loss account: gross profit (where the lessor is also the dealer)
interest charge relating to the period

Balance sheet: current asset; net investment in finance leases (being the lease payments, less the interest charge, due within the next twelve months)
fixed asset; net investment in finance lease (being lease payments less interest charges receivable in more than twelve months time)

Bills of exchange

When goods are sold on credit the seller is normally paid sometime later by the purchaser through the medium of a cheque. However, particularly with foreign trading, it is not uncommon for a bill of exchange to be used as the medium of exchange. A bill of exchange operates as follows:

(a)   The seller 'draws' a bill of exchange (a legal document) on the buyer who signifies 'acceptance' of the bill by signing it, and returning it to the seller.
(b)   The seller (or drawer) can then:
(i)   Wait until the bill matures and then present it to the buyer (drawee) for acceptance.
or   (ii)   Discount the bill before maturity with a bank. The bank will then hold the bill until maturity, meanwhile making a charge to the seller (drawer) for the service it provides (the discounting charge).
or   (iii)   Negotiate (transfer) the bill to a third party in satisfaction of a debt, who can then further negotiate if desired. The person holding the bill at maturity (i.e. the date the bill becomes payable) will present it to the drawee for payment.

To the person holding the bill it is known as a bill receivable, to the drawee a bill payable.

Drawer's books

Example 12.5
A draws a bill of exchange on B (who accepts it) on 1 January 19X3 for
£1,000 in respect of goods sold. The date of maturity is 31 March 19X3.

(*a*)   Assume A holds the bill until maturity when B pays.

B account

1 January Sales	1,000	1 January Bills receivable	1,000

Bills receivable

1 January B	1,000	31 March Bank	1,000

(*b*)   Assume A negotiates the bill to X on 27 January 19X3.

B account

1 January Sales	1,000	1 January Bills receivable	1,000

Bills receivable account

1 January B	1,000	27 January X	1,000

(*c*)   Assume A discounts the bill with Z bank on 28 February 19X3, the
discounting charge being £18.

B account

1 January Sales	1,000	1 January Bills receivable	1,000

Bills receivable account

1 January B	1,000	28 February Bank	1,000

Bank

28 February Bills receivable	1,000	28 February Discounting charges	18

Discounting charges account

28 February Bank	18

Drawee's books

In each of the three situations above the drawee's position (or strictly
speaking the acceptor's after he has accepted the bill by signing it) is
the same, i.e. he has accepted the bill and he has paid it.

A account

1 January Bills payable	1,000	1 January Purchases	1,000

Bills payable account

31 March Bank	1,000	1 January A	1,000

Royalties

A royalty is a payment made in exchange for the use of an asset owned
by another party, the amount of the payment being determined by the

use made of that asset. Such payments are frequently encountered in the extraction of minerals from the ground, where the owner of the mineral rights (called the landlord) may allow another person (called the lessee) to extract the minerals, the amount of the payment being based on the amount of the mineral extracted, e.g. £1 per tonne. Similarly, the publisher of a book may make royalty payments to the author based upon the number of books sold.

The contract entered into by the landlord and the lessee will normally contain details concerning the following:

(a) The amount of the royalty payment – this will normally be based upon the use made of the asset by the lessee, e.g. £10 per ton of mineral extracted, £1 per book sold.
(b) Minimum rental – the landlord may insist on a minimum rental being paid each year. This obviously protects his interests should the lessee's use of the asset fall below an acceptable level.
(c) Short workings – where a minimum rental clause is contained in the agreement, the lessee is frequently given the right to offset short workings payments against excess payments in future years. This right may be restricted to a specific number of future years. After this period the short workings are no longer recoverable.

Thus the following accounts are required to deal with royalty transactions:

(a) Royalties payable/receivable – this account records the royalties payable/receivable during the accounting period.
(b) Landlord/lessee – these are personal accounts and record the indebtedness and payments made between the landlord and lessee.
(c) Shortworkings – this account records the amount of any shortworkings recoverable, recovered and written off.

Example 12.6
The lessee of a gravel pit is to pay a royalty of £1 per tonne of gravel extracted. The minimum rent is £1,000 per annum. Short workings can be recovered in the two years following that in which they arose. The extraction rates are as follows:

19X1   800 tonnes
19X2 1,050 tonnes
19X3 1,100 tonnes
19X4 1,200 tonnes

Show the ledger accounts in the books of the lessee. When answering royalty questions it is suggested that a tabulation similar to Table 12.1 should first be prepared.

Table 12.1

Year	Tonnes extracted (a)	Payable (b) £	Minimun rent (c) £	Short working recoverable (d) £	Recovered (e) £	Irrecoverable (f) £
1	800	800	1,000	200		
2	1,050	1,050	1,000		50	
3	1,100	1,100	1,000		100	50
4	1,200	1,200	1,000			

Column (b) shows the amount payable based upon the quantity extracted.
Column (c) shows the minimum rent payment for each year.
Column (d) shows the amount of short working (i.e. the minimum rent less the royalty payable).
Column (e) shows the amount of short workings recovered in the year. In this case £50 in year 2 and £100 in year 3 as this is the amount by which the royalty payable exceeds the minimum rent.
Column (f) shows the amount of short workings not recovered at the end of the recoverable period, and which must therefore be treated as irrecoverable and written off.

Lessee's books

Royalties

		£			£
19X1	Landlord	800	19X1	Profit and loss	800
19X2	Landlord	1,050	19X2	Profit and loss	1,050
19X3	Landlord	1,100	19X3	Profit and loss	1,100
19X4	Landlord	1,200	19X4	Profit and loss	1,200

Short workings

		£			£
19X1	Landlord	200	19X2	Landlord	50
				Balance	150
		200			200
19X3	Balance	150	19X3	Landlord	100
				Profit and loss	50
		150			150

Landlord

		£			£
19X1	Bank	1,000	19X1	Royalties	800
				Short workings	200
		1,000			1,000

	£			£
19X2 Short workings (recovered)	50	19X2	Royalties	1,050
Bank	1,000			
	1,050			1,050
19X3 Short workings (recovered)	100	19X3	Royalties	1,100
Bank	1,000			
	1,100			1,100
19X4 Bank	1,200	19X4	Royalties	1,200

Profit and loss account (extract)

		£
19X1	Royalties	800
19X2	Royalties	1,050
19X3	Royalties	1,100
	Short workings	50
19X4	Royalties	1,200

Notes:
(*i*) The balance on the short workings account at the end of 19X2 is similar to a pre-payment and would be treated as a current asset in the balance sheet at the end of 19X2.
(*ii*) In the ledger of the landlord the accounts would simply be reversed (see below)

Sub-leases

The lessee may have the right to sub-let the lease of a quarry, mine, etc. The terms of the sub lease will normally contain provisions relating to minimum rent and short workings in the same way as the main lease.

In this situation the landlord will normally receive royalties based on the *total* quantity of minerals extracted, while the lessee will receive royalty payments from the sub-lease. Thus the lessee will effectively act as landlord to the sub-lessee, and at the same time will have to account to his landlord for the total quantity extracted by himself and the sub-lessee.

Example 12.7
A Ltd was granted by B Ltd a right to extract sand and gravel at a royalty of £1 per tonne. The minimum rent was fixed at £5,000 per annum with A Ltd having the right to recoup short workings in the two years following that in which they arose.

A Ltd granted a sub-lease to X Ltd to extract gravel at a royalty of £1.50 per tonne. The minimum rent was fixed at £3,000 per annum, and short workings are recoverable in the two years following that in which they arose.

Extraction rates were as follows:

	A Ltd	B Ltd
19X1	1000 tonnes	1600 tonnes
19X2	2200 tonnes	1300 tonnes
19X3	3000 tonnes	2800 tonnes
19X4	3200 tonnes	2900 tonnes
19X5	3300 tonnes	2700 tonnes

The accounts in the books of A Ltd would be as follows:

Royalties payable by A Ltd

Year	Tonnes Extracted A Ltd	B Ltd	Royalties payable £	Minimum rent £	Short workings Recovered £	Recovered £	Irrecoverable £
19X1	1000	1600	2,600	5,000	2,400		
19X2	2200	1300	3,500	5,000	1,500		
19X3	3000	2800	5,800	5,000		800	1,600
19X4	3200	2900	6,100	5,000		1,100	
19X5	3300	2700	6,000	5,000		400	

Royalties receivable by A Ltd

Year	A Ltd	B Ltd	Royalties payable £	Minimum rent £	Short workings Recovered £	Recovered £	Irrecoverable £
19X1	–	1,600	2,400	3,000	600		
19X2	–	1,300	1,950	3,000	1,050		
19X3	–	2,800	4,200	3,000		1,200	
19X4	–	2,900	4,350	3,000		450	
19X5	–	2,700	4,050	3,000			

Royalties payable

19X1	Landlord	2,600		19X1	Profit and loss	2,600
19X2	Landlord	3,500		19X2	Profit and loss	3,500
19X3	Landlord	5,800		19X3	Profit and loss	5,800
19X4	Landlord	6,100		19X4	Profit and loss	6,100
19X5	Landlord	6,000		19X5	Profit and loss	6,000

Short workings (main lease)

		£			£
19X1	Landlord	2,400	19X3	Landlord	800
19X2	Landlord	1,500	19X3	Profit and loss	1,600
				Balance	1,500
		3,900			3,900
	Balance	1,500	19X4	Landlord	1,100
			19X5	Landlord	400
		1,500			1,500

Landlord (B Ltd)

		£			£
19X1	Bank	5,000	19X1	Royalties	2,600
				Short workings	2,400
		5,000			5,000

		£			
19X2	Bank	5,000	19X2	Royalties	3,500
				Short workings	1,500
		5,000			5,000
19X3	Short workings	800	19X3	Royalties	5,800
	Bank	5,000			
		5,800			5,800
19X4	Short workings	1,100	19X4	Royalties	6,100
	Bank	5,000			
		6,100			6,100
19X5	Short workings	400	19X5	Royalties	6,000
	Bank	5,600			
		6,000			6,000

Royalties receivable

		£			£
19X1	Profit and loss	2,400	19X1	Lessee	2,400
19X2	Profit and loss	1,950	19X2	Lessee	1,950
19X3	Profit and loss	4,200	19X3	Lessee	4,200
19X4	Profit and loss	4,350	19X4	Lessee	4,350
19X5	Profit and loss	4,050	19X5	Lessee	4,050

Short workings (sub-lease)

		£			£
19X3	Lessee	1,200	19X1	Lessee	600
19X4	Lessee	450	19X2	Lessee	1,050
		1,650			1,650

Lessee (X Ltd)

		£			£
19X1	Royalties receivable	2,400	19X1	Bank	3,000
	Short workings	600			
		3,000			3,000
19X2	Royalties receivable	1,950	19X2	Bank	3,000
	Short workings	1,050			
		3,000			3,000
19X3	Royalties receivable	4,200	19X3	Short workings	1,200
				Bank	3,000
		4,200			4,200
19X4	Royalties receivable	4,350	19X4	Short workings	450
				Bank	3,900
		4,350			4,350
19X5	Lessee	4,050	19X5	Bank	4,050

Containers

Goods may be despatched to customers in containers on which a deposit is charged, the customer being credited with the deposit on return of the container. Thus it is necessary to record the movement of containers to and from customers, and also the stock of containers at a given time.

Example 12.8
A Ltd delivers its goods to customers in containers. A deposit is charged to customers on delivery which is refunded on return of the container.
   During the year ended 31 December 19X1 the following transactions took place.

(a)   100 containers were purchased for £80 each.
(b)   322 containers were sent to customers who were charged a deposit of £100 on each container.
(c)   260 containers were returned by customers who were credited with £100 in respect of each container retained.
(d)   Three containers were damaged and sold for £10 each.
(e)   Twelve containers were retained by customers who forfeited their deposit.
(f)   On 31 December 19X1 there were fifty returnable crates with customers and thirty-five crates in stock at A Ltd warehouse.

The stock of cases at the end of Decembr 19X1 are to be valued at £60 each.

Containers stock

	Rate £	Qty	Value £		Rate £	Qty	Value £
Bank (purchases)	80	100	8,000	Containers suspense – kept by customers	100	12	1,200
				Bank – damaged containers	10	3	30
				P & L – cost of containers used			1,670
				Stock – with customers	60	50	3,000
				– on hand	60	35	2,100
		100	8,000			100	8,000

	Rate		Qty	Value
Stock – with customers	60		50	3,000
– on hand	60		35	2,100

Containers suspense

	Rate £	Qty	Value £		Rate £	Qty	Value £
Debtors – containers returned	100	260	26,000	Debtors – containers charged out	100	322	32,200
Containers stock – kept by customers	100	12	1,200				
Stock (deposits on cases returnable)	100	50	5,000				
		322	32,200			322	32,200
				Stock	100	50	5,000

Note:

(a) The transfer to the profit and loss account is the balancing figure on the containers stock account.

(b) In the balance sheet at the end of December 19X1 the stock of crates valued at £5,100 would appear as a current asset; the balance on the containers suspense accounts which represents deposits still returnable would appear as a current liability.

Where the customer is credited with cases returned at a price lower than the original charge the difference represents a hiring charge. Taking the above illustration, and assuming that cases returned are credited at £80 the accounts will appear as follows.

Containers suspense

	Rate £	Qty	Value £		Rate £	Qty	Value £
Debtors – containers returned	80	260	20,800	Debtors – customers charged out	100	322	32,200
Containers stock – kept by customers	80	12	960				
Containers stock – hiring charge			6,440				
Stock (deposits on cases returnable)	80	50	4,000				
		322	32,200			322	32,200
				Stock	80	50	4,000

Containers stock

	Rate £	Qty	Value £		Rate £	Qty	Value £
Bank	80	100	8,000	Containers suspense – kept by customers	80	12	960
				Bank	10	3	30
Profit and loss – profit on container usage			4,530	Containers suspense – hiring charge			6,440
				Stock – with customers	60	50	3,000
				– on hand	60	35	2,100
		100	12,530			100	12,530
Stock – with customers	60	50	3,000				
– on hand	60	35	2,100				

Joint ventures

Joint ventures are business ventures entered into by two or more persons together. It is important to note that the individuals are not partners since their joining together is normally for one business venture only. Consequently, no separate books of account are opened, instead the venturers merely record in their own books (in a joint venture account) details of the transactions with which they have been concerned. On completion of the venture a *memorandum* joint venture account is opened to calculate the profit or loss on the venture. Cash is then transferred between the venturers as a final settlement.

Example 12.9
Jones and Smith agree to enter into a joint venture to grow and sell flowers. The following transactions took place:

19X1

January 1	Jones purchased seed, compost and plant pots costing £250.
February 9	Jones paid heating costs of £180.
March 12	Jones paid £100 for casual labour.
April 13	Smith paid £25 for transport expenses.
April 20	Smith paid £10 for hire of market stall.
May 19	Smith sold plants for £655.
May 25	Jones sold plants for £90.

On 31 May the joint venture ended and settlement was made between the partners.

Show the joint venture accounts in the books of Jones and of Smith, and the joint venture memorandum account. The venturers agree to share profits equally.

Jones' books

Joint venture with Smith

19X1	£	19X1	£
January 1 Bank – purchase of seeds etc.	250	May 25　Bank – sales	90
February 1 Bank – heating costs	180	May 31 Bank – received from Smith	530
March 12 Bank – casual labour	100		
May 31 P&L – share of profit	90		
	620		620

Smith's books

Joint venture with Jones

19X1	£	19X1	£
April 13 Bank – transport	25	May 19 Bank – sales	655
April 20 Bank – market stall	10		
May 31 P&L – share of profit	90		
May 31 Bank – payment to Jones	530		
	655		655

Memorandum joint venture

	£		£
Expenses – seeds	250	Sales	90
heating	180	Sales	655
labour	100		
transport	25		
market stall	10		
Profit – Jones	90		
Smith	90		
	745		745

Note carefully the entry of the profit in the respective joint venture accounts and also the transfer of cash between the venturers to balance the accounts and effect final settlement.

It should be noted that goods transferred between venturers would not be recorded unless they were taken over at the end of the venture. In such a case, the value of goods taken over would be credited to the joint venture account of the venturer taking over stock, with a corresponding debit to purchases.

Questions

1   Hallows plc sells photocopiers to small companies. Hallows buys the photocopiers from the manufacturers for £750 each and adds in a standard profit mark up of 33.1/3% to arrive at a basic selling price. This price is charged on cash sales. Hallows also sells photocopiers on credit and by hire purchase. A standard credit agreement is used by the company. This agreement involves a deposit of £165 followed by twelve monthly payments of £90 beginning the month after delivery of goods. The hire purchase agreement used by Hallows also requires a deposit of £165 and payments of £50 per month for twenty-four months, the first payment beginning the month after delivery of goods. Recently, Hallows has also begun to lease photocopiers. Its lease requires a monthly rental of £30 for five years, with the first three months rentals payable in advance. The photocopiers have an economic life of five years with no residual value. Hallows engaged in the following transactions over the last three months:

Month	Number of photocopiers purchased	Number of photocopiers dispatched			
		Cash	Credit	Hire purchase	Lease
January	100	40	20	20	10
February	130	30	24	52	20
March	140	28	40	56	24

You are required to show how the above transactions should be recorded in Hallows accounts at 31 March.

2   Washbrook Ltd is a finance company which arranges hire purchase finance for industrial washing machines. The company calculates its finance charge as a flat annual percentage. The precise rate depends upon the type of washing machine involved. Washbrook uses HP agreements for either twelve or twenty-four months duration. All its HP agreements involve equal monthly instalment payments. The value of these instalments is calculated as follows: the customer's deposit is deducted from the cost of the washing machine purchased; the finance charge is calculated by applying the flat annual percentage rate to the balance of cost; the charge is added to the balance of cost and the total is liquidated by equal monthly instalments. The total finance charges contained in the last three years' volume of hire purchase transactions is given below:

Year ended	12 months term £	24 months term £
31 December 19X5	249,600	882,200
31 December 19X6	323,856	1,046,400
31 December 19X7	360,672	1,084,800

It is to be assumed that all HP agreements are entered into on 1 May in each year and finance charges are to be taken into account as they are earned and are based upon the date of inception of the agreements on 1 May.

You are required to set out the appropriate hire charges accounts in the accounting records of Washbrook for the three years ended on 21 December 19X7.

3 Busby Ltd holds the mineral rights on a deposit on lease from Edwards Ltd. Under the terms of the lease Busby Ltd pays a royalty of 60p per ton of mineral sold, merging with a minimum rent of £4,800 per year. Busby Ltd has granted a sub-lease of the rights to Atkinson and this provides for royalty of 90p per ton of mineral extracted, merging with a minimum rent of £1,400 per year. Both the head lease and sub-lease provide that, should the royalties for any calendar year be less than the specified minimum the deficiency may be recouped out of royalties, in excess of the minimum, for either of the two next following calendar years.

In addition the following information is relevant:

	Busby Ltd		*Atkinson Ltd*	
		Stock at		*Stock at*
	Sales	*31 December*	*Sales*	*31 December*
	tons	*tons*	*tons*	*tons*
19X5	5,600	800	2,200	700
19X6	7,200	900	2,750	250
19X7	6,500	500	3,400	650

Settlement of the royalties due is made annually on 31 December.

You are required to record the above transactions in the books of Busby Ltd for each of the years 19X5, 19X6 and 19X7 closing the accounts at 31 December each year. (You may ignore taxation.)

4 O'Farrell Ltd manufactures a standard product which is distributed to the hotel trade in uniform packing. The product is charged to customers at cost plus 150 per cent. If the packing is returned, full credit is given to the customer and any packing in the hands of customers at the year end is valued at cost less 20 per cent.

You are required to show in ledger account form how the following information would appear in the books of O'Farrell and discuss the balance sheet presentation of the balances remaining at the end of the year:

	£
Stock of cases, 1 January, 19X4	25,800
Cases in hands of customers at	
1 January 19X4	42,000
Cases charged to customers	157,000
Materials used	1,900
Wages for manufacturing and repairing	
cases	7,800

	£
Cases returned by customers	163,000
Cases paid for by customers	7,000
Stock of cases in factory	
31 December, 19X4	14,000

5   Law and Best entered into a joint venture to buy and sell a quantity of crockery. It was agreed that Law should receive a commission of 2.1/2 per cent on all sales in return for which he was to bear all losses from bad debts. Subject to this arrangement profits and losses were to be shared equally.

On 12 February 19X1 Law purchased goods for 13,600 for which he paid £9,600 in cash, and accepted bills of exchange for £1,600 and £2,400.

On 13 February, Law dispatched goods to Best which had cost £5,500, and Best paid £7,700 to Law.

On 19 February Law sold goods to Charlton for £840 and to Pereira for £500 and he accepted bills of exchange for the amounts respectively due from them. Law endorsed both these bills over to Best, who discounted them.

On 13 March Law sold goods for £3,600. On delivery the customer rejected goods invoiced at £180 and these goods were collected by Best, who sold them to another customer for £220.

On 21 March Charlton met his bill, but Pereira's bill was dishonoured. Pereira was insolvent with no assets.

On 15 April, Best paid the bill for £1,600 which had been accepted by Law and Law paid the second bill, £2,400.

During April 19X1 Law sold the remainder of the crockery in his possession for £5,820 and Best's sales amounted to £6,800. Bad debts (apart from the amount due from Pereira) were £84, of which £60 was in respect of sales by Law, and £24 in respect of sales by Best.

On 30 May 19X1 the venture was closed. Best took over the stock in his possession at a valuation of £1,000, and the sum required to settle accounts between the venturers was paid by the party accountable.

You are required to prepare:

(*a*)   The accounts which would appear in the books of Law and Best to record the joint venture.
(*b*)   A memorandum joint venture account showing the net profit.

(You may ignore charges for discounting bills of exchange.)

6   On 1 January 19X1 Crerand Ltd, sent goods costing £4,800 on consignment to GOT Ltd in Scotland. Crerand Ltd paid freight of £184 and insurance of £152 on the goods. A bill drawn by Crerand on GOT payable in three months time for £2,400 was discounted by Crerand Ltd for £2,364.

On 31 March 19X1 Crerand Ltd received an account of sales from

GOT showing sales £6,020, commission £180 and expenses £74. Stock remaining unsold in the hands of GOT was £820 at original cost.

GOT Ltd settled the balance due for goods by means of a two-month bill. Crerand Ltd discounted the bill with its bank, which deducted £34 from its face value for charges.

You are required to show the ledger accounts (excluding cash) recording the above transactions in the books of Crerand Ltd and GOT Ltd.

13 Analysis of accounting statements

In other chapters we have discussed in detail the preparation of published financial statements. In particular we have set out the detailed reporting requirements of company law and accounting standards and have examined financial reporting by organizations in the public sector. In so doing we have concentrated upon the supply of accounting reports. As we saw in Chapter 1, there is another very important aspect to financial reporting – the users of financial statements and the uses to which they put the information contained in those statements. The influence of users has already been apparent in what we have said about the preparation of financial statements, whether as a general concern, or more specifically in the emphasis placed upon reporting to the owners of a business in company law and in the emphasis on comparability between companies in accounting standards. Here we consider in detail how users of financial statements may interpret the data provided by those statements.

Financial statements may be used by a number of different groups of users. These groups include shareholders, investment analysts, creditors, suppliers of resources, competitors, employees, customers, government and its agencies, and the general public. Table 13.1 shows some of the decisions which different groups of users may need to make.

Not all these groups will necessarily be interested in every organization's financial statements since, for example, nationalized industries do not have shareholders nor would creditors of nationalized industries be particularly concerned with assessing bankruptcy risk. However, groups do need to make assessments of, and decisions about, all organizations and a key source of data for those decisions is the organization's financial statements.

In this chapter we concentrate upon financial decisions rather than those of a broader economic or social character, although information on such matters is readily available in accounting reports, either be-

Table 13.1

User group	Decisions
Shareholders	Share purchase or sale decisions; takeovers and mergers; assessing management performance.
Investment analysts	Analysis for advising clients on share purchase or sale decisions, takeovers and mergers; assessing management performance.
Creditors and other suppliers	Credit granting decisions: bankruptcy risk assessments; terms for credit.
Competitors	Assessment of financial performance for competitive advantage.
Employees	Collective bargaining decisions: wages and conditions; security of employment.
Customers	Continuity of supply; assessment of economic and financial performance
Government and its agencies	Taxation and subsidy policy; regulatory policy; employment and macroeconomic policy; environmental impact; financial performance.
Public	Social responsibility, environmental impact.

cause of statutory disclosure requirements or voluntary disclosures. The method which we shall use is financial. This involves the calculation of key ratios from combinations of items from ratio analysis and the financial statements. Another very important source of information for decisions is the analysis of cash flow and funds flow. This was discussed in Chapter 7.

Financial ratio analysis

The purpose of financial ratio analysis is the derivation of relative rather than absolute measures. In order to assess performance it is necessary to have a basis of assessment. For example, it may be superficially impressive to learn that a company's annual profit was £100,000. However, in terms of *performance* that figure is put into a very different perspective when related to capital employed or turnover. If the former is £50 million and the latter £80 million, the company is not doing very well. Thus, financial ratio analysis involves comparisons of items from different financial statements (profit and capital employed) and comparisons of items within the same statement (profit and turn-over). Thus other types of comparison are regularly made in financial ratio analysis. One is comparison through time: comparing ratios derived from an organization's financial statements for different accounting periods. This type of comparison is essential if trends or changes are sought. The other is the comparison of specific financial ratios for one organization with those of other, similar organizations, or with ratios which represent group averages or norms. Variables such as financial structure will have an important bearing on the comparability of organizations. Industry or group norms or averages are very important for comparability. Comparison of a company's rate of return of capital employed with the average for the industry in which it operates will indicate something of its performance relative to all its peers.

All these comparisons need to be made with caution. There are several problems which may be encountered. One is the frequent use of absolute standards for making comparisons. For example, many textbooks state that firms should aim for a ratio of current assets to current liabilities of 2:1. It is dangerous to assume that there are hard and fast absolute norms such as this. The process of deciding whether ratios are satisfactory or not depends on many circumstances which involve judgement. A second problem concerns extraneous factors which may invalidate comparisons if not taken into account. If comparisons of ratios are made through time it is important to identify (and if possible correct for) any changes which have taken place in the environment in which an organization operates, or in the accounting policies which it adopts. If the inflation rate has doubled, or if a government has introduced legal restraints on dividend payments by companies, accounting data will not be comparable. Likewise, if a company has altered its accounting treatment of important items such as stock valuation or leases, comparisons will be invalid unless the items are adjusted to a common base. The same problem exists for inter-firm comparisons. If companies adopt different accounting policies comparisons are difficult. The accounting standards programme aims to ease this difficulty by standardizing accounting methods or, through SSAP2, ensuring that sufficient information is disclosed to enable users to identify material differences in accounting treatment.

Types of ratios

A great many financial ratios can be calculated from a typical set of financial statements. It is convenient to organize these ratios under headings as follows:

(a)   *Liquidity ratios*, concerned with an organization's present financial position, that is its ability to meet its current financial obligations.

(b)   *Long-term solvency ratios*, concerned with an organization's long-term financial position, that is its financial structure and ability to meet its long-term financial obligations.

(c) *Financial and operating performance ratios,* concerned with the effectiveness with which an organization's operations are being managed.
(d) *Stock market ratios,* concerned with the stock market performance of companies.

We will illustrate the calculation of these ratios using the following specimen set of company accounts for Pollard plc.

Pollard plc

Profit and loss account for the year ended 31 December 19X7

		(£000s)	
		Year ended 31 December 19X7	Year ended 31 December 19X6
Notes:			
2	Turnover	13,125	12,240
3	Cost of sales	(9,565)	(9,154)
	Gross profit	3,560	3,086
3	Distribution costs	(930)	(698)
3	Administrative expenses	(1,010)	(998)
3	Other operating costs	(220)	(178)
	Operating profit	1,400	1,212
4	Investment income	20	0
4	Interest payable	(20)	(12)
	Profit on ordinary activities before taxation	1,400	1,200
5	Taxation on profit on ordinary activities	(730)	(600)
	Profit on ordinary activities after taxation	670	600
	Extraordinary items after taxation	(60)	(10)
	Profit for the year	610	590
	Dividends	(335)	(266)
	Retained profit for the year	275	324
	Earnings per share		

Balance sheet as at 31 December 19X7

	31 December 19X7			31 December 19X6		
	£000s	£000s	£000s	£000s	£000s	£000s
Fixed assets:						
Intangible assets		750			616	
Tangible assets						
Freehold land and buildings	2,952			2,358		

	31 December 19X7			31 December 19X6		
	£000s	£000s	£000s	£000s	£000s	£000s
Leasehold land and buildings		189			196	
Plant and machinery		3,545	6,286		2,839	5,393
Current assets:						
Stock and work-in-progress		1,900			1,408	
Debtors and prepayments		1,920			1,960	
Short-term investments		300			0	
Cash in hand and at bank		876			3	
		4,996			3,371	
Creditors falling due within one year:						
Overdraft	0			182		
Trade creditors	837			532		
Taxes	297			526		
Dividends proposed	621	(1,755)		524	(1,764)	
Net current assets			3,241			1,607
Total assets less Current liabilities:			10,677			7,616
Creditors falling due outside one year:						
Debentures 12%		(900)			0	
Taxation		(627)	(1,527)		(504)	(504)
Provision for liabilities:						
Deferred taxation			(420)			(84)
			8,370			7,028
Called up share capital						
Ordinary shares of 25p each			6,000			5,040
Preference shares of £1 each (10%)			600			600
			6,600			5,640
Share premium		750			560	
Revaluation reserve		360			0	
General reserve		600			600	
Profit and loss account		60			228	
			1,770			
			8,370			7,028

Extract from notes to the accounts
1   *Accounting policies:*
   (a)   Stocks and work-in-progress. Raw materials are valued on the
         FIFO basis. Work-in-progress and finished goods are valued at
         standard cost, adjusted for changes in prices and wages subse-
         quent to setting standards.

(b) Tangible fixed assets are depreciated on a straight line basis.
(c) Research and development expenditure is written off as incurred.

2 *Turnover:*
The analysis of company turnover and profit is as follows:
Turnover:

	Year ended 31 December 19X7 £000	*Year ended 31 December 19X6* £000
Class of business		
Hand tools	5,250	5,508
Kitchen ware	4,594	3,672
Kitchen fittings	3,281	3,060
	13,125	12,240
Geographic analysis:		
UK	6,825	5,998
EEC (excluding UK)	2,132	2,416
North America	2,188	2,260
Africa	1,980	1,566
	13,125	12,240
Operating profit:		
Class of business:		
Hand tools	392	384
Kitchen ware	560	528
Kitchen fittings	448	288
	1,400	1,200

3 Cost of sales is composed as follows:

Depreciation	490	384
Hire of plant	25	17
Goodwill written off	70	58
Other costs	8,980	8,695
	9,565	9,154

Distribution costs are composed as follows:

Depreciation	120	98
Other costs	810	600
	930	698

Administrative expenses are composed as follows:

Auditor's fees	8	6
Depreciation	75	60
Other expenses	927	932
	1,010	998

		(£000s)	
		Year ended	*Year ended*
		31 December 19X7	*31 December 19X6*
	Other operating costs:	£	£
	Research and development costs	220	178
4	Investment income and interest payable:		
	Income from listed securities	20	0
	Interest payable:		
	On overdrafts	(5)	(12)
	On debentures repayable beyond five years	(15)	0
		0	(12)
5	*Taxation on ordinary activities:*		
	Corporation tax		
	Deferred tax		
	Tax credit on franked investment income		
		730	600
6	Employees and directors:		
	Staff and workers		
	The average number of workers on a weekly basis was:		
	Management and office	120	90
	Hand tools	680	534
	Kitchen ware	380	290
	Kitchen fittings	690	630
		1,770	1,544
	Salaries wages and other costs:		
	Wages and salaries	4,535	3,516
	Social security costs	708	488
	Other pension costs	508	435
		5,751	4,439

Liquidity ratios

The liquidity of an organization is of great importance to anyone who commits resources to that organization. Two ratios in particular are used to assess short-term liquidity:

Current ratio
This ratio (also known as the working capital ratio) measures the adequacy of current assets to meet current liabilities. The ratio is normally expressed as $\dfrac{\text{current assets for the period}}{\text{current liabilities for the period}}$.

Thus, for Pollard it is:

	31 December 19X7	31 December 19X6
Current assets (£000s)	4,996	3,371
Current liabilities (£000s)	1,755	1,764
Current assets – current liabilities	2.85	1.91

In the current year Pollard appears to have ample current assets out of which to meet its current commitments and has improved its financial position over the previous year. Earlier, we cast doubt on the use of absolute benchmarks for ratios, but implicitly some absolute standards are borne in mind. In the case of the current ratio a value of one would seem an important benchmark, implying just sufficient assets to meet liabilities. Better than one means greater security from a cushion of assets; less than one insufficient assets and hence risks. However, as we noted, the operating characteristics of different industries will impose their own benchmarks. For example, companies operating supermarkets will have low current ratios because they buy on credit but do not extend it to their customers. Engineering firms tend to have high current ratios since they sell on credit and hold valuable stocks and work-in-progress. With this in mind we should compare Pollard's current ratio with the industry norm.

It should be remembered that the adage 'the bigger the better' does not necessarily apply to ratios such as the current ratio. A very large value of the ratio may indicate not just a high level of security but, perhaps, over investment or under-utilization of the financing represented by creditor items. A fundamental problem with the current ratio is that it may not measure very accurately the ability of an organization to meet its immediate commitments. There are two reasons for this. One is a problem of the accounting conventions adopted. Conventionally, stock is valued at the lower of cost or net realizable value. If realizable value is lower than cost then stock does reflect liquidatable value. However, if cost is lower than realizable value (the normal case) stock's ability to provide liquidity is underestimated. This deficiency could be remedied by using estimates of realizable values for ratio analysis. This problem is less serious if the accounts are based upon current cost rather than historic cost.

The second problem is that both current assets and liabilities include items of ranging degrees of liquidity. Certain current assets may not be readily realizable in the normal course of business nor in an emergency. Likewise, not all current liabilities represent immediate obligations. This leads to the next ratio.

Acid test (or quick ratio)
This ratio may be calculated in two ways:

(a) $\dfrac{\text{Quick assets at the end of the period}}{\text{Current liabilities at the end of the period.}}$

(b) $\dfrac{\text{Quick assets at the end of the period}}{\text{Immediate liabilities at the end of the period.}}$

Two quickly liquidatable assets can be identified: cash and short-term investments. Whether other current assets are included as 'quick' depends upon judgement of the commercial circumstances. Stock could be liquidated but it is unlikely that this could be on favourable terms. Moreover, disposing of stock would only be warranted by extreme circumstances. We shall thus exclude stock from quick assets. Debtors could also be liquidated, either by selling debtors to a financial institution for cash or in the normal course of business as debts are settled. Under normal circumstances only the second should be considered for ratio analysis purposes. The 'quickness' of debtors as a source of cash can be gauged from their relationship with sales. We can introduce another ratio to show this relationship, the debtors' turnover ratio:

$$\frac{\text{Debtors at the end of the period}}{\text{Annual turnover}} \times 365 \text{ days}$$

For Pollard this is: $\dfrac{£1,920,000}{£13,125,000} \times 365 \text{ days} = 53 \text{ days}$

Thus, if the above relationship holds for the immediate future, Pollard could expect all its closing debtors to be turned into cash within fifty-three days. Strictly, one should relate debtors to credit sales to obtain the debtors turnover ratio, so we shall assume in retrospect that all Pollard's sales are on credit. We shall also judge seven weeks to be an acceptable degree of 'quickness' for debtors. This gives quick ratios based on version (*a*) above of:

(£000)

	Year ended 31 December 19X7	Year ended 31 December 19X6
Cash	876	3
Short-term investments	300	0
Debtors	1,920	1,960
Total quick assets	3,096	1,963
Current liabilities	1,755	1,764
Quick ratio	1.76	1.11

This ratio shows less asset cover than did the current ratio, but sufficient liquidity appears present, and the ratio has increased over the previous year. However, as before, we would need to make comparisons outside the organization to judge this ratio properly.

A more conservative assessment of immediate liquidity would be obtained if we excluded debtors from quick assets. Other things being equal this would produce ratios of $\dfrac{£1,176,000}{£1,755,000} = 0.67$, for 19X7 and $\dfrac{£3,000}{£1,764,000} = 0.002$ for 19X6. By any standards, 19X6 would have caused concern and 19X7 shows great improvement and probably reflects sufficient liquidity for practical purposes.

We may argue that the calculations based on version (*a*) overstate the need for liquidity by including all current liabilities. If we concentrate on only immediate liabilities we should get a more realistic, if less prudent, picture. Bank overdrafts are repayable on demand and are thus immediate. Trade creditors will be due for payment on whatever terms have been agreed and we shall assume that this means in the immediate future. The immediacy of taxes depends on when they are due, as does dividends. Without other information we shall assume that taxes are due shortly, but that dividends are payable in three months' time. Hence, immediate liabilities comprise overdrafts, creditors and taxes (£1,134,000 for 19X7, £1,240,000 for 19X6), and when related to quick assets including debtors gives ratios of 2.73 for 19X7 and 1.58 for 19X6. Excluding debtors from quick assets gives ratios of 1.03 for 19X7 and 0.002 for 19X6.

From these ratios we may conclude that Pollard's short-term liquidity has improved significantly from that of the previous year and that its present position is relatively secure. This does not, of course, reflect its position relative to comparable companies.

Long-term solvency ratios

These ratios relate to an organization's ability to survive and operate in the long term. They give indications of the organization's fitness for future trading and are concerned with the long-term financial structure of the organization.

The chief indicators of long-term financial position are the gearing ratios which show the relationship between shareholders' funds and fixed charge capital. Gearing ratios may be calculated on either book values or market values of securities. Here, we consider book values only. Companies are considered highly geared if a relatively large proportion of capital is in forms which carry fixed charges, and low geared if the reverse applies. The significance of gearing is that it introduces financial risk to both a company and its shareholders. One aspect of this is the risk of bankruptcy. Fixed charges attaching to capital, . example interest on debentures, are contractual obligations whic , if not met, could result in bankruptcy. This clearly presents a risk to both company and shareholders. The second aspect of financial risk is the extra variability in earnings to shareholders which results from gearing. Earnings to shareholders are the residual in the profit and loss account and their value depends upon earnings from operations and deductions therefrom, including fixed charges. To illustrate this, consider the example of a company which has £1 million of 10 per cent debentures as its only long-term fixed charge capital and earnings net of non-interest expenses of £250,000. Corporation tax is charged at 50 per cent. The abbreviated profit and loss account is:

	£000
Pre-tax earnings net of non-interest expenses	250
Interest on debentures (£1 m × 10%)	(100)
Net earnings before tax	150
Corporation tax (at 50%)	(75)
Earnings attributable to shareholders	75

The effect of this company's gearing is felt if operating earnings (represented by pre-tax earnings net of non-interest expenses) vary: earnings to shareholders will vary more. Below we illustrate the effects of the stated percentage changes in operating earnings on shareholders' income:

	Decrease in operating earnings from base of:			Increase in operating earnings from base of:	
	20%	*10%*	*Base (£000)*	*10%*	*20%*
Pre-tax operating earnings	200	225	250	275	300
Interest	(100)	(100)	(100)	(100)	(100)
Pre-tax earnings	100	125	150	175	200
Corporation tax (at 50%)	(50)	(62.5)	(75)	(87.5)	(100)
Earnings to shareholders	50	62.5	75	87.5	100
% change in earnings to shareholders from base.	33	17		17	33

Because of gearing, earnings to shareholders fall by 17 per cent when operating earnings fall by 10. This differential change would be greater, the greater the gearing. Gearing is not wholly disadvantageous as the examples of growing earnings show: shareholders benefit more than proportionately from growth.

Several ratios are available for the assessment of gearing from a company's balance sheet:

(a) $\dfrac{\text{Prior charge capital (A)}}{\text{Total capital in issue plus reserves (B)}}$

(b) $\dfrac{\text{Total borrowings (C)}}{\text{Total capital in issue plus reserves}}$

(c) $\dfrac{\text{Prior charge capital plus borrowings}}{\text{Total capital in issue plus reserves}}$

Note:
A: preference shares and debentures
B: A plus equity capital and reserves
C: long-term and short-term borrowings

All the above may be calculated with two alternative denominators: total long-term assets employed (giving the same value as in B above), and shareholders' funds. The above ratios are calculated as follows:

		(£000)	*19X7*	*19X6*

(a) $\dfrac{\text{Prior charge capital}}{\text{Total capital in issue plus reserves}}$ $\dfrac{600 + 900}{(600+900) + (8370-600)} = 0.16$

		(£000)	19X7	19X6
		$\dfrac{600 + 0}{600 + (7028-600)}$		= 0.09

(b) $\dfrac{\text{Total borrowings}}{\text{Total capital in issue plus reserves}}$ $\dfrac{900 + 0^{(1)}}{(600+900) + (8370-600)} = 0.10$

$$\dfrac{0 + 182^{(1)}}{600 + (7028-600)} = 0.03$$

(c) $\dfrac{\text{Prior charge capital plus borrowings}}{\text{Total capital in issue plus reserves}}$ $\dfrac{600 + 900 + 0^{(1)}}{(600+900) + (8370-600)} = 0.16$

$$\dfrac{600 + 182}{600 + (7028-600)} = 0.11$$

(d) $\dfrac{\text{Prior charge capital}}{\text{Shareholders funds}}$ $\dfrac{600 + 900}{8370} = 0.18$

$$\dfrac{600 + 0}{7028} = 0.09$$

$\underline{\text{Total borrowings}}$ $\dfrac{900 + 0^{(1)}}{8370} - 0.11$

$$\dfrac{0 + 182^{(1)}}{7028} = 0.03$$

$\dfrac{\text{Prior charge capital plus borrowings}}{\text{Shareholders' funds}}$ $\dfrac{600 + 900 + 0^{(1)}}{8370} = 0.18$

$$\dfrac{600 + 182}{7028} = 0.11$$

Note: (1) = Short-term borrowings in the form of overdrafts

It is not necessary to calculate all the above measures of gearing in order to assess long-term financial structure but it is useful to test the sensitivity of gearing to changes in its definition. Under all the definitions Pollard appears to be low geared and hence its shareholders and creditors, both long and short-term, face limited financial risk. Indeed, it might be argued that too little use is made by the company of geared finance. Not all companies are suitable for effective use of significant degrees of gearing. Companies with stable earnings or good prospects for earnings growth can readily absorb geared finance and gain from its use. For example, property investment companies generally have stable earnings and usually have significant levels of gearing. Such companies also have sufficient assets which are suitable for securing loans, itself an important consideration. Assets subject to rapid depreciation or obsolescence are clearly not suitable to support material levels of gearing.

An alternative way of indicating the effects of financial structure and its attendent risks is found by using figures from the profit and loss account to calculate the interest cover ratio:

$$\frac{\text{Operating profit before interest and tax}}{\text{Interest payable net of interest receivable}}$$

From Pollard's profit and loss account the values of this ratio are:

	31 December 19X7	31 December 19X6
$\dfrac{£1,400,000}{£0}$	$= \quad \infty$	
$\dfrac{£1,212,000}{£12,000}$		$= \quad 101 \text{ times}$

Clearly, interest is more than adequately covered in Pollard.

Financial and operating performance ratios

The purpose of these ratios is to aid the assessment of an organization's performance. Since an organization's performance can only be assessed against objectives, it is necessary first to identify the latter. Having done this we may next identify a key ratio which measures performance towards the identified objective or objectives. Thereafter, analysis of performance may proceed by calculating other ratios which relate to aspects of performance and which are derived from the key ratio.

The matter of organizational objectives is a complicated one. Different types of organization will have different objectives, and even within a class of organizations objectives will vary. Not all companies, for example, can be assumed to be the profit maximizers of economic theory. The pursuit of satisfactory profit, or of multiple objectives which include profit, are certainly more practical alternatives. For our present purposes we shall assume that the pursuit of profit is the most important objective and that companies, including our example, set themselves periodic profit targets. The most widely recognized ratio for setting and assessing profit targets is the rate of return on capital employed (ROCE) which, in general terms, is expressed as:

$$\frac{\text{Profit per period}}{\text{Capital employed}} = \%$$

Absolute profit alone is a poor measure, but when related to capital employed this indicates the scale of resources committed (thereby facilitating comparisons). If ROCE is accepted as the key performance ratio we may now consider other ratios which relate to aspects of operations contributing to overall performance. These subsidiary ratios may be presented in the form of a pyramid. Figure 13.1 contains two such ratio pyramids, one for a manufacturing company, the other for a retailer.

(a) *Manufacturing company*

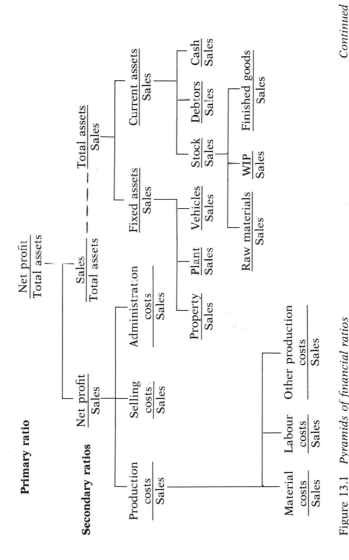

Figure 13.1 *Pyramids of financial ratios*

Continued

Figure 13.1 – *continued*

(b) *Retail trading company*

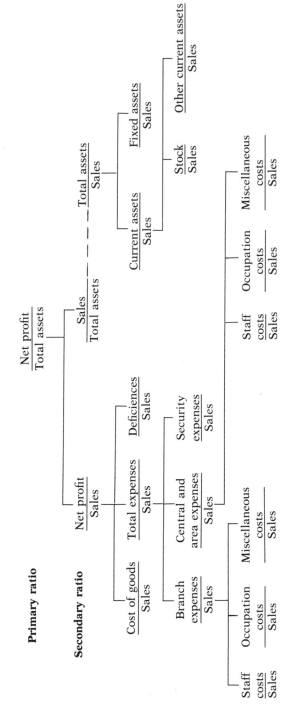

Figure 13.1 *Pyramids of financial ratios*

Each of the pyramids has at its apex ROCE. The version of this ratio given in Figure 13.1 is rather more specific that the general definitional one on page 312. To be more specific still, we may define ROCE for computational purposes as:

$$\frac{\text{Profit before interest and tax}}{\text{Total assets for the period}} = \%$$

Capital employed is thus measured by total assets and this is frequently averaged over opening and closing balance sheet values to obtain a more representative value for the year by avoiding any distortions contained in year end figures. Thus, from Pollard's accounts, average total assets are:

	(£000)	
	19X7	*19X6*
Fixed assets	6,286	5,393
Current assets	4,996	3,371
Total assets	11,282	8,764
Average total assets		
	10,023	

Giving a ROCE for 19X7 of: $\dfrac{£1,400,000}{£10,023,000} \times 100 = 14\%$

A comparative figure for ROCE for 19X6 calculated on this basis requires a closing balance sheet for 19X5. We shall assume that the corresponding value of total assets for 19X5 was £7,985,000, giving an average value for total assets for 19X6 of:

$$\frac{£8,764,000 + £7,985,000}{2} = £8,374,500, \text{ and a ROCE for 19X6 of:}$$

$$\frac{£1,212,000}{£8,364,000} \times 100 = 0.14$$

On a year end basis for total assets ROCE is:

	19X7	*19X6*
$\dfrac{£1,400,000}{£11,282,000} =$	0.124	
$\dfrac{£1,212,000}{£8,764,000} =$		0.138

The ROCE ratio could also be calculated in other ways, particularly as regards the denominator. This could be expressed as long-term capital employed (shareholders funds plus creditors falling due outside one year) or its equivalent, total net assets employed (fixed assets plus current assets less current liabilities). These would produce a numerically different result to those above but, if used consistently in comparisons they would provide useful information.

ROCE, however calculated, is an indicator of overall business performance and may be compared with the company's past performance, the targets currently set for it by management, or the ROCEs of other companies. Its usefulness as a general indicator is also a weakness: it gives no indication of the sources of the good or bad performance which may be indicated by it. This weakness is remedied by moving down the pyramid. In each version of the pyramid in Figure 13.1 the secondary ratios are the same. The secondary ratios together make up the primary ratio thus:

Primary ratio: *Secondary ratios:*

$$\frac{\text{Net profit}}{\text{Total assets}} = \frac{\text{Net profit}}{\text{Sales}} \times \frac{\text{Sales}}{\text{Total assets}}$$

Cancelling out sales in each secondary ratio allows the primary ratio to be derived. The ratio of net profit to sales measures the company's gross profit margin on sales whilst sales to total assets measures asset turnover, or the extent to which the company's assets have generated sales. The former measures the ability of sales to generate profits and the latter the ability of the company's assets to generate sales. Arithmetically, the two ratios may be combined in many ways to produce a given value of ROCE. A ROCE of 14 per cent for example may be generated by:

ROCE (%)	Profit margin (%)	×	Asset turnover
14	14		1
14	9.33		1.5
14	7		2
14	5.6		2.5

As one moves down the profit margin column, profit margin is reduced, due perhaps to lower pricing, more competitive markets, or higher costs. Moving down the asset turnover column indicates increasing profits by effective use of assets in generating sales. The former suggests poorer performance, the latter better performance, although together they produce the same ROCE. Hence, it is important to separate these two components. In Pollard's case, the ROCEs based on average total assets of 14 per cent are composed as follows:

		19X7		*19X6*
$\frac{\text{Net profit}}{\text{Sales}} =$	$\frac{£1,400,000}{£13,125,000} =$	0.107	$\frac{£1,212,000}{£12,240,000} =$	0.098
		×		×
$\frac{\text{Sales}}{\text{Total assets}} =$	$\frac{£13,125,000}{£10,023,000} =$	1.309	$\frac{£12,240,000}{£8,374,500} =$	1.462
ROCE		14%		14%

Should ROCE change over time, analysis of its two chief components indicates the source of change. Or, should ROCE not change, as in

Pollard's case, this disaggregation prevents the analyst from assuming that nothing has changed. In fact, Pollard's net profit margin has improved slightly whilst its asset turnover has declined. The latter may have resulted from the policies which led to the former if, for example, the margin has been increased by raising selling prices with an adverse effect on sales volume.

The same principle of disaggregation of ratios to obtain further information applies to the rest of the pyramids of Figure 13.1. We shall treat Pollard as a manufacturing company (see the sales data in note (*b*) to the company's accounts) and utilize the appropriate pyramid for such a company as far as possible given the information in the accounts. The ratios shown in Figure 13.1 represent those which might usefully be calculated, not those which can be. For example, these ratios necessitate an analysis of costs, but such data may not be fully available. It is frequently necessary, as with all standard ratios, to modify them to a usable form. For example, examination of Pollard's accounts shows that production costs and material costs are not reported separately. However, administration costs, selling costs (termed 'distribution costs' in the accounts), labour costs and other production costs are reported and ratios can be calculated as follows:

(£000)

	19X7		19X6	
$\dfrac{\text{Distribution costs}}{\text{Sales}}$	$\dfrac{£930}{£13,125}$	= 0.071	$\dfrac{£9,154}{£12,240}$	= 0.057
$\dfrac{\text{Administration costs}}{\text{Sales}}$	$\dfrac{£1,010}{£13,125}$	= 0.077	$\dfrac{£998}{£12,240}$	= 0.082
$\dfrac{\text{Other operating costs}}{\text{Sales}}$	$\dfrac{£220}{£13,125}$	= 0.017	$\dfrac{£178}{£12,240}$	= 0.015
$\dfrac{\text{Labour costs}}{\text{Sales}}$	$\dfrac{£5,571}{£13,125}$	= 0.42	$\dfrac{£4,439}{£12,240}$	= 0.036

The data on labour costs is obtained from note 6 to the accounts and data for the other ratios from the face of the profit and loss account. Cost of sales is reported in Pollard's profit and loss account and can serve as an approximation to production costs giving the following values:

	19X7		19X6	
$\dfrac{\text{Cost of sales}}{\text{Sales}}$	$\dfrac{£9,565}{£13,125}$	= 0.73	$\dfrac{£9,154}{£12,240}$	= 0.75

These ratios show the relationship of costs and profit to turnover. We can express the major components of the profit and loss account as relative measures (in the form of ratios) rather than as absolute values. If we calculate one further ratio, that of the gross profit margin, we can re-express Pollard's profit and loss account in ratio form. The gross profit margin is:

(£000)

	19X7			19X6	
$\dfrac{\text{Gross profit}}{\text{Sales}}$	$\dfrac{£3,560}{£13,125}$	=	0.271	$\dfrac{£3,086}{£12,240}$	= 0.252

The various profit margin and costs ratios may be combined as follows:

	19X7		19X6	
	(£000)	*Ratios to sales*	*(£000)*	*Ratios to sales*
Turnover	13,125	1.000	12,240	1.00
Cost of sales	(9,565)	(0.729)	(9,154)	(0.748)
Gross profit	3,560	0.271	3,086	0.252
Distribution costs	(930)	(0.071)	(698)	(0.057)
Administrative expenses	(1,010)	(0.077)	(998)	(0.082)
Other operating costs	(220)	(0.017)	(178)	(0.015)
Net profit	1,400	0.167	1,212	0.098

Comparison of the two columns of ratios shows profit margins to have improved slightly in 19X7 due to a reduction in the cost of sales ratio not entirely offset by increases in ratios of the other costs.

We shall turn next to the other secondary ratio, asset turnover. For 19X7 we calculated this as $\dfrac{£13,125,000}{£10,023,000} = 1.309$, indicating that each £1 worth of Pollard's assets generated £1.31 worth of sales. The two accounting items which make up this ratio can be inverted to present an alternative view of the same relationship, although no longer contributing to ROCE, thus:

$$\frac{\text{Total assets}}{\text{Sales}} = \frac{£10,023,000}{£13,125,000} = 0.764$$

This ratio measures the extent of the investment in total operating assets required to generate sales. In this case £764 of operating assets generate £1,000 of sales in 19X7. A similar process of disaggregation can be applied to the asset turnover ratio (and its reciprocal) as was applied to the profit margin, as Figure 13.1 shows. Indeed, it is the reciprocal which is conventionally used for this purpose. To illustrate other asset ratios we shall use year end values for assets. Recalculating the overall asset ratio on this basis gives:

	19X7			19X6	
$\dfrac{\text{Total year end assets}}{\text{Sales}}$	$\dfrac{£11,282,000}{£13,125,000}$	=	0.860	$\dfrac{£8,764,000}{£12,240,000}$	= 0.716

The first disaggregation is into fixed and current assets:

(£000)

	19X7			19X6	
$\dfrac{\text{Fixed assets}}{\text{Sales}}$	$\dfrac{£6,286}{£13,125}$	=	0.479	$\dfrac{£5,393}{£12,240}$	= 0.381

(£000)

	19X7			19X6	
$\dfrac{\text{Current assets}}{\text{Sales}}$	$\dfrac{£4,996}{£13,125}$	$=$	0.381	$\dfrac{£3,371}{£12,240}$	$= 0.257$

Both classes of asset have experienced additional investment which is not yet associated with a proportionate increase in sales. On the data available, two of the three fixed asset ratios of Figure 13.1 can be calculated and both show the same pattern:

(£000)

	19X7			19X6	
$\dfrac{\text{Property}}{\text{Sales}}$	$\dfrac{3,141}{13,125}$	$=$	0.239	$\dfrac{2,554}{12,240}$	$= 0.209$
$\dfrac{\text{Plant}}{\text{Sales}}$	$\dfrac{3,545}{13,125}$	$=$	0.270	$\dfrac{2,839}{12,240}$	$= 0.232$

An additional fixed asset ratio, relating to intangible assets, can be calculated in addition to the above. This shows little change:

(£000)

	19X7			19X6	
$\dfrac{\text{Intangible fixed assets}}{\text{Sales}}$	$\dfrac{750}{13,125}$	$=$	0.057	$\dfrac{616}{12,240}$	$= 0.050$

The three current asset ratios of Figure 13.1, supplemented by one for short-term investments are:

(£000)

	19X7			19X6	
$\dfrac{\text{Stocks and work in progress}}{\text{Sales}}$	$\dfrac{1,900}{13,125}$	$=$	0.145	$\dfrac{1,408}{12,240}$	$= 0.115$
$\dfrac{\text{Debtors and prepayments}}{\text{Sales}}$	$\dfrac{1,920}{13,125}$	$=$	0.146	$\dfrac{1,960}{12,240}$	$= 0.160$
$\dfrac{\text{Short-term investments}}{\text{Sales}}$	$\dfrac{300}{13,125}$	$=$	0.023	$\dfrac{0}{12,240}$	$= 0$
$\dfrac{\text{Cash}}{\text{Sales}}$	$\dfrac{876}{13,125}$	$=$	0.067	$\dfrac{3}{12,240}$	$= 0$

These show significant changes in the pattern of current asset investment. The final disaggregation into the various components of stock is not possible in the case of Pollard due to lack of data. If this data was made available these ratios would give further indications of Pollard's policies on asset investment and their success in generating sales.

Certain of these ratios of assets to sales can be viewed in a different way. Consider the ratio of stocks to sales just calculated. In this form it shows the fraction of annual sales represented by stock. When it is related to the number of days in a year thus:

$$\frac{\text{Stock}}{\text{Annual sales}} \times 365 \text{ days}$$

it shows the number of days work of sales which are maintained in stock. This indicates how long sales might be sustained without production. For Pollard these values are:

19X7

$$\frac{£1,900,000}{£13,125,000} \times 365 \text{ days} = 52.8 \text{ days}$$

19X6

$$\frac{£1,408,000}{£12,240,000} \times 365 \text{ days} = 42.0 \text{ days}$$

This ratio is an imperfect measure since its numerator (stock) is valued at cost or net realizable value whilst its denominator is measured at selling price.

A similar ratio can be calculated by relating debtors to sales. Ideally, debtors should be related to sales on credit, indicating the debtors outstanding in terms of periodic credit sales, or, if expressed in days, the number of days of credit sales outstanding. In the absence of credit sales data total sales may be used, thus:

$$\frac{\text{Debtors outstanding}}{\text{Sales for the period}} \times 365 \text{ days}$$

For Pollard the ratio is valued at:

19X7

$$\frac{£1,920,000}{£13,125,000} \times 365 \text{ days} = 53.4 \text{ days}$$

19X6

$$\frac{£1,960,000}{£12,240,000} \times 365 \text{ days} = 58.4 \text{ days}$$

Stock market ratios

All the ratios so far considered have emphasized aspects of the liquidity, solvency or operating performance of the company, and have been presented as being useful to those with decisions to make concerning the company. An important group of decision makers are shareholders both actual and potential. Whilst they will undoubtedly have an interest in the ratios in the first three categories, their major concern is likely to be with stock market ratios. Stock market ratios are different from those in the other three categories in that they utilize company information with an external rather than an internal perspective. All of the stock market ratios are concerned with company performance but in a purely financial sense, unlike those ratios which measure aspects of operating performance. Obviously, operating performance will be related to financial performance, and it might be argued that stock market ratios are the ultimate reflection of all the other ratios: a sound liquidity position and good operating performance make a company's shares an attractive investment. Hence, working backwards, attractive stock market ratios may indicate a well-run and soundly financed company. Perhaps this is placing too much reliance on stock market ratios as summaries and certainly there is no suggestion that they are the only ratios which need to be calculated. However, much may be read into them and they do represent how the stock market views the company. When one recalls that the stock market consists not simply of small shareholders with limited financial knowledge but also of financial institutions whose investment analysts will put considerable time, effort and skill into company analysis, the market's view is worth considering seriously. Two warnings must be given at this point. The first is that the market may not always be right. One purpose in analysing stock market ratios may be to identify shares in which a gain can be made by 'beating the market'. The second warning is that whilst the sophisticated investment analysts referred to above may set the market for some shares, they do not do so for all companies' shares. Given the thousands of companies whose shares are listed on the Stock Exchange or are traded on the Unlisted Securities Market, this would be impossible. Thus there are very many companies for which a thorough analysis of all ratios, both stock market and non-stock market, would be necessary if informed decisions were to be made. The following are the most frequently calculated stock market ratios.

Earnings per share
Earnings per share (EPS) is an accounting ratio which is widely used in shareholder investment decisions in itself, and as an input into other ratios. Its importance is indicated by the existence of an accounting standard, SSAP3, devoted to standardizing accounting practice relating to its calculation and disclosure. The requirements of SSAP3 go beyond the scope of this book and are considered in detail in the companion volume, *Advanced Financial Accounting*. For present purposes we may define EPS as:

$$\frac{\text{Attributable equity profit for the period}}{\text{Number of equity shares in issue and ranking for dividend}}$$

Attributable equity profit for the period is defined by SSAP3 as the consolidated (where appropriate) profit of the period after tax and after deducting minority interests (where appropriate), but before taking into account extraordinary items. Thus, from Pollard's profit and loss account, attributable earnings are determined as follows:

	(£000)	
	19X7	*19X6*
Profit for the year	610	590
Less preference dividends	(60)	(60)
Profits attributable to equity shareholders	550	530

The figures for dividends in Pollard's accounts include dividends on preference shares and hence these must be deducted separately to arrive at equity earnings. Pollard's issued share capital was £6 million in 19X7 and £5.04 million in 19X6, both in units of 25p, giving shares in issue (and we shall assume, ranking for dividend) of 24 million in 19X7 and 20.16 million in 19X6. Thus EPS is:

$$\frac{£550,000}{24,000,000 \text{ shares}} = 2.29 \text{ pence per share} \qquad \frac{£530,000}{20,160,000 \text{ shares}} = 2.63 \text{ pence per share}$$

19X7   *19X6*

This indicates how much Pollard has provided for each of its shares over the two years. Earnings include both dividends paid and profits retained, and the total return attributable to a share in the business. Expressed as EPS it is an absolute amount of return, and whilst the trend of EPS may be of interest, as may its relationship to EPS for other comparable companies' shares, it is perhaps more informative if shown as a yield.

Earnings yield
This ratio is defined as:

$$\frac{\text{EPS}}{\text{Current market price of the share}} \%$$

If we discover Pollard's price per share currently to be 35 pence and to have been 42 pence on 31st December 19X6, earnings yields are:

19X7   *19X6*

$$\frac{2.29}{35} \times 100 = 6.5\% \qquad \frac{2.63}{42} \times 100 = 6.3\%$$

This trend over the two years should be compared with that for the stock market as a whole, or the industrial sector in which Pollard operates, or with specific companies, if the worthwhileness of the investment is to be judged.

Price earnings ratio
The data making up the earnings yield may be used to calculate the price earnings ratio (PER) as follows:

$$\text{PER} = \frac{\text{Current market price of the share}}{\text{EPS}}$$

Thus, PER is the reciprocal of the earnings yield and for Pollard is valued at:

19X7   *19X6*

$$\frac{35p}{2.29p} = 15.3 \text{ times} \qquad \frac{42p}{2.63p} = 16.0 \text{ times}$$

PER expresses current share price as a multiple of current EPS: the number of times share price exceeds current earnings. This implies that if the current rate of EPS were maintained it would take over fifteen years to repay the cost of investing in one of Pollard's shares at their current market value. Of course the pay back period is actually rather longer since all of Pollard's earnings are not distributed. An investment with such a pay back period would not be acceptable to most companies, or, indeed, most shareholders, but high PERs are generally viewed as better than low ones by the stock market. This apparent paradox is easily resolved if one recalls that share investment decisions are forward looking and are based upon expectations of future earnings and dividends. Thus, current EPS is less significant than judgements of what EPS will be in the future. Pollard's high PER means that current share price is high relative to current EPS but this may be because EPS is forecast to grow significantly from its present low level and this has perhaps stimulated demand for Pollard's shares, thereby forcing up their price. Hence, low current EPS and high current share price may be quite consistent.

Both earnings yield and PER contain EPS and whilst earnings yield is a measure of the total yield of a share it may not be of great interest to the investor who is chiefly concerned with dividend income. In such cases dividend yield may be a better ratio.

Dividend yield
Dividend yield is:

$$\frac{\text{Net dividend per share}}{\text{Current market price per share}} \%$$

'Net dividend' is the usual description of actual dividend paid, net of imputed tax (tax credit). Thus gross dividend would be obtained by adding back the imputed tax. Dividends paid per ordinary share are determined from Pollard's accounts as follows:

	19X7	19X6
Dividends as disclosed	£335,000	£266,000
Less preference dividends	(60,000)	(60,000)
Dividends to ordinary shares	£275,000	£206,000
Ordinary shares in issue and ranking for dividends	24,000,000	20,160,000
Dividends per share	1.15 pence	1.02 pence

With the share prices as above, dividends yields are:

19X7	*19X6*
$\frac{1.15}{35} \times 100 = 3.3\%$	$\frac{1.02}{42} \times 100 = 2.4\%$

An alternative version of dividend yield is obtained if dividends are grossed up for the income tax deducted at source by companies. If we take the rate of income tax payable on dividends to be 29 per cent, then Pollard's net dividend of 1.98 pence per share in 19X7 represents 71 pence of the gross dividend. Thus, the gross dividend can be calculated as:

$$1.15 \text{ pence} \times \frac{100}{71} = 1.62 \text{ pence}$$

and for 19X6,

$$1.02 \text{ pence} \times \frac{100}{71} = 1.44 \text{ pence}$$

The gross dividend yield is thus:

	19X7		*19X6*
$\dfrac{1.62 \text{ pence}}{35 \text{ pence}} \times 100 = 4.6\%$		$\dfrac{1.44 \text{ pence}}{42 \text{ pence}} \times 100 = 3.4\%$	

Dividend cover
Another ratio involving dividends is dividend cover. This ratio is defined as:

$$\frac{\text{EPS}}{\text{Net dividend per share}}$$

For Pollard, its value is:

	19X7		*19X6*
$\dfrac{2.29\text{p}}{1.15\text{p}} = 1.99 \text{ times}$		$\dfrac{2.63\text{p}}{1.02\text{p}} = 2.58 \text{ times}$	

This ratio indicates the number of times the earnings attributable to the equity shareholders cover the actual net dividends payable for the period and is a measure of the cushion available to maintain dividends if earnings fall. An alternative view of the earnings-dividends relationship is given by inverting the ratio thus:

$$\frac{\text{Net dividend per share}}{\text{EPS}}$$

which measures the dividend pay out rate, the proportion of earnings distributed to shareholders. For Pollard the dividend payout rates are:

	19X7		*19X6*
$\dfrac{1.15\text{p}}{2.29\text{p}} = 0.50$		$\dfrac{1.02\text{p}}{2.63\text{p}} = 0.39$	

Thus, Pollard's policy is to pay out most of the firm's earnings to shareholders.

The relationships between the various stock market ratios are shown in Figure 13.2, with calculations for 19X7 as illustrations.

Questions

1   J. Supply Company Limited is a manufacturer of dental supplies and equipment. It has been plagued, in recent years, with relatively low profitability and as the result of changes in the board of directors, a new chief executive has been appointed to improve the situation. He has asked you to make an analysis of the company's financial situation and has supplied you with the company's most recent

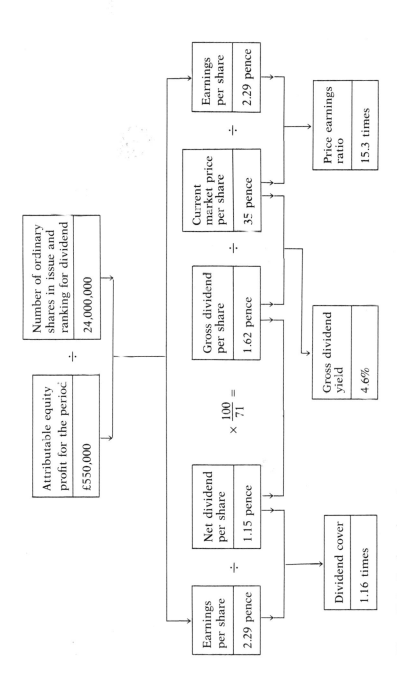

Figure 13.2 Stock market ratios

financial statements which are reproduced in Schedule I below. You have also obtained data relating to the sector of industry in which the company operates: this is given in Schedule II.

Schedule I   J. Supply Company Ltd.
Profit and loss account for the year ended 31 December 19X5

	£000	£000
Sales		26,500
Cost of sales		(22,250)
		4,250
Gross profit		
*Distribution cost	(2,085)	
*Administration expenses	(800)	
		(2,885)
		1,365
Operating profit		
Investment income	100	
Interest receivable	150	
		250
Interest payable		(115)
Profit on ordinary activities before taxation		1,500
Taxation on profit (at 50%)		(750)
Profit for the financial year		750

*Included in these headings are:
  Depreciation   £400,000
  Hire of vehicles   £67,000

Statement of retained earnings

	£000
Balance as at 1 January 19X5	5,950
Profit for the year	750
Balance as at 31 December 19X5	6,700

Balance sheet as at 31 December 19X5

	£000	£000
Tangible fixed assets:		
Plant and machinery, at cost		7,500
Less: depreciation		2,600
		4,900
		1,100
Listed investments		
Current assets:		
Stocks	5,300	
Debtors	2,200	
Cash	1,500	
	9,000	

	£	£
Creditors – amounts falling due within one year:		
Loan repayable	(1,500)	
Trade creditors	(1,500)	
Other creditors	(700)	
	(3,700)	
Net current assets		5,300
Total assets *less* current liabilities		11,300
Creditors – amounts falling due after more than one year: Debentures		(800)
		10,500
Capital and reserves:		£000
Called up ordinary share capital		3,800
Profit and loss account		6,700
		10,500

Schedule II

	Industry average ratios
Current ratio	2:1
Quick ratio	1:1
*Debt to total assets	30%
Times interest earned	7 times
Fixed charges coverage	5 times
Stock turnover	10 times
Average collection period	15 days
Fixed asset turnover	6 times
Total asset turnover	3 times
Net profit (after tax) to sales	3%
Return on total assets	9%
Return on net worth	12.8%

*Debt includes current liabilities and *all* loans

You are required to prepare a short report to the chief executive, giving your observations on the latest results.   (*20 marks*)

Chartered Institute of Management Accountants, Professional Stage Part 1, Financial Accounting 2

2 When a business has insufficient resources, particularly of a liquid nature, to maintain its existing level of operation, it may be said to be in a position of overtrading. This situation may arise through internal mismanagement, or through external factors, or a combination of both.

You are required to identify and discuss briefly the ways in which such a situation may arise. Your answer should deal with:

(a) those factors internal, and   (*10 marks*)
(b) those factors external to the business   (*10 marks*)
                                                                    (*Total: 20 marks*)

Chartered Institute of Management Accountants, Professional Stage Part 1,
Financial Accounting 2

3   Maximize plc operates a small chain of wholesale food and clothing
    warehouses and has traded profitably for a number of years. The
    company's policy is to seek maximum market share by increasing its
    number of trading outlets. At the start of 19X2 further units were
    brought into operation and this was financed by the issue of addi-
    tional shares.
        Accounts for the two years ended 31 December 19X1 and 19X2 are
    as follows:

Trading and profit and loss accounts

	19X1		19X2	
	£000	£000	£000	£000
Sales cash		500		400
credit		5,500		6,600
		6,000		7,000
Cost of goods sold		4,680		5,530
		1,320		1,470
Expenses				
Administration	300		310	
Selling and distribution	675		815	
		975		1,125
		345		355
Dividends ordinary	200		145	
preference	50		110	
		250		255
Retained for year		95		100

Balance sheet as at 31 December

	19X1		19X2	
	£000	£000	£000	£000
Fixed assets				
Land and buildings				
cost	200		200	
depreciation	20	180	24	176
Fixtures and fittings				
cost	500		700	
depreciation	130	370	161	539
		550		715
Current assets				
Stock	1,360		1,500	
Debtors	960		1,560	
Bank	20		20	
	2,340		3,080	

	19X1		19X2	
	£000	£000	£000	£000
Current liabilities				
Creditors	640		845	
Net current assets		1,700		2,235
		2,250		2,950
Financed by:				
Share capital ordinary		1,000		1,000
preference		500		1,100
Profit and loss account		750		850
		2,250		2,950

A director comments that the recent expansion has only resulted in the ordinary dividend being reduced and should not have been undertaken.

You are required to prepare a report for the director assessing the company's performance and the effects of the expansion.

(20 marks)

Chartered Institute of Public Finance and Accountancy, Professional Examination 1, Financial Accounting and Auditing

14 Auditing for internal control

At various points in other chapters we have encountered auditing as an activity relevant to the financial accounting and reporting of enterprises. This has been primarily the external auditing of company accounts to comply with the requirements of the Companies Acts. In this chapter we consider another type of auditing activity, namely internal audit. Internal audit may be defined as:

> Internal auditing is an independent appraisal function established within an organization to examine and evaluate its activities as a service to the organization. The objective of internal auditing is to assist members of the organization in the effective discharge of their responsibilities. To this end, internal auditing furnishes them with analyses, appraisals, recommendations, counsel, and information concerning the activities reviewed. (*Institute of Internal Auditors*)

It is thus different from the external audit, whose function, according to the Auditing Standards which prescribe the basic principles and practices which auditors are expected to follow, is:

> ... the independent examination and expression of opinion on the financial statements of an enterprise by an appointed auditor in pursuance of that appointment and in compliance with any relevant statutory obligation.

The main differences between internal and external audits are apparant from comparing these definitions. The external audit is a statutory requirement and hence has the purpose of ensuring that financial statements meet their statutory objectives. In the case of limited companies this means giving an opinion on whether those statements present a true and fair view. The external audit therefore serves the external users of financial statements, in particular shareholders in the case of companies. Internal audit on the other hand is an activity which facilitates the control of the organization and therefore aids management and is established by the decision of management rather than by statute.

330

External audit relates to financial statements whilst internal audit has broader concerns, extending beyond the financial. Both require independence on the part of the auditor, but the requirement that the external auditor be independent is formally recognized by company law, whereas independence is a desirable property of the internal audit if it is to achieve its purposes.

This property may be difficult to achieve since the internal auditors are employees of the organization which they are auditing. Consequently, it is necessary to consider the venture of independence as it applies to the internal audit process. CIPFA, in its *Statements on Internal Audit Practice – Public Sector*, identifies a number of properties which should be striven for in internal auditing. These properties, which are appropriate to enterprises in both the public and private sectors are:

(*a*)   The internal auditor should have access to all department heads, the chief executive and the board of directors or managers.

(*b*)   The internal audit should be independent of the personnel engaged in the operations under examination.

(*c*)   The internal audit should be completely independent of financial systems operating in the organization.

(*d*)   The chief internal auditor should be able to report directly without editing in his own name.

(*e*)   The chief internal auditor should have the right to report directly on any aspect of financial activities, including those of the finance department.

Despite the difficulties of ensuring the independence of the internal auditor, its work demands as much integrity and ethical responsibility as should be exercised by the external auditor.

Internal audit can be seen as relating to five aspects of an organization's activities, as follows:

(*a*)   *Financial accounting*, involving the verification of financial accounting information periodically supplied to management, and the testing of its suitability for its purposes. This will involve examining and reporting on:

- periodic management reports on profit and financial position
- periodic cash flow and credit positions
- periodic inventory positions

(*b*)   *Management accounting*, involving the verification, testing and reporting on the suitability of periodic management accounting information supplied to management. This includes:

- periodic budgets, statements of standard costs and variances
- periodic forecasts of cash flow

(*c*)   *Internal accounting control*, involving the verification and testing of the enterprises control system, with special regard to the procedures operating to prevent the loss of the enterprise's assets as well as to ensure the effectiveness of the enterprise's accounting systems.

(d) *Operational effectiveness*, involving the verification, testing and reporting on the effectiveness of the enterprise's operations which implement its policies and decisions relating to those operations. This aspect of the internal audit relates primarily to non-accounting activities and non-accounting personel.

(e) *Managerial efficiency*, involving the verification, testing and reporting on the efficiency of company management, especially the manner in which it formulates plans and implements decisions.

Clearly some aspects of internal audit are concerned with the same data and processes as is the external audit, both specifically, as in the case of (*a*) above, and generally since both are part of the overall system of organizational control. This latter point means that the internal audit function will need to be examined by the external auditor.

Role and objectives

The above discussion indicates something of its general role and objectives within organizations. However, we can consider this more specifically by examining particular roles which internal audit may fulfill. Some of the more important of these are discussed below.

Detection and prevention of fraud

In the nineteenth century the focus of auditing was the detection of fraud. The Auditing Practices Committee of the CCAB has stated the current position as far as the external audit is concerned as follows:

> ... the responsibility for the prevention and detection of irregularities and fraud rests with (management). However, we will endeavour to plan our audit so that we have a reasonable expectation of detecting material misstatements in the financial statements from irregularities or fraud but our examination should not be relied upon to disclose irregularities and fraud which may exist. (APC, 1984)

This appears to place the onus on the internal audit, as a support to management, to detect fraud. However, this places too much emphasis upon the internal auditor as policeman. Rather, the primary duty of the internal auditor is to encourage management to introduce and maintain effective internal control procedures. Management, particularly line management, remains responsible for detecting fraud and the auditor can serve as an advisor in this function. There is evidence which suggests that management control procedures in many organizations are not the major means of discovering fraud. Other means, such as confession and accidental discovery, uncover fraud. This suggests that much needs to be done in many organizations to strengthen internal control.

Analysis and development of systems

Organizations are composed of many systems. A system can be described as a service of interrelated procedures designed to achieve some objective. Three in particular are of interest in the present context: the organization's accounting system, its management information system, and the management control system. The accounting system collects and records accounting data, the management information system collects, records and reports accounting and other data to management, and the management control system uses management information to make evaluations and decisions concerning organizational operations. It is important to isolate systems from each other to enable each to be analysed.

Accounting systems and records should be designed to record the transactions and other activities of an organization in order to facilitate the effective and efficient running of the operations which achieve the organization's objectives. In addition, accounting systems should facilitate the preparation of reports to those external to the organization who have rights to such reports. Thus, accounting information systems provide part of management information as well as information for external reporting. Such systems will be as good as the skill and care with which they have been designed and implemented, and with which they are operated. The accounting records produced will depend upon the accuracy and strength of the accounting systems and the skills and experience of those responsible for turning accounting data into reports.

The analysis and development of accounting systems is clearly of great importance to the operation of an organization and its management and is hence a vital part of the internal audit function. It is also important for the external audit especially since the Companies Acts require auditors to form an opinion on whether proper books of account or accounting records have been kept. Similar statutory requirements are laid on the auditors of other types of organization, for example trades unions, building societies, and housing associations.

An essential part of the audit of accounting systems is the ascertainment and recording of the systems in operation within an organization. Following from this is the analysis of the operation of the system, in terms of its objectives, costs and other characteristics, and an evaluation of it with a view to its development. The same considerations apply to management information and control systems.

Various aspects of the analysis and design of systems are considered later in this chapter. Whilst it is important to be able to draw boundaries between systems to isolate them for analysis, it is vital to remember that not only do the components of a particular system interact, but also systems interact with each other. This means that modifications cannot be made to parts of one system without affecting other systems. The auditor must ensure that each system is achieving its objectives but that there is a comprehensive control system covering all the organization's activities and that systems are coordinated and linked.

Testing of statements

Accounting and management information systems, as well as recording data, prepare statements for purposes of accountability and decision making. Obviously, the annual published accounts of a company are the best known example of such a statement, but many others are provided on a periodic basis, such as stock returns and management performance reports. The role of an audit is to test and report upon the quality of accounting and other information in statements. This may involve forming opinions on the truth and fairness and compliance with law (in the case of company accounts) or the accuracy and usefulness of internal accounting or management statements.

Investigations

Much of audit activity, both internal and external, might be described as routine. This is not to imply that it is carried on in an unthinking or uncritical fashion, but that it is regular and repeated. Routine accounting procedures will involve investigations of particular parts of organizational systems and activities. Just as the external auditor may be asked to undertake special investigations, say in connection with the proposed purchase of a business, or in support of a bank advance, so too may the internal auditor find it necessary to carry out special investigations or enquiries, for example a survey on the practicalities and relevance of introducing a standard costing system.

Management control

Above, we made some observations on the responsibilities of the auditor with regard to organizational systems, and referred to the management control system. We may characterize an organization's management control system as the whole system of controls, financial and otherwise, which have been established by management in order to carry on the activities of the organization in a manner appropriate to its objectives. The latter involves ensuring adherence to the policies of the organization, safeguarding its resources, controlling its commitments, and securing the accuracy and completeness of its accounting and other records. The responsibility for introducing and maintaining an adequate system of management control rests with management itself. The external auditor is not a substitute for effective management control, nor is the internal auditor. However, both external and internal auditors may be asked to advise on the adequacy of control systems. Indeed the interest of the internal auditor in an organization's management control system is likely to be (and should be) much greater than merely providing advice on request, as we shall see below when internal control and systems are discussed in detail.

Operational audit

Earlier in the chapter we referred to five aspects of organizational activity in which the internal audit would have an interest. Two of these, operational effectiveness and management efficiency relate to the operational audit. The operational audit is concerned with assessing how well an organization is managed, how far it achieves its objectives, and evaluating the means by which it achieves its objectives. The operational audit seeks evidence on these characteristics of operations and management, economy, efficiency and effectiveness. These three terms may be defined as follows:

(a) *Economy:* The terms under which an organization acquires resources. An economical operation acquires resources in appropriate quality and quantity at lowest cost.
(b) *Efficiency:* The relationship between the inputs of resources and the outputs of goods and services which they produce. Efficient operations produce maximum output for given input levels, or minimum input for a given level of output.
(c) *Effectiveness:* The extent and manner in which an activity or programme achieves its intended objectives or effects.

The investigation and assessment of these three operating characteristics present different problems for the auditor. Economy and efficiency, being more readily quantifiable, are less difficult to assess than effectiveness. This is particularly true of economy, where the primary concern is with cost. Thus, departments with excessive staffing levels or over-qualified staff would be considered uneconomic. The assessment of efficiency requires the identification of both input and output. In some activities, particularly intermediate organizational processes (e.g. the accounts department or vehicle maintenance) output may be implicit and difficult to measure. In such cases concern may be with costs: if the same level of service can be provided at lower cost (by computerizing accounts or re-organizing the maintenance shop) then an efficiency gain will be made. For other activities, output may be quite readily measurable, as in departments providing the organization's ultimate outputs, or in some intermediate activities, for example the operation of a factory or office heating system. In such cases ratios of output to input can be calculated.

The review of effectiveness is where auditors are likely to experience greatest difficulty. Effectiveness is concerned with success or otherwise in achieving an organization's ultimate objectives. The most fundamental danger is in appearing to question the objectives or policies themselves or in making political judgements. At a more practical level the auditor will face problems if objectives are not clearly stated. Even where they are clearly stated there is usually scope for interpretation and agreed criteria must be identified. Such criteria may have to be established by the auditor, usually in conjunction with management, or if a public sector organization is involved as is more likely to be the case, with the policy makers. Effectiveness, like efficiency, is not an absolute measure. The critical feature of effectiveness is that it is concerned only with outputs, and not with inputs, their relationship to output, or cost considerations.

From the above discussion it is apparent that the scope of internal audit is very wide and encompasses issues of considerable complexity and difficulty whereas the external auditor's responsibilities are limited by statute. There is no similar limitation placed on the internal audit function. Its purpose is to serve the organization and its members. As the organization, its membership, and their problems and needs evolve, so too does internal audit.

Internal control and systems

Earlier in the chapter we outlined the nature of management control and its relevance to internal audit. In this section of the chapter we examine auditing for internal control in more detail and consider in particular the audit of systems.

An internal control is any measure established by an organization's management to ensure that organizational objectives are achieved. Various types of internal control may be identified. An organization's personnel practices effect internal control. Staff should be competent and skilled in the tasks which they are expected to fulfil. Likewise the duties of staff should be clearly designated by job descriptions, manuals and other documentation and duties should be segregated. Also clear identification of function should ensure that no tasks are omitted and internal control correspondingly weakened. Supervision should be provided to ensure duties are carried out properly. Related to this is the introduction of dual control into internal control systems. Dual control means the assignment of more than one person to a given task. This is designed to check the worth of one against that of the other. An internal control system should contain effectively designed and utilized documentation. Thus, forms and other supporting documents should contain appropriate information and should provide space to allow the indication that all supporting documentation has been properly collated and checked and that, where appropriate, authorization has been given. The pre-numbering of forms is an illustration. This allows the ready checking of the sequence in which documents (and the transactions to which they relate) have been processed. Procedures to ensure the approval and authorization of transactions should be present, as should controls and checks to ensure that authorization has been granted. Unauthorized actions should be prevented. Finally, accounting systems should contain controls which confirm or query the reliability of recorded data. In this section of the chapter we shall concentrate upon accounting systems as the objects of internal auditor's investigations of internal control procedures.

In investigating the accounting systems of an organization an internal auditor must first ascertain and record the systems in force. In recording the systems in force the auditor must sub-divide the overall accounting routines in appropriate sub-divisions for ease of understanding and analysis.

For a company, a typical sub-division of accounting systems might include the following:

(a) Organizational and general matters.
(b) Purchase and accounts payable.
(c) Stocks and costing.
(d) Payroll matters.
(e) Sales and accounts receivable, despatch of goods.
(f) Bank and cash balances, receipts and payments.
(g) Investments and investment income.

The sub-divisions will differ for specific types of organization in the company sector, and for public sector organizations.

The above accounting systems will contain several common features relating to internal control. Accounting systems should contain accounting controls which ensure that:

(a) Transactions have been properly authorized: there are authorization procedures.
(b) All authorized transactions proceed through the system.
(c) Information recording details of the transaction is transferred to source documents.
(d) Information concerning the transaction is transferred from source documents to other documents.
(e) The physical location of documents and information is organized.
(f) Procedures exist to check operations performed in the accounting system, to check details on the documents generated by the transaction.

The compiling of system information is to enable the auditor to evaluate the adequacy of the systems and the internal controls incorporated in them. This involves:

(a) Determining whether the existing system satisfies existing requirements.
(b) Determining whether existing requirements remain relevant in the context of management's future objectives and needs.
(c) Identifying alternative systems which would meet present and future needs if existing systems do not.

This is the systems audit. In auditing the accounting control systems, an internal auditor should:

(a) Apply sample tests to ensure that accounting systems operate as they are described in the organization's manuals or according to the internal auditor's own recording of the system.

(*b*)   Identify points of apparent strength and weakness in the accounting system, thus evaluating the efficiency of the control system and the extent to which reliance can be placed on it.

(*c*)   Construct and execute a programme of audit work which seeks to assess the level of reliance which can be placed on the accounting system.

Despite its importance, formal techniques for the review of internal control systems are lacking. One important exception to this generalization is the internal control questionnaire (ICQ). ICQs are guides to auditors which seek to ensure that a systems review does not omit major areas of importance. They call for descriptive answers to questions which indicate whether an adequate degree of internal control is present. Thus, an ICQ for the purchases and accounts payable accounting system might appear as follows.

Purchases and accounts payable
1   Can goods be ordered without authorization?
   (*a*)   Are requisitions approved by responsible authority?
   (*b*)   Are there limits to authority?
   (*c*)   Is purchase documentation issued only to responsible staff?
   (*d*)   Are requisition forms required for all purchases?
   (*e*)   Are requisition forms pre-numbered?
   (*f*)   Are all numbers accounted for?
   (*g*)   Are all requisition forms completed with details of purchase terms?
   (*h*)   Are orders checked?
   (*i*)   Are values compared with budgets?

2   Can liabilities for goods be incurred but not recorded?
   (*a*)   Are goods received at one location?
   (*b*)   Are goods received forms completed on receipt of goods?
      (*i*)   Are goods-received forms pre-numbered?
      (*ii*)   Are all forms accounted for?
      (*iii*)   Are forms used to keep stock records up to date?

3   Are goods examined on receipt?
   (*a*)   For quantity?
   (*b*)   For quality?
   (*c*)   Are controls available to ensure examination takes place?

4   Are goods-received forms passed on promptly to other departments?
   (*a*)   Accounts
   (*b*)   Purchasing
   (*c*)   Stock records
   (*d*)   Other (give details)

5   Are goods-returns properly authorized?

6   Are goods-returned forms prepared?
   (*a*)   When goods are returned to suppliers?

(b)   Are forms pre-numbered?
(c)   Are all forms accounted for?
(d)   Are forms used to keep stock records up to date

7   Are accounting records regularly checked?
(a)   Are purchase records examined for items for which no invoices have been received?
(i)   Are discrepancies investigated?
(b)   Are goods-received records examined for items for which no invoices have been received?
(i)   Are discrepancies investigated?
(c)   Are invoices which have been received approved before passing through the accounting system?
(d)   Are suppliers' statements checked against records to ensure all items have been passed into the accounting system?
(i)   Are discrepancies investigated?
(e)   Are suppliers' statements checked against purchase ledger?
(i)   Are discrepancies investigated?
(f)   Are goods-returned records checked to ensure receipt of credit notes?
(i)   Are discrepancies investigated?

8   Can goods not received be paid for?
(a)   Are suppliers' invoices and credit notes
(i)   Pre-numbered?
(ii)   All accounted for?
(iii)   Compared with requisition for order characteristics?
(b)   Are discrepancies investigated?
(i)   Compared with goods-received forms?
(ii)   Checked for arithmetic errors?
(iii)   Approved by an authorized person?
(iv)   Entered only when authorized?
Similar ICQs could be set out for the other accounting systems.

Once an ICQ has been completed it should be reviewed to aid the identification of strengths and weaknesses in the accounting system. In undertaking this review the auditor should bear in mind that other controls may exist elsewhere in the accounting system which may make good a weakness identified in some other section.

Once the strengths and weaknesses of the internal control system have been identified, the internal auditor may next begin the task of testing the system. Various types of audit test are available and may be considered appropriate in different circumstances. These tests will now be considered.

Where the evaluation of the accounting system has found the controls to be apparently strong and generally reliable the auditor will engage in compliance testing.

Compliance testing

Compliance testing is designed to establish a reasonable level of reassurance that controls are functioning effectively and can be relied upon. Compliance tests are designed to test aspects of the system which are significant for its control function and hence the tests should be directed towards those parts of the system which are important for its efficient and effective operation. If the tests disclose parts of the system which are not working properly this may be interpreted to mean that the system, despite the initial evaluation of its comparative strength, after all contains weaknesses. This presumes, of course, that the weaknesses identified are considered material. Materiality is fundamental to the whole audit process. Unfortunately, as the ICAEW have concluded in the context of the external audit, materiality is not subject to precise definition. The same comment applies to internal audit: materiality is determined by circumstances and depends upon the professional judgement and experience of the auditor. On the other hand, if no weaknesses are discovered in practice, the auditor may conclude that reliance may be placed on the effective functioning of the internal controls which have been tested.

Since the precise details of any auditing exercise will be determined by the circumstances of the investigation it is difficult to be too specific about compliance testing. However, in general four types of audit test may be recognized:

Inspection
The auditor may inspect written evidence on the performance of an internal control, prepared perhaps by the staff member responsible for it, or by his superior. Also, accounting records, source or other documents, or assets themselves may be inspected.

Observation
The auditor may observe a procedure being performed, or the operation of a part of the system.

Inquiries
The auditor may inquire of appropriate persons how the control is working.

Computation
The auditor may make computations or re-computations in order to check the accuracy of accounting records.

Such tests may be undertaken in many different ways and correspondingly, different types of evidence of compliance will be forthcoming. *The Auditing Guideline on Audit Evidence* produced by the Auditing Practices Committee makes certain observations regarding the reliability of various types of audit evidence: documentary evidence, is more reliable than oral evidence; and evidence originated by the auditor by means such as analysis and physical inspection is more reliable than evidence obtained from others. Continuing the example given above of the purchases and accounts payable accounting system, the following are examples of compliance tests which might be applied:

(*a*) Test the sequence of purchase orders.
(*b*) Test the approvals given to purchase requisitions.
(*c*) Test the sequence of goods-received records.
(*d*) Test that purchase invoices have been arithmetically checked.

Substantive testing

The other major type of audit test is substantive testing. Substantive testing is the testing of transactions and balances which provides evidence as to the completeness, accuracy, and validity of the information contained in accounting records or financial statements. The extent and character of substantive testing utilized by the auditor depends in large measure upon the extent of reliance which the auditor feels able to place upon the internal controls after testing for strengths and weaknesses. Where reliance was strong we noted a progression to compliance testing. Had reliance been weak, it would have been appropriate for the auditor to proceed to substantive testing had the likelihood of significant errors due to weak control have been judged likely. Likewise, had compliance testing proved unsatisfactory, then a progression to substantive testing would be appropriate. Indeed, even following satisfactory compliance testing, the application of restricted substantive testing would generally be pursued.

Substantive tests may be divided into detailed substantive tests (tests of transactions and balances making up financial statement figures) and analytical review procedures. In detailed substantive testing the auditor can evaluate any evidence providing that it is capable of substantiating individual transactions and balances. Such tests are normally conducted by taking a sample of transactions or balances and evaluating evidence in support of the sampled items. There are numerous statistical sampling techniques which are applied to auditing problems. Each of these techniques involve a method for evaluating the data in the sample. Methods of sample selection normally involve the use of some random sampling technique. Two of the most generally utilized sampling techniques are stratified variable sampling and monetary unit sampling. The former involves the auditor in stratifying the population into strata according to the value of the items. The sample is allocated to the various strata according to a pre-determined formula and random samples of the specified sizes are selected from the various strata.

In monetary unit sampling, on the other hand, the monetary value of the population is the basis of the sample. Consider for example a population of invoices valued at £100,000. This would be regarded as 100,000 £1 monetary units. Each of these units is assigned a unique indicator card and a sample of monetary units is drawn randomly from the sample. Since random selection means that each monetary unit has an equal chance of selection, and since large valued invoices have most monetary units in them, they have the largest chance of selection. Given the economic importance of large invoices the sampling methods emphasis upon them introduces the notion of key element sampling into the proceedings.

The selection of the sample provides the auditor with evidence. This evidence may be examined by the auditor without the use of formal statistical evaluation and a judgement may be arrived at concerning the degree of assurance which may be attached to the population from which it is drawn. Such a judgement is subjective and as such, needs to be treated with care. The subjectivity attached to such judgements may be reduced if the sample is evaluated using a statistical technique designed to assess the confidence which may be placed in sample values. The advantage of formal statistical evaluation is the apparent objectivity which it brings to the assessment of the sample, expressed perhaps as confidence intervals or probabilities.

Above we note that substantive testing consists of analytical review in addition to detailed substantive testing. Analytical review in general involves the prediction of one variable on the basis of an expected relationship with another. By condoning such a relationship as the basis of prevention the auditor is in effect establishing a model of the behaviour of the variable to be predicted. If there is a discrepancy between a predicted value and its actual value, the auditor may investigate the variance and seek an explanation for it. The predictive process may be quite formal (and thus be based upon a formal model of the relationship between two variables) as would be the case if a statistical technique such as linear regression were used. Alternatively, less formal prediction methods may be employed. These might involve the auditor's judgement based upon observations of trends in variables. For example, sales might be subjected to analytical review. An informal prediction of the level of sales in the month under investigation might be derived by applying the company's average profit make up to that month's cost of sales. More formally, the trend of sales might be established by regressing monthly sales against a time variable. If predicted and actual sales diverge in either case the auditor might concentrate his investigations on sales for that month and in addition such an explanation of why the postulated relationship (based on profit mark up or linear time trend) did not apply in the month in question. The auditor may discover that during the month production was disrupted, or a change in production mix occurred, or that changes in selling prices occurred.

Verification of assets and liabilities

One of the most basic purposes of any audit, whether external or internal, is to resolve uncertainty about something on behalf of those who are not capable of resolving it themselves. Accounting reports contain data on assets and liabilities and it is necessary for an auditor to undertake procedures to verify that the data represents the underlying assets and liabilities. Verification procedures for important categories of assets and liabilities are considered below:

Assets

Plant and machinery
The auditor should consult the plant register or detailed schedules of plant and machinery in order to verify the amounts recorded in the financial statements. In addition, the capital transactions for the period should be checked and physical checks should be undertaken of selected items or selected sites where plant and machinery is located. Where appropriate the basis upon which provisions for depreciation have been estimated should be investigated. The auditor's chief concern in this case is to determine whether accounting judgements on depreciation have been made on a proper basis as regards principles and consistency, and that provisions made appear reasonable and sufficient.

Land and buildings
The auditor must verify that, where property is owned, title deeds are in the possession of the organization and that those deeds appear to be in order. If property is held under leases the lease documents should be checked.

Investments
To verify this category of assets, the auditor should obtain a schedule of investments and compare the detail with balances shown in financial statements. In addition, titles to ownership should be verified by physical inspection and, if necessary, with reference to third parties, and calculations of gains or losses on disposal and valuations should be checked.

Stocks and work-in-progress
The significance of this item both for the determination of profit or loss, and for the appearance of the balance sheet makes its verification of critical importance to an auditor. Several sources of error may be recognized:

(*a*) Including in accounting reports valuations of stock which do not exist.
(*b*) Including in stock items which have already been sold.
(*c*) The omission or suppression of data relating to stocks.
(*d*) Including in stocks items for which invoices have not been passed through purchases.
(*e*) Including valuations or prices which are incorrect.
(*f*) Failure to provide for diminution in value where stock is obsolete, damaged, etc.
(*g*) Arithmetic errors.

If proper stock records and control procedures are present these may be used by the auditor for checking stock. The auditor must verify that counting and inspection of stock items, together with recording and pricing has been carried out correctly. A physical check of a portion of the stock should be carried out. Work-in-progress may present particular problems of verification, especially in complicated production processes where products may go through numerous stages when costs are added. If appropriate management accounting systems are in operation they should provide the auditor with the basis of checking stock valuation. However, an important part of the internal audit process will be the testing of the management accounting system including that related to stock control and valuation.

Debtors
The most effective audit test for this item is direct confirmation of the whole or a proportion of the trade debtors. This may be done by direct contact with customers who are asked to agree or disagree with stated balances. The auditor should take care in selecting which debtor accounts to circulate and the number and type chosen will depend upon the total number of debtors, the relationship of debtors to other assets, and the degree of internal control. Choice should be random, perhaps on a stratified basis.

Cash and bank balances
The auditors should check the petty cash book and count cash, and should compare the sums to ensure that all cash is accounted for and is subject to appropriate controls. Bank reconciliation statements should be checked and bank balances confirmed directly with banks.

Liabilities

Share capital
The balances in share registers should be checked against issued share capital, and the total issued share capital checked against the Memorandum and Articles of Association and share transfers should be checked, as should the payment of dividends.

Reserves
All movements on reserves should be checked and it should be confirmed that no amounts taken directly to reserves should have been properly dealt with in other ways.

Taxation
Tax computations should be checked and movements on tax accounts should be reviewed. Also, checks should be made on computations for deferred taxation to ensure that they are in accordance with the organization's accounting policies.

Debentures and loans
The auditor should check borrowing powers to ensure that these have not been exceeded and the trust deeds of debenture issues need to be examined to ascertain the terms of issue and to verify that they have been met. The payment of interest should similarly be verified.

Creditors
The auditor must verify that liabilities are fairly stated and complete and that the basis of accounting for creditors is acceptable and consistent with stated policies. The invoice file for the period should be checked to ensure that items have been correctly charged to the period. The auditor should check that suppliers' invoices have been recognized and included by direct circularization of suppliers with a request for a statement of balances. All the main expense accounts e.g. employment costs, advertising, rent and rates, etc., should be examined to determine whether appropriate charges for the period have been made.

Planning the audit programme

Like any activity, an internal audit requires planning if it is to prove effective. The plan will include an outline of the sequence of activities involved in the audit, a statement of the approach to be adopted and the emphasis to be given at each stage in the audit process. An outline of a general approach to an audit is set out in Figure 14.1.

As in an external audit, an important part of the audit process is documentation. The key elements in audit documentation are working papers and audit files. Working papers represent a permanent record of the information obtained by the audit, the methods adopted by the auditor, and the work which has been done in the audit. The objectives of audit working papers are to communicate what is to be done and to provide evidence of what has been done. Thus, they provide a link between the audit plan and the audit work to be undertaken. They should ensure that work is conducted systematically and with continuity as audit staff change. Audit working papers record evidence of the work which has been done and what conclusions have been drawn and how they have been drawn. Given their roles of communication and record, it is essential to ensure that the information contained in the working papers is accessible and cross-referenced. Working papers related to current audit activity are normally filed separately from those relating to previous audit or those which are permanent records used as reference material. The former is the current working papers file and the latter is the permanent audit file.

Computer systems audit

The general objective of internal auditing is not affected by the introduction of computerized information systems. Consequently, the internal

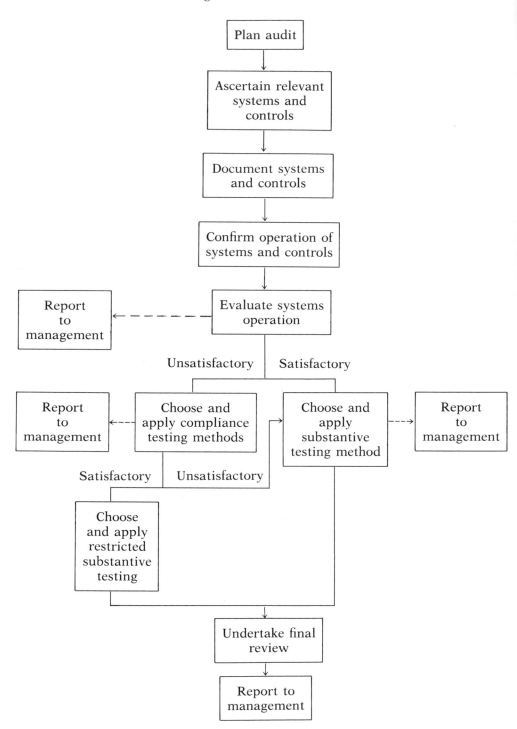

Figure 14.1 *General approach to an audit*

audit of such systems involves ascertaining the characteristics of the system, and evaluating and testing the controls in the system. However, computer systems do present different problems from non-computer systems since they record and process transactions in a significantly different manner than manual systems. In more detail we may observe:

(a) The ability of computers to store and process information, and the specialized nature of their operation, means that there is a tendency for the concentration of activities upon them.

(b) Although computers process accounting information, computer systems are not necessarily operated by accounting staff. This may tend to weaken internal control features.

(c) The technology of computing means that formality replaces the mix of formality and informality which is present in manual systems. Informal controls may be a valuable feature of control systems.

(d) The operation of computing systems will be critically dependent upon systems design and implementation. The system will continue to operate, albeit inefficiently, if poorly designed systems have been installed. Manual systems are likely to be more adaptive.

(e) Data held in computer systems may be more easy to manipulate than that in manual system, and more difficult to access independently by auditors.

Consequently, the auditor, external or internal, will need to take into account additional factors in relation to the techniques available to him. In particular, the auditor will need to consider the timing of his work, the form in which accounting records are maintained, the internal controls existing, the availability of data and the length of time it is maintained in a usable form.

During the early years of computer based systems audit methods required little adaptation from those applied to manual systems. The overriding method used in computers was batch processing (the submission and processing of batches of transactions to be dealt with in a computer run). This allows the processing activity to be largely ignored in the audit. Audit effort is concentrated on the input and output of the system. Source documents containing input may be inspected and processed manually so that they may be compared to output. As batches are processed totals are accumulated for rejected and accepted items and hence auditors may investigate rejected items and evaluate them.

An alternative approach to computer audit is to use the computer in the audit process. This may involve the preparation of a test pack of data (both valid and invalid) which is input to test the system. The computer output from this test pack input can be compared with manual output based on the same data. If the results are different the auditor can attempt to determine the cause of the discrepancy. This method has limitations in that it can only be used on one program at once. Also the test pack may become obsolete if the computer program changes.

Furthermore, the auditor must be assured that the program which is tested is that which is used regularly in the system. A potential weakness of the approach is that the test pack cannot cover all combinations which may be faced in practice.

A development of the test pack is the use of an integrated test facility. This requires the extraction of selected transactions from the normal processing activity and their use in the generation of results which can be checked against pre-determined figures.

A more common audit technique is the use of generalized audit software which is capable of performing audit tests on the operation of the computer system and its proceedural controls. These audit software packages are the computer adaptation of manual audit techniques involving the selection of items and then comparison with pre-determined values, the resorting of files, the sampling of populations of transactions, the statistical evaluation of samples and the summarizing of files. Test packs and audit software packages are examples of computer assisted audit techniques (CAATs).

A modern development in computer systems is data base management. Data base management systems maintain a common data base for several applications which is organized in a hierarchical fashion. This complicates the entering of the system by the auditor and the retrieval of data.

Internal controls in computer systems

Internal controls over computer systems can be divided into two categories:

(a)   *Application controls*. These refer to the specific controls applying to specific computer functions within the accounting system. Their objectives are to ensure that accounting records are complete and accurate and that the entries within accounting systems are valid.

(b)   *General controls*. These concern the environment within which the computer based accounting systems are developed, maintained and operated. They apply to all functions within the computer system and aim to ensure the proper development and implementation of computer applications, the integrity of programme and data files, and the integrity of computer operations.

Both types of controls may be either manual or programmed. Although the two types of control may be distinguished from each other, they are interrelated. Weak general controls may undermine application controls, and strong general controls may increase confidence in application controls. The internal auditor will need to determine whether the application and general controls meet the objectives of the system, the standards set for internal control, and whether they can be relied upon. In its guideline on auditing in a computer environment, the APC stated that in assessing the reliability of internal controls the auditor will be informed by the cost effectiveness of audit methods and the ease of testing computer systems. Hence, where application controls are entirely manual the auditor may decide to apply compliance tests only to application controls rather than rely on general controls. When application controls involve computer programs the auditor needs to test whether the programs have operated properly. This may be done by evaluating relevant general controls or particular aspects of the specific computer programs involved.

On some occasions a computer programmer accounting procedure may not be subject to effective application controls. The auditor may decide to apply compliance tests to general controls in order to determine whether the controls have operated properly. As with manual systems, if compliance tests do not show controls to be reliable, substantive tests should be applied.

The investigation of general controls may assume a regular part of audit work since one of the functions of general controls is the prevention of systematic recurring errors. Such errors may be an expected feature of computer systems because of the potential for program faults or problems with computer hardware.

Whatever pattern of testing of general or application controls the auditor adopts, the audit of computer systems must exhibit certain features if it is to be effective. Perhaps the most basic and obvious of them is that audit staff should possess an appropriate level of technical knowledge and skill with computer systems. Equally, audit tests will be either manual or may be performed by a computer (CAATs, as indicated elsewhere in this section). The auditor will need to determine the appropriate mix of manual and CAATs in planning and implementing the audit. For many aspects of an audit, the auditor may have the choice between manual and CAATs. The criteria to be applied in making such a choice will include the relative effectiveness of the two types of tests, their respective costs, and the extent of compliance or substantive testing achieved by each. However, since computer systems frequently leave no concrete evidence of the functions which they have performed, there may be an effective limit to the application of manual tests. In similar vein, the relative speed of CAATs compared with manual tests may bias the auditor in favour of their use. Their use does pre-suppose the availability of computer facilities, computer files and programs. The internal auditor may be able to overcome the problems of ensuring that such resources are available more readily than his external counterpart. A particular need if CAATs are utilized is to ensure that audit working papers should indicate the tasks performed by the CAATs, the technical problems overcome, the results of the CAATs and the auditor's conclusions drawn from them.

Auditing standards

The accountancy profession in the UK began to issue statements on external auditing in 1961 when the ICAEW published Statement UI,

General Principles of Auditing. It was not until 1976, when the Consultative Committee of Accountancy Bodies (CCAB) established a sub-committee, the Auditing Practices Committee (APC), that the accountancy profession began to take a collective approach to the regulation of auditing. The APC was set up specifically to consider the setting of auditing standards but it was only in 1980 that a definition statement on standards emerged in *Auditing Standards and Guidelines*. Auditing standards are defined by the APC as 'basic principles and practices which members are expected to follow in the conduct of an audit' although they have no status in law. In addition auditing guidelines are issued and these give auditors guidance on which auditing procedures to adopt, how to apply auditing standards, how to deal with problems posed in particular industries, and latest techniques. To date auditing standards have been issued, together with guidelines. In addition several other documents are either in the process of being developed or have a status yet to be determined.

As we noted, the APC's interest lies chiefly with the external auditor. However, the work of the APC concerns internal audit in three ways. First, the APC's work programme includes a guideline *Reliance on Internal Audit*, which gives guidance on the matters which need to be considered and the procedures which need to be followed by external auditors when placing reliance on internal audit. Second, the APC has issued a guideline entitled *Internal Controls* which gives guidance on the external audit's ascertainment and evaluation of internal controls. Third, at the initiative of the Chartered Institute of Public Finance and Accountancy (which became a governing member of the APC in 1982). the APC has undertaken research projects into the development of value for money work and internal audit. Although these projects remitted from a public sector initiative it was intended that guidance developed would have general application to both public and private sectors.

Questions

1 M plc has a number of companies engaged in manufacturing and wholesaling. It is proposing to establish an internal audit department which will report directly to the managing director.

You are required to:

(a) State what you consider to be the function of such a department.   (*10 marks*)
(b) Discuss, briefly, why this activity is gaining in importance.
(*5 marks*)
(*Total: 15 marks*)

Institute of Cost and Management Accountants, Professional Stage Part 1, Financial Accounting 2

2 You are the recently appointed internal auditor of Z Limited and one of your first tasks is to investigate the procedure with regard to the receipt of customers' orders and the dispatch of goods to them.

Your investigation reveals the following procedures, which are the only ones concerning the receipt and dispatch of customers' orders. The orders arrive daily by post, either directly from the customer, or via the company's representatives. These go to the Sales Office where a pre-printed two-part unnumbered sales order set is made out for each incoming order. The Sales Office staff attach the second copy of the set to the original order and file this in alphabetical sequence.

The top copy is sent initially to the Credit Controller for approval. He checks it against a computer print-out of the current balances on the debtors' ledger and/or credit 'black list' reports. If credit is approved, the top copy is then sent to the Finished Goods Warehouse where the items on the order are checked for availability.

If they are available, the Warehouse Foreman then raises an un-numbered four-part pre-printed invoice/dispatch note set. The individual copies of this set are distributed as follows. The top copy, valued by the Warehouse, is sent to the customer as an invoice. The second copy goes to the Accounts Department to update the debtors' ledger. The third copy, unvalued, is used as a dispatch advice note and included with the goods. The dispatch clerk checks that no goods leave the company without this third copy. Finally, the fourth copy is retained on the Warehouse file attached to the sales order copy.

You are required to:

(a) Identify the internal control weaknesses of this system.
                                                                  (*10 marks*)
(b) Suggest improvements to overcome them.   (*10 marks*)
                                                      (*Total: 20 marks*)

Chartered Institute of Management Accountants, Stage 2, Financial Accounting, Specimen Examination Paper (New Syllabus)

3 (a) Define internal control and identify the essential elements of good internal control.   (*5 marks*)
   (b) Outline a procedure for the control of the purchase of raw materials by a manufacturing company identifying the controls at each stage through to the eventual payment for the materials.   (*15 marks*)
                                                      (*Total: 20 marks*)

Chartered Institute of Public Finance and Accountancy, Professional Examination 1, Financial Accounting and Auditing

4 You are Chief Internal Auditor of a large public sector organization. The 19X4–X5 budget provision for the Internal Audit Section is

£465,500. The Director of Finance is under considerable pressure from the Chairman of the Finance Committee to rationalize his department to secure savings and, at the same time, obtain better value for money. Various proposals have been put forward by the Chairman, some of which are aimed specifically at Internal Audit, namely:

(a) A review of the Internal Audit Section with a view to reducing costs by 25 per cent over the next two years.

(b) Potential savings from increased economy, efficiency and effectiveness could far exceed those arising from the prevention of fraud. He has, therefore, proposed a switch in emphasis from 'probity' or 'regularity audit' to 'Value for Money Audit'.

(c) The possible privatization of internal audit which would involve the entire internal audit function being undertaken by a private firm.

You are asked to report to the Director of Finance on the proposals.   (*20 marks*)

Chartered Institute of Public Finance and Accountancy, Professional Examination 2, Auditing and Control

5 You have been appointed computer auditor in a large public sector organization that owns and operates a mainframe computer installation. The installation supports a variety of batch and on-line applications, but the audit plan does not call for the review of individual applications until later in the year; instead your first task is to review the general controls in operation at the installation, working to the following terms of reference:

'To review the adequacy of the general controls to ensure that they provide secure, safe and efficient day-to-day operation of the installation.'

You are required to:

(a) State the areas that you would want to examine and, for each, set out the controls that you would want to see.   (*15 marks*)

(b) Outline the advantages and disadvantages of appraising the general controls before looking at individual applications.
(*5 marks*)
(*Totals: 20 marks*)

Chartered Institute of Public Finance and Accountancy, Professional Examination 2, Auditing and Control

Index